The Anglican Church in Singapore

ANGLICAN STUDIES

Series Editor: Sheryl A. Kujawa-Holbrook, Claremont School of Theology

This series responds to the growing need for high-quality and innovative research in Anglican Studies made available to the scholarly and ecclesial communities. Anglican Studies as expressed here is an interdisciplinary field, including Anglican history, theology, liturgy, preaching, postcolonial studies, ecclesiology, spirituality, literature, missiology, ethics/moral theology, ministry, pastoral care, ecumenism, and interreligious studies. Studies that engage global Anglicanism, as well as studies related to individual contexts are welcome. The series seeks monographs and edited volumes which explore contemporary issues and forge new directions in interdisciplinary research.

Titles in the series

The Anglican Church in Singapore: Mission and Multiculture, Renewal and Realignment, by Edward Jarvis

The Huguenot-Anglican Refuge in Virginia: Empire, Land, and Religion in the Rappahannock Region, by Lonnie H. Lee

The Goldilocks God: Searching for the via media, by Guy Collins

Sacramental Poetics in Richard Hooker and George Herbert: Exploring the Abundance of God, by Brian Douglas

Ministry in the Anglican Tradition from Henry VIII to 1900, by John L. Kater

A Eucharist-shaped Church: Prayer, Theology, and Mission, edited by Daniel J. Handschy, Donna R. Hawk-Reinhard, and Marshall E. Crossnoe

The Anglican Church in Singapore

Mission and Multiculture, Renewal and Realignment

Edward Jarvis

LEXINGTON BOOKS/FORTRESS ACADEMIC
Lanham • Boulder • New York • London

Published by Lexington Books/Fortress Academic
Lexington Books is an imprint of The Rowman & Littlefield Publishing Group, Inc.
4501 Forbes Boulevard, Suite 200, Lanham, Maryland 20706
www.rowman.com

86-90 Paul Street, London EC2A 4NE, United Kingdom

Copyright © 2024 by The Rowman & Littlefield Publishing Group, Inc.

All rights reserved. No part of this book may be reproduced in any form or by any electronic or mechanical means, including information storage and retrieval systems, without written permission from the publisher, except by a reviewer who may quote passages in a review.

British Library Cataloguing in Publication Information Available

Library of Congress Cataloging-in-Publication Data

Names: Jarvis, Edward, 1975– author.
Title: The Anglican Church in Singapore : mission and multiculture, renewal and realignment / Edward Jarvis.
Description: [Lanham] : [Lexington Books/Fortress Academic], [2024] | Series: Anglican studies | Includes bibliographical references and index. | Summary: "The Anglican Church in Singapore examines the church from multiple perspectives, expositing its unique place within world Christianity. This book documents the Church's two-hundred-year history, from the conflicts and contradictions of British colonialism to the crucial and controversial disputes that currently divide Anglican Christians worldwide"— Provided by publisher.
Identifiers: LCCN 2024006265 (print) | LCCN 2024006266 (ebook) | ISBN 9781978716988 (cloth) | ISBN 9781978716995 (epub)
Subjects: LCSH: Anglican Communion—Singapore—History. | Anglican Communion—Political aspects—Singapore. | Singapore—Church history.
Classification: LCC BR1205 .J37 2024 (print) | LCC BR1205 (ebook) | DDC 283/.5957—dc23/eng/20240213
LC record available at https://lccn.loc.gov/2024006265
LC ebook record available at https://lccn.loc.gov/2024006266

∞™ The paper used in this publication meets the minimum requirements of American National Standard for Information Sciences—Permanence of Paper for Printed Library Materials, ANSI/NISO Z39.48-1992.

Contents

Foreword *by Robbie B. H. Goh*	vii
Acknowledgments	ix
Abbreviations	xi
Introduction	1
Chapter One: "To Pave the Way for Better Things": The Arrival of Church and Empire in Southeast Asia and Singapore	11
Chapter Two: "Desiring to Enter the Fold of Christ": Struggling to Balance Priorities in a Missionary Church	31
Chapter Three: "Wherever the Sun Shines": From the Victorian Mission Boom to the End of Empire's Golden Era	51
Chapter Four: "Between What Is Christian and What Is Western": Evolving Outlooks in an Age of Change	71
Chapter Five: "The Church in Times of Suffering and Persecution": The Second World War, the Japanese Occupation, and the Aftermath	93
Chapter Six: "More Fruitful and Urgent Tasks": The Postwar Church amidst Conflict, Controversy, and Merdeka	113
Chapter Seven: "The Deepening and Renewal of Her Spiritual Life": Tension and Transformation in Singapore's Anglican Church	133
Chapter Eight: "Indifferent to the Agenda of the Western Theological Intelligentsia": Singapore's Anglican Church: Realization and Realignment	153

Conclusion	173
Bibliography	183
Index	193
About the Author	197

Foreword

The Anglican Church has had a long history in Singapore—longer than any Christian body save the Catholics. It has left a lasting impact, for example in education—with two of the oldest mission schools in Singapore, St. Margaret's School for girls, established in 1842, and St. Andrew's School for boys, established in 1862. Its lasting impact can also be seen in the architecture of heritage buildings like St. Andrew's cathedral in Singapore's civic district, in the social welfare organizations operated by the Anglican Church, its role in the founding and operation of the Trinity Theological College (one of the leading seminaries in Asia), and of course in the communities of Anglican worshippers—one of the largest and most vibrant Christian denominations operating in Singapore today.

In the present volume, Edward Jarvis has performed a considerable service, not just to the history of Anglicanism in this part of the world (which needs telling) but also to the cultural and religious history of Singapore, in which the Anglican Church has played a significant role. Jarvis's account of the origins and early days of the Anglican presence in Singapore is meticulously researched and far more detailed than that of existing studies. Not simply a dry account of dates and numbers, it provides color and insight, detailing the difficulties faced by early workers in the field, the attitudes of colonial-era churchmen to the native society and culture of the time, dramatic episodes like the wartime baptism of a Chinese prisoner of war just minutes before he was executed by the Japanese, and even accounts of "profligate" church workers and other "scandalous" and "controversial" incidents. The historical color in Jarvis's book also extends at times to the native attitudes to missionaries and the early Christian community, which ranged from acceptance and appreciation to hostility and even violence.

While the attitudes of the pioneering Anglicans included, of course, sentiments which may be considered inappropriate today, it is important to remember their historical context, and to see them as expressions of the zeal with which they regarded their work in this region. This zeal, Jarvis's work reminds us, persisted in spite of considerable early difficulties, and the lack of adequate support from sending organizations.

One of the main points made in this volume is worth reiterating; that the Anglican missionaries and clergy were by no means uncritically aligned with colonial administrators, but often held differing views, attitudes, and agendas. Like the missionaries of other denominations operating in various parts of Asia, the Anglicans in Singapore had to defy and work around the East India Company's (EIC) prohibition on evangelism (prior to the revision of the Company charter), strategize its evangelical work in the face of the colonial government's policy of non-interference in native cultures and religions, as well as work in the gaps and lapses of the social services that the colonial administration generally was not interested in providing for the native population.

In the closing chapters, Jarvis's book also provides an account of Singapore Anglicanism's interface with Pentecostalism, a feature which *prima facie* seems to contradict the "High Church" character of the former, and certainly marks a long and interesting transformation from its early "Anglo-Catholic" sympathies. Here Jarvis is certainly correct in noting the uneven distribution of Pentecostal elements in the Singapore Church's various churches, leaders and agencies—an unevenness that can be seen even among the different services held at St Andrew's cathedral, which range from the more openly charismatic to the more traditional. The sections on Pentecostalism may be a bit too far-reaching for some readers. Again, however, Jarvis provides color and insight, noting how Anglicanism's receptivity to Pentecostalism was in large part shaped by the personalities and experiences of Bishops Chiu and Tay, and at times created conflict with other Anglicans of differing theologies.

In the final analysis, the present volume is a fascinating story of how, in Jarvis's words, an "autocephalous national Church" developed one part of its global export model in this region, and the adaptations and accommodations necessary for the development of this global model. It would indeed be too limiting to see the present challenges and conflicts within Singapore's Anglican Church as postcolonial legacies; much better to see them as consequences of the evolution of Christianity within the development of Singapore as an independent and modern nation, with a national character blending pragmatism with conservatism, inherited Asian values with a global economic outlook. Christianity in Singapore, including the Anglican Church, has had to evolve within the development of this national character and national positioning, and to position itself accordingly.

Robbie B. H. Goh
Professor and Provost of Singapore University of Social Sciences (SUSS)

Acknowledgments

I would like to express my profound gratitude to all who have helped to bring this project to completion with their support, assistance, and encouragement: to the Diocese of Singapore, for generously granting me permission to access their archives, and to my friends, colleagues, acquaintances, and consultees in the Churches in Singapore, in other parts of Southeast Asia, in the United Kingdom, and in Europe; for various reasons it is not possible or practical to name them all individually, for which I apologize.

I am very grateful to Robbie B. H. Goh for his support and for kindly providing the Foreword to this book. I have benefited greatly, during my research at York St. John University, from the input and insights of Sue Yore and James Lorenz; many thanks also to Esther McIntosh at York St. John, and to Wayne Morris at the University of Chester, for their advice and guidance. Special thanks to Kevin Ward for his suggestions and encouragement.

The outstanding team at Lexington Books/Fortress Academic, an imprint of Rowman & Littlefield, Anglican Studies Series, have made the realization of this project as smooth as can be; heartfelt thanks to series editor Sheryl Kujawa-Holbrook and associate editors Gayla Freeman and Zachary Nycum for their unfailing support.

As well as the archive team at the Diocese of Singapore, I am indebted to the National Archives and National Library Board of Singapore, the Bodleian Libraries, Oxford, and, in London, The National Archives, the Imperial War Museum, the Royal Asiatic Society, and the Royal Historical Society. Not for the first time, I owe a special vote of thanks to Richard Mammana for the scholarship and resources provided by him and his wonderful Project Canterbury.

As ever, the constant support of near ones and dear ones ensures that everything works out; thanks to the brothers of the Divine Compassion Friary of the Society of St. Francis and the rest of the Anglican Franciscan family;

thanks to David Potts for his encouragement and for sharing his recollections of Singapore and Malaya; and thanks to my family and friends, especially Rachanee Surintharat for her inexhaustible patience and understanding.

Abbreviations

AC	Anglican Communion
ACS	Anglo-Chinese School
AMiA	Anglican Mission in the Americas
BA	British Advisor
BEIC	see EIC
BMA	British Military Administration
CBE	Commander of the Order of the British Empire
CCA	Christian Conference of Asia
CCM	Council of Churches of Malaysia
CCMS	Council of Churches of Malaysia and Singapore
CIBC	Church of India, Burma, and Ceylon (1930–1947)
CIPBC	Church of India, Pakistan, Burma, and Ceylon (after 1947)
CMS	Church Missionary Society (renamed Church Mission Society in 1995)
CO	Colonial Office (London)
CPM	Communist Party of Malaya
CSI	Church of South India
EACC	East Asia Christian Conference
EIC	East India Company
FCC	Federation of Christian Churches (of Malaya)
FCO	Foreign and Commonwealth Office
FoM	Federation of Malaya
GAFCON	Global Fellowship of Confessing Anglicans / Global Anglican Future Conference (also "Gafcon")
GSFA	Global South Fellowship of Anglican Churches / of Anglicans
LMS	London Missionary Society
MBE	Member of the Order of the British Empire
MC	Military Cross

MCC	Malayan Christian Council
MPAJA	Malayan People's Anti-Japanese Army
MRHA	Maintenance of Religious Harmony Act (1990)
NAS	National Archives of Singapore
NCCS	National Council of Churches of Singapore
OBE	Officer of the Order of the British Empire
PBS	Pingat Bakti Setia (Singaporean Long Service Award)
PSEA	(Church of the) Province of South East Asia
QC	Queen's Counsel (senior trial lawyer)
SACM	St. Andrew's Church Mission
SDA	Singapore Diocesan Association
SDM	*Singapore Diocesan Magazine*
SEACC	South East Asia Church Council
SIM	Singapore Industrial Mission
SPCK	Society for Promoting Christian Knowledge
SPG	Society for the Propagation of the Gospel in Foreign Parts, renamed United Society for the Propagation of the Gospel (USPG) in 1965, renamed United Society Partners in the Gospel (USPG) in 2016
TNA	The National Archives (London)
TTC	Trinity Theological College
USPG	See SPG
WCC	World Council of Churches

Introduction

This story unfolds in one of the most remarkable and fascinating countries in the world. It is also one of the richest countries in the world; according to some reports it is the second richest, according to others the third, and it has the second-highest proportion of millionaires per capita. Singapore is, in addition, believed to be the second most densely populated sovereign state in the world. All of this amounts to a complex experience for the island nation's six million inhabitants, and all of the numbers and proportions mentioned here are headed upward. Another part of this complexity is the high rate of religious affiliation among Singapore's population; conflicting calculations show that between 80 and 99 percent of Singaporeans follow a religion. Singapore has also been named the world's most religiously diverse country, with seven religions each claiming adherence from at least 1 percent of the population. Up to 36 percent of the population adhere to traditional Chinese religions, which, by some calculations, does not include at least 15 percent who are solely Buddhist, though these groups are not usually considered to be mutually exclusive. All of these calculations, in fact, come with an important caveat; they can be useful for giving rough indications but they quickly reveal their limitations, and this attests to the complexity of the situation. Between 19 and 22 percent of the population are Christian and this proportion may already have increased by the time of publication. Sixteen to 18 percent are Muslim, 5 to 8 percent are Hindu, and around 5 percent are agnostic, with the remainder being either followers of a minority religion or unaffiliated, which includes those who privately believe in a spiritual being or beings. With at least 80 percent of the population looking to a world religion to guide and inform their lives, and an unclear number of unaffiliated Singaporeans being personally religious in some way, it is fair to say that Singapore is overwhelmingly religious (Zurlo et al. 2022: 73; Musa 2023: 1).

Notable on this religious landscape is the proportion of adherents to Singapore's fastest-growing religion, Christianity, which is set to exceed 22 percent of the population. This is a remarkable increase since the year 2000, when the proportion was 14.6 percent, which was already significantly higher than Singapore's regional neighboring countries (Goh 2005: 35). Compared to other religions, Christianity is a relative newcomer to Southeast Asia, and even one hundred years ago, at the height of British colonial rule, only 5 percent of Singapore's population were Christians. Understanding Christian expansion in Singapore is an area of study in itself, but Christianity's gain is generally acknowledged to be at the expense of traditional Chinese religions. The latter's followers, it is widely believed, turn to Christianity in search of a modern, rational alternative to what are seen as the superstitious and illogical tenets of Taoism and Buddhism, though some also reject Christianity for the same reasons, it must be noted. Most Singaporean Christians and most Singaporeans in general are ethnic-Chinese, who are the most heterogeneous ethnic group, and while some of them attempt to approach traditional religion rationally, others have no religious affiliation at all, but residual attachment to elements of Buddhist may persist across all subgroups. Their rational approach to traditional religion may be described as the intellectualization of religion, or it may simply be understood as a search for something to believe in that is compatible with a modern urban context of globalization and a high-tech knowledge economy (Kuo 2016: 22; Chin 2017: 3–6). Christianity's tendency toward lively corporate worship may contrast positively with religious traditions that promote silent, solitary prayer, especially for urban citizens who already feel starved of human interaction. In rural parts of Southeast Asia, by comparison, young people have tended to see in Christianity a potential escape from restrictive traditional customs, rites, and expectations, especially concerning marriage, career, and life choices (Koepping 2006: 60–65).

Singapore is often proposed as an ideal case study for investigating social trends in Asia, and this clearly includes religious trends, especially the growth of Christianity (Chin 2017: 82). In his foreword to this book, Robbie B. H. Goh points out the Anglican Church's undeniable material impact on colonial Singapore, most visibly its landmark buildings such as St Andrew's cathedral, lauded as "the finest east of Suez" (*Singapore Diocesan Magazine*, vol. XII, no. 47, August 1922: 1). The Church has, at first glance, endowed Singapore with renowned institutions, prestigious schools, pioneering hospitals, and exceptional individuals who helped to build the modern nation. Less visible are what might be called the reverse processes, such as what the Church gained in return for its ostensible generosity, how the Church in Singapore reconfigured itself through and after national independence, and how Anglicans in this small and unique island state have impacted global Anglicanism, the world's third-largest communion of Christian Churches after Roman Catholicism and Eastern Orthodoxy. These dialogues and their wider implications provide the subject matter of this book, interwoven with a chronological historical narrative that explains how it all came to pass. Modern Singapore is often described as the brainchild of Sir Stamford Raffles

(1781–1826), a British colonial administrator who intuited the strategic potential of this then-almost-uninhabited island and arranged its colonization in 1819. Raffles, in common with other colonial pioneers such as Sir James Brooke in Borneo, was little more than nominally Christian, but he had a high regard for broadly Christian values and, crucially, he foresaw the benefits of involving the Church in establishing his new colony. Only the Church, Raffles realized, could encompass such tasks as founding schools and colleges, relieving the immediate effects of poverty, and providing a credible moral framework for this fledgling society. The presence, specifically, of England's Established Church seemed to confer status and validate the perception of Singapore as an ordered, stratified, and faithful scale replica of England itself.

Before arriving in Singapore, Britain and the other imperial powers had introduced Christianity into Southeast Asia over a roughly two hundred-year period, as part of the colonization process. Many decades later, the process of decolonization also had significant religious dimensions; the region's Christian inheritance was reevaluated, revised, and rejected in parts. Local critiques of imported Christianity probed the supposed connections between Western, Christian, civilized, and rational, without necessarily taking for granted that the lived reality of colonial Christianity was in fact irredeemably Western (Chin 2017: 3–6). Aspects of colonial baggage were challenged and rejected, certainly, but Western-inspired forms of Christianity retained their appeal in many parts of Southeast Asia. This is, therefore, not a predictable story of empire-era expansion and postcolonial decline in a now-decrepit branch of the English Church. The present-day Church of the Province of South East Asia (PSEA), of which the Diocese of Singapore forms part, is less than thirty years old, but it quickly earned a reputation for growth, dynamism, and cohesiveness, with its member dioceses united by the common experience of being surrounded on all sides by pluralism. Western observers soon noted that the PSEA's performance outstripped that of the various Anglican provinces in Britain, where the Church has been present for nearly two thousand years instead of only two hundred. The comparison may seem contrived but it is not entirely unfair; both Singapore and Britain are urban, industrialized, pluralistic, and densely populated, with institutions founded on near-identical principles. Both countries faced mammoth postwar-era challenges, with Singapore extricating itself from British control in a demoralized state, bereft of resources, plagued by corruption, and teetering on the brink of interethnic unrest (Green 2001: 1–3).

The geographical and historical parameters of this book's scope are inevitably quite strange; the sphere of operations and influence of the Anglican Church in Singapore has never been limited to the island of Singapore itself, which has been a fully independent state only since 1965. The story frequently overlaps with that of the modern-day territory of Malaysia and its Church, but the peculiarity of the Anglican presence in Singapore and its significance as part of the wider phenomenon of Singaporean Christianity, especially after the turning point of 1965 and full decolonization, will certainly become clear. There are several perspectives from which to examine this history, but the temptation to reduce these viewpoints to two opposing "sides" of colonialism, and other binary analyses, should be resisted. Historical events themselves may seem to invite binary critiques, but there are strong arguments for rejecting them. Western paradigms have, predictably, permeated the interpretation and transmission of Southeast Asian history in general, generating simplistic narratives populated by receptive Chinese and hostile Malays. Mission history, as Jeffrey Cox pointed out, has been riddled with binary analyses; British and native, civilized and savage, godly and heathen, and so on. Some categorizations are roundly repudiated, but others are so well-rooted that they seem unavoidable. Binary narratives may also contain grains of truth, but they can obscure the complexity of the colonial experience, overlooking crucial factors like gender, prejudice, fraught processes of integration and localization, and painstaking transitions to real local ownership. Steps toward a more nuanced, multilateral discussion may include comparing colonial life's various marginal experiences to cognate experiences at the centers of colonial activity, considering three- and four-way interethnic relations, and seeking multiple perspectives on issues of gender and identity (Cox 2008: 5–6).

There is also a lurking danger of attributing too much to colonialism (Chen 2010: 1–2). Today's Anglican Church in Singapore is not simply the old colonial Church on life support, nor is it a contemporary reboot struggling to distance itself from its colonial ancestor. Colonial history may be relevant to today's Singaporean Christians, but it does not define them; a more significant source for Asian Christians would be Asianness itself, which Peter Phan called "their context of being Christian" (Phan 2000: 218). The quest to pin down a shared understanding of Asianness has a checkered history; it fed into a highly influential "Asian values" philosophy, which in turn developed into a major political ideology centered upon Singapore. The colonial Church, curiously enough, played an important role in fostering and developing Asian identity, and this has undoubtedly contributed to the evolution of the Singaporean Christianity observable today. Mostly as a matter of strategy rather than magnanimity, it may be said, the colonial Church tolerated considerable local diversity in Christian expression, and this was actually inspired by the legislation underpinning the colonial Church itself. The East India Company Act of 1813, also known as the Charter Act, had extended the Established Church's domain to Britain's growing colonial possessions, and Church leaders, grateful for these powers, cautiously entrusted the colonial Church to bishops who were moderates with no particular agenda to advance. This reflected the practice for appointments in the home dioceses of the Church of England, where moderate bishops, who might in retrospect be called liberals, were increasingly seen as being the most capable of holding the Church's conflicting factions together (Wilson 1863: 7). As the nineteenth century progressed, factional influences did impact the colonial Church, thanks to Evangelical- and Catholic-leaning missionary societies, but their areas of influence did not usually overlap and serious clashes were avoided (O'Donovan 2008: 4–5). The missionary societies' effect was subtle, however; as they were effectively promoting their own diverse and sometimes unconventional takes on Christian worship, they in turn exercised patience with different local expressions as these developed. Singapore, like much of Southeast Asia, came under Anglo-Catholic influence, which, as a non-mainstream expression of worship diversity, helped to normalize further worship diversity. The familiar spectrum of theological and liturgical traditions was and still is observable in Southeast Asia, but it integrates a wide variety of local, regional, global, and experimental influences (Kuo 2016: 21–22).

Diversity in general is a feature of Singapore's Christian community, which brings together individuals from a range of ethnic, social, and economic backgrounds, but it is perhaps not the most striking feature. Singaporean Christians tend to be well-educated and young; over 40 percent of them are graduates and more than 70 percent of new converts are under thirty (Chin 2017: 4). This is consistent with the comparative youthfulness of the general population, within which the number of Christians has increased more than fivefold since 1970. Christian growth has especially benefited independent, contemporary, charismatic churches, suggesting younger generations' estrangement from traditional denominations and their conventional methods; within those historic denominations, too, the most successful churches are those that embraced contemporary and charismatic worship styles. The influence of Pentecostalism both upon and from within the historic denominations in Singapore, including the Anglican Church, has been immense (Goh 2005: 16). Pentecostal "megachurches" with four- and five-figure Sunday attendances are frequently accused of preaching a false "prosperity gospel" focused on materialist aspiration, but these accusations themselves have also been criticized; they have been called knee-jerk assessments that disparage authentic attempts to contextualize the gospel, in a fast-paced, high-cost, wealth-focused environment, which speak directly to people's immediate concerns as they perceive them (Kuo 2016: 22). Closer examination of the Christian community has revealed an even more eclectic combination of consistency, conformity, individualism, and convention-breaking than expected, leading Terence Chong and Yew-Foong Hui, in their landmark survey for the Institute of Southeast Asian Studies (ISEAS), to describe Christianity in Singapore as a "heterogeneous middle class faith" with a broadly conservative membership. These descriptors may seem to clash with the spontaneous worship, spectacular healings, and high-adrenaline preaching of Pentecostal Christianity, and while this apparent paradox has been challenging for the historic denominations, they have by no means completely failed to meet that challenge (Chong and Hui 2013: 14–15, 20–21).

From its beginnings as part of the original colonial plan of the great visionary Raffles, the Anglican Church in Singapore replicated the British Empire's ability to adapt and diversify. Converting the locals was, perhaps surprisingly, never a central part of the plan, and for much of the nineteenth-century evangelism was officially discouraged. Negative interpretations of the colonial Church fostered an image of Victorian missionaries as overzealous "converters" who made "conversion" synonymous with "coercion." The topic remains controversial, but proactive conversion efforts are very much part of the current Singaporean and Southeast Asian Christian experience, even though the context may make it unpopular, divisive, or even legally problematic to change religion. Coercive or incentivized conversion tactics are generally eschewed, and charitable works must be strictly "no strings attached" (Green 2001: 26–27); such tactics would arguably fool few people in twenty-first-century Singapore anyway (Ballard and Pritchard 2006: 149). Christians agree that genuinely motivated conversions are both desirable and, fortunately for the Churches, still happening, but everything else surrounding the question of conversion is subject to a debate that is as old as Christianity itself (Walls 2004: 2). Understandings of conversion may follow denominational lines, but a variety of conversion theologies can coexist within a denomination, as is the case within Anglicanism. Some traditions see conversion as a "punctiliar" event, whether a spiritual "seeing the light" moment or a sacramental rite of passage, but time-specific or "crisis" conversions may not lead to an enduring commitment; lasting conversion tends to be a process rather than an event (Green 2001: 27). For many new Christians, conversion is most effectively achieved through the kind of informal, supportive, communitarian program at which contemporary churches often excel. The current "growth" Christian traditions, such as Pentecostalism, emphasize outreach based on processes of befriending, personal connections, and one-to-one evangelization, though without excluding the possibility of "thunderbolt" conversions (Peace 2004: 9–13).

The troubling image of the coercive, convert-seeking Victorian missionary, which was not a universal reality, and the corresponding perception of missionary work as mere complicity in colonial expansion have strongly influenced scholarship, which explains why mission was often overlooked in conventional histories of British religion (Cox 2008: 3–7). It has been taken for granted that beyond what Andrew Porter called the "complicity paradigm" there is little to say about nineteenth-century mission, unless the intention is to exonerate or rehabilitate the Victorian Church; this assumption encouraged a perception of mission history as a denominational rather than scholarly activity (Porter 2004: 2–6). These common misapprehensions, and the occasional emergence of an actual apologist for colonialism, have impeded a fuller understanding of colonial Church history, and relevant scholarship has struggled to find its place. In related fields, such as postcolonial studies, mission was generally ignored because the field is so avowedly secular, while some Church historians misinterpreted overseas mission as a simple extension of the Church's philanthropic activity. Gradually, however, the boundaries between colonial history, Church history, and mission studies broke down (Cox 2008: 4–6). Even so, some regions, such as Southeast Asia, still failed to attract scholarly attention in favor of the vaster British imperial topics of India and Africa (Porter 2004: 2–3).

One of the difficulties in examining religion in Southeast Asia is that there is, historically, neither a long tradition nor a strong tradition of reliable data collection. This problem has its roots in colonial times, when records were either inadvertently skewed by bias and prejudice or deliberately manipulated to serve certain interests, but analogous difficulties have persisted in recent decades, in the form of cautiousness in the face of authority and a fear of challenging official versions of events (Goh 2005: 14–15). Clampdowns on activism in the 1970s, anti-government conspiracy scares in the 1980s, and the inflexible Maintenance of Religious Harmony Act in the 1990s all placed pressure on Christian scholars and transformed data gathering into a suspect activity, dogged by reservations and circumspection (Chong and Hui 2013: 2–7). These factors add to the predictable challenges of monitoring a movement in rapid evolution like Christianity in Singapore, meaning that studies struggle to stay up to date. In estimating the number of Singaporean Anglicans, even more fundamental difficulties arise, such as the absence of agreed definitions, criteria, and metrics for assessing belonging; these are the classic problems of measuring religious affiliation or membership, enhanced by different cultural understandings of these concepts. The four dioceses of the PSEA, including Singapore, are widely believed to have, collectively, between 100,000 and 125,000 loosely defined members, with around a fifth of these in Singapore. However, modes of participation and meanings of belonging vary hugely; there are cases of dual and triple religious affiliation, cases of casual attendance but not official belonging, and cases of non-attendance but heartfelt belonging, which all combine to make a reliable estimate appear unachievable (Jarvis 2022: 160). It seems fair to say, in any case, that the Anglican Church's impact and contribution outweigh its size (Goh 2005: 15). Numbers, furthermore, do not express the cultural significance and social collateral of being Christian in Singapore. Just as the importance of Singapore itself is in vast disproportion to its small size, the same may be said of its Anglican Church (Goh 2005: 35).

The study of the Anglican Church in Singapore is impeded by some significant difficulties but facilitated by a range of excellent resources. The SPG (Society for the Propagation of the Gospel in Foreign Parts) papers at Oxford's Bodleian Libraries, the Colonial Office Archives at The National Archives (TNA), and Bishop John Leonard Wilson's papers at the Imperial War Museum are all invaluable. Of special relevance are the *Singapore Church Record Books*, held by the outstanding National Archives (NAS) at the National Library in Singapore. These so-called books are actually a kind of unpublished miscellany, a vast and eclectic collection of correspondence, notes, pamphlets, minutes, accounts, and assorted ephemera, which have been preserved and bound ad hoc in nine roughly chronological volumes with no systematic page numbering. The NAS also curates the archives of the Diocese of Singapore, accessible with individual item-by-item permission from the diocese. The loss of archive materials due to deterioration, destruction, and environmental factors is a recurring feature of researching Southeast Asia; even one hundred years ago, humidity and white ants were found to have devoured diocesan records (*Singapore Church Record Book* vol. 7, 1902–15: 251). There are also qualitative problems with nineteenth-century sources; missionary society records, for example, can be rich in minutiae and thoroughly preoccupied with the inner workings of the organization (Cox 2002: 3); there is much pride, propaganda, and prejudice to wade through (Maughan 2014: 16). The question of sources presents serious obstacles, therefore, but the situation is not hopeless. Many old, interesting, and previously difficult-to-access sources, including older published items, are now accessible thanks to free online collections. Outstanding among these is Project Canterbury (anglicanhistory.org), an indispensable, digitalized, intercontinental collection of old and out-of-print Anglican documents, brainchild of the multitalented Richard Mammana. The Internet Archive (archive.org) is also a goldmine of elusive older works, such as the early published correspondence of Sir Stamford Raffles. To all of these institutions, curators, and facilitators, past and present, a huge debt of gratitude is owed.

The time is ripe to reappraise the Anglican Church's engagement with the British Empire and the cognate phenomena of colonial and postcolonial Christianity, especially in Asia. Scholars in diverse fields seek a more comprehensive understanding of all things Asian and global-south; meanwhile, global-north and Western societies strive to balance uncomfortable colonial pasts with their current, ethical self-understandings. Growth in both religious allegiance and religious diversity worldwide have defied the direst twentieth-century predictions; the world is becoming more religious and more religiously diverse, developments fueled by a litany of political and geopolitical upheavals over the past four decades (Zurlo et al. 2022: 72). The study of world religions and religion in Asia, and of world Christianity and Christianity in Asia are, in consequence, vibrant and expanding fields, especially as increasing interaction between scholars and stakeholders enhances and internationalizes the conversation. Some Christian organizations may still struggle to break free from obsolete Eurocentric, West-centric, and global-north-centric mindsets, within which notions of a "normative" Christianity endure; the idea that Asia may now be performing, within Christianity, the defining role once enjoyed by Europe may be viscerally resisted. Attachments to the idea of a normative Christianity tend to be partnered with a certain worldview that has its own default package of values, economic relations, and conceptions of being "civilized" (or, the preferred euphemism, "developed"), just as these attachments did in colonial times. In Europe and North America, Church leaders and Church members seek to comprehend and contain an intensifying north-south tension (or divide) in global Christianity, amidst the creeping realization that this division may expose the true nature of the postcolonial dynamic between former colonizer and former colonized. These real and consequential concerns point to a story that needs to be told (Chong and Hui 2013: 2; Johnson and Zurlo 2017: 49–51; Musa 2023: 1).

Chapter One

"To Pave the Way for Better Things"

The Arrival of Church and Empire in Southeast Asia and Singapore

Christianity in Southeast Asia may be described as a relatively recent phenomenon, especially in terms of having a significant impact, but, as with many aspects of the region, the Southeast Asian religious landscape is more complex than first impressions suggest. Southeast Asia consists of eleven nations lying to the east and southeast of the Indian subcontinent and to the south and southwest of mainland China. It is made up of the modern-day states (in alphabetical order) Brunei, Cambodia, East Timor, Indonesia, Laos, Malaysia, Myanmar (or Burma), the Philippines, Singapore, Thailand, and Vietnam. These nations have a number of things in common, not least that they have all been profoundly influenced and shaped by their interactions with the old Western colonial powers; nearly all of Southeast Asia was once under colonial control. The Western powers' interest in Southeast Asia was initially due to the prospect of acquiring valuable and highly-prized natural products; first spices, and then metals, gems, rubber, and teak. Trading posts turned into colonies, whence further explorations and conquests could be made. All of the colonizing powers in Southeast Asia brought Christianity with them, beginning in the early sixteenth century with the Portuguese in modern-day peninsular Malaysia and the Spanish in the Philippines (Goh 2005: 1–2).

Another common inheritance of the Southeast Asian nations is that prior to their encounters with the European colonial powers and Christianity, they were exposed to Asia's own powerful cultural, philosophical, and religious influences; from India in the west came Hinduism and Buddhism, and from China in the north came Taoism (or Daoism) and Confucianism. The

European colonial powers, therefore, in bringing Christianity to Southeast Asia, entered an already well-occupied, fairly stable, and quite complex religious arena. Alongside these important influences from other parts of Asia, each nation of the region also developed its own range of religious customs, belief systems, spiritualities, and hybrids of two or more of these. This complexity did not make any of the local religions easy to supplant. Deep-rooted beliefs "in spirits of earth or air or water" and in one "life force" being present in all living things and in objects such as leaves and stones, would defy missionaries' teachings, even after ostensible conversion to Christianity, and they persisted among many Muslims "beneath a veneer" of Islam, along with their associated rites of passage (Ferguson-Davie 1921: 16). This situation did not make lasting conversions impossible but it did test the incoming religions' capacity to accommodate and adapt; instead of superseding local religious traditions they fused with them. This fusion tended to be most effective when core values such as understandings of leadership and governance, as well as basic religious principles, found affirmation and validation in the other belief system, exemplified by the arrival of Islam in the Malay Archipelago in the thirteenth century; Islam showed surprising flexibility in accommodating spirit beliefs and even elements of Hinduism (Goh et al. 2021: 7). The result is that none of the world religions present in Southeast Asia, whether Islam, Christianity, or Buddhism, is a monolith (Gomes 1911: 175–77; Ponniah 2000: 32). Identifiable shared values, crowned by endorsement from a stable ruler, proved to be a highly effective combination, conducive to peace and trade, and apparently impossible to dislodge.

European colonization, however, was not primarily about converting people to Christianity. The main motivations for colonizing were economic and commercial, not religious, nor even ideological (Roxborogh 2014: 98). The Western powers' pursuit of wealth, and the enriching potential of Southeast Asia, meant that control over the region was contested from outside and resisted from within. Achieving and retaining control, it was believed, demanded comprehensive cultural dominion, with the diffusion and normalization of Western values, and the Church's involvement in this was seen as highly advantageous. The Western powers' economic representatives faced a similar challenge to the spiritual representatives, however; neither would find, in the local populations, a tabula rasa upon which to inscribe their values and precepts. The situation was particularly disillusioning for those missionaries with a highly developed sense of their own divine authority to enlighten unbelievers; only very gradually would they begin to understand the process of introducing new religious ideas as a negotiation rather than an imposition (Koepping 2006: 59). Faced with apparent indifference from resident populations, Church leaders were at times dismissive and at times openly hostile, deriding local belief systems as "ignorance, pollution, [and] enmity against God and holiness," in the words of Daniel Wilson (1778–1858), fifth Bishop of Calcutta, whose jurisdiction included Singapore (Wilson 1863: 13). Christian missionaries would eventually realize that Christianity could only ever gain ground if it was perceived as being not in conflict with, and potentially harmonious with, previously established beliefs and customs. Harmonious coexistence of local belief systems with Christianity was indeed possible, as it was with Islam. Meetings of two religions, the missionaries learned, do not have to trigger a fight for hegemony, especially when the communities' primary social concerns of "food, fiancées and funerals" can be mutually acknowledged and respected (Koepping 2006: 60).

Harmonious coexistence of religions may have sounded like syncretism to some missionaries' ears, but it was already a well-established phenomenon outside of Southeast Asia; Christianity itself, since its beginnings, mutated and melded as it crossed cultural and physical borders. In today's Christian-influenced Western world, non-Christian religions are frequently discussed according to Christian terminology such as congregation and worship, even when these terms are not strictly accurate or appropriate. Non-Christian theologies are often evaluated according to Christian concepts, such as revelation and salvation, and other religions' sacred texts are presumed to have the same kind of role and centrality as the Bible has for Christians (Hoskins 2014: S302). In Southeast Asia, similarly, the major world religions have often been observed through a local lens and interpreted according to local concepts, to arrive at a communicable popular form of each religion. How exactly this happens, how boundaries are negotiated, and how breaches of those boundaries are managed, varies from place to place. Ultimately, however, Christianity in a supposed pure form, whatever that might mean, is not to be found; this has universal implications for discussing "true" Christianity. The most successful missionaries were arguably those who accepted that Christianity complements the religious landscape of Southeast Asia rather than competing with it, resulting in what has been called a symbiosis of religions, rather than religions eclipsing or merging with one another (Pieris 2004: 261–63).

DENOMINATIONAL AND POLITICAL CONTRASTS AND CONFLICTS

From the political point of view, the need to tolerate and accommodate local belief systems, as described above, was not seen as an impediment to the dissemination of Christian and Western values, but as a realistic method of spreading them in locally acceptable forms. The diplomatic, harmonious approach to introducing Christianity was appreciated by colonial administrators; whether personally devout, religiously indifferent, or even anticlerical, they recognized religion's usefulness for promoting their cultural and moral values, while also providing justification for their economic and military presence. Once the immediate goals of colonial expansion were achieved, religion could be utilized in a number of ways to help develop a lasting, influential, and socially integrated presence in Southeast Asia. Colonial officials were therefore generally supportive of the goal of introducing Christianity, but they did not necessarily appreciate the difficulties faced by missionaries, such as dealing with pre-established local beliefs. Among the Christian denominations, the extent of this difficulty varied; Roman Catholic missionaries had the challenging task of introducing a complex institutional heritage and a set of intricate rituals, but they had convincing symbols of authority and considerable corporate experience of mission in their toolkit. The Catholic combination of moral authority and empire building, in a Christendom-inspired society governed by parallel spiritual and secular powers, was a well-established and exportable societal vision, but it also presented Catholic missionaries with problems that Protestant missionaries did not face (Bell 2004: 425). Catholic missionaries on the ground were generally open to accommodating local customs and beliefs, and they were flexible with regard to who could convert, whether individuals or whole ethnic communities, but these generous approaches would never be officially endorsed by their hierarchy. Colonial expansion, from the sixteenth century onwards, was contemporaneous with increasingly strict centralization in the Catholic Church and consolidation of papal control, but new Catholic converts in the colonies could hardly be expected to develop a strong sense of veneration for alien institutions in unknown, faraway lands (Keith 2012: 24–26).

The institutional commitment technically being demanded of Catholic converts may therefore be considered unrealistic, and the path to conversion presented by Protestants and Anglicans might be expected to allow for looser forms of adherence. Anglican mission thinking, however, was only at the beginning of a long process of evolution in the first half of the nineteenth century, during which the colonial Church's objective would go from ministering solely to colonists to evangelizing the whole human race. Eventual Protestant revival movements, furthermore, tended to not only energize the Church's mission but infuse it with a sense of urgency, whereas the centuries-old Catholic missionary mindset tended to have its gaze fixed on the long term. A variety of attitudes would therefore be observed among Anglican missionaries, with some of them committed to toleration and accommodation, while others insisted on the exclusive and dogmatic adoption of Christianity. Neither approach guaranteed success, but it would become very difficult to deny that demanding absolutely exclusive adherence only succeeded in dividing communities (Koepping 2006: 60).

The colonial experience in the Protestant-ruled Dutch East Indies, Borneo, Burma, Malaya, and Singapore, though far from a uniform experience, was observably different from the colonial experience in regions under Roman Catholic colonizers. The confessional differences between Protestant Holland and Britain, and the Roman Catholic powers of Spain, Portugal, and France, were reflected in political rivalry, commercial competition, and in their different approaches to colonization. The Protestant Dutch, and especially the British, prioritized trade and subjugated all other objectives to it; good trading relations meant keeping the peace, and consequently they aimed to avoid clashes with local religions. The presence of missionaries in the colonies was certainly allowed and appreciated, but under quite strict conditions, such as those established in the late eighteenth and early nineteenth centuries by the powerful British East India Company (EIC). The EIC was a private company to which administration of Britain's eastern colonies had been granted. Successive generations of missionaries would assess the EIC's conditions, which effectively prohibited serious evangelization, as being overly restrictive, and some blamed the EIC's rules for smothering the early development of the local Churches; others placed the blame on insufficient Church oversight, because places like Singapore and Malaya were not granted their own bishop(s) for such a long time; both accusations contain some truth, and the reasons behind them are interrelated (Loh 1963: 3–4). Some Anglican clergy were critical of what they saw as their Church's lackluster approach to evangelization, complaining that its leaders, lulled into indifference by comfortable lives back home, fundamentally lacked passion for the divine mission (Buckley 1902, vol. 2: 660–61).

Already hindered by restrictions on missionary work, Anglicans were also acutely aware of being late starters on the Christian scene in Southeast Asia, compared to the Roman Catholics. Some Anglican missionaries admired the zeal of their Catholic counterparts, but they were critical of the coercive conversion tactics rumored to have been used by them, and they generally saw themselves as wholly different and better-motivated than the Catholics (Strong 2007: 11). Anglicanism was, after all, greatly influenced by the Protestant belief in freedom of conscience; it was considered anathema to enforce Christianity with threats or legislation, and it was perhaps hard to see how this could ultimately benefit the empire anyway. Missionaries were also aware, however, that it was not up to any of them to set the priorities; the Church's endeavors were heavily dependent on its relationship with the colonial administration, as dysfunctional, frustrating, and inconclusive as that relationship was turning out to be (Cox 2008: 10–11).

The EIC's prohibition of aggressive missionary work could be seen as justifiable caution, prompted by fears of real or imagined Roman Catholic-style coercive conversion tactics; this caution seemed to make commercial sense, and it also sat well with the Protestant ethic of freedom of conscience. The Anglican Church would bear the brunt of the EIC's prohibition, because the two organizations were official representatives of one and the same empire, and they worked under each other's watchful eye. Later, when the EIC's restrictions began to be relaxed, the prohibitive ethos remained in the form of indifference, wariness, and sometimes hostility in official circles with regard to spreading the word of God, with received wisdom still dictating that robust missionary work was simply bad for business. This conflictive reality contrasts with the perception of Christian missionaries as outright accomplices of the colonizers, part of an "unholy alliance" between Christianity and colonialism (Pieris 2004: 256). There certainly were instances of missionaries cooperating too closely with the colonial masters; some of them enjoyed excessive material comfort, some were too quick to call for the military when faced with local resistance, and others were overly keen on adventurism and swashbuckling, but it is erroneous to conclude that all Christian missionary activity was just part and parcel of Western colonialist ambition (Evers 2014: 68). The relationship between religion and empire, however, was chronically ill-defined and unstable; imperial authorities tended to see individual missionaries, at best, as inconsequential figures, and at worst they denigrated them as cranks and misfits. This further challenges the idea of an unholy alliance. British missionaries did come from a position of considerable security, but this security did not necessarily stem from, or translate into, privileges conferred by the empire. The nineteenth century witnessed a religious revival in Britain, encouraging the belief that a propitious historical moment for spreading Christianity had arrived. This timing provided outgoing colonial missionaries with a confidence boost; the age of colonial expansion and the occurrence of a Christian revival coincided chronologically, but this coincidence should not be mistaken for correlation (Cox 2008: 3–4).

FORMALIZING THE BRITISH COLONIAL RELIGIOUS INVESTMENT

Long before the Victorian colonial boom, influential Evangelical Anglicans had drawn positive links between Protestantism, colonialism, and mission. The British government was highly receptive to this thinking, as demonstrated by its support for the foundation, in 1701, of the Society for the Propagation of the Gospel in Foreign Parts (SPG), which eventually came to be identified with the Catholic tradition within Anglicanism, rather than the Evangelical one (Strong 2007: 2–10). Before 1701, the Church of England did conduct some foreign mission work, but not in an organized way. Shortly after the Church's separation from Rome, Archbishop of Canterbury Thomas

Cranmer hastened to provide two chaplains for the French port of Calais, at that time (1534–35) Britain's only foreign possession. Forty-three years later, on May 31, 1578, when seafarer Martin Frobisher sailed in search of the northwest passage to India, a chaplain, named Robert Wolfall, was officially appointed to accompany the expedition; Wolfall had the privilege of being the first cleric of the reformed Church of England to minister on American shores. To "discover and to plant Christian inhabitants in places convenient" in America was the main objective of the expedition of Sir Humphrey Gilbert, who took possession of Newfoundland in 1583, and to whom was granted, by Queen Elizabeth I, the first charter for the founding of an English colony. Similar powers were given, in 1584, to Gilbert's half-brother, Sir Walter Raleigh; Wingandacoa was discovered in that year and renamed Virginia (it is now within North Carolina). The first band of colonists sent there included the astronomer and ethnographer Thomas Harriot (1560–1621), who has been described as the first Anglican missionary to America (Pascoe 1895: 1).

Early English colonization in all its aspects was clearly focused on America, and Anglican missionary efforts in that direction grew to be extensive and more overtly dedicated to wholesale evangelization than they would later be in Asia. The introduction of Christianity into Southeast Asia, including future British possessions, also began in an earnest way in the sixteenth century, though not under the English. The Portuguese established a presence in Melaka (Malacca) in 1511, though it is likely that small trading settlements in the area had already included pockets of Christians for around two hundred years (Gillman and Klimkeit 1999: 311–12). There are, in fact, archeological indications of Christian settlements in the northwest of the Malay Peninsula as early as the seventh century, but very little is known about them (Goh 2005: 1–2). Melaka passed from the Portuguese to the Dutch in 1641, but Portuguese influence lives on in many Malay words, including the word for church, gereja, and the region's oldest surviving gerejas are found in Melaka. The first British presence dates to 1786, with the arrival of an expedition to seize Pulau Pinang (the island of Penang), which the British named Prince of Wales Island. Anglicans were no doubt present among traders who subsequently based themselves in Penang, and from around 1795 they were also present in Dutch-held Melaka, which the British wanted to take control of. Penang had its first ordained Anglican minister in 1805, and its first church, St. George's, was completed in 1818 (Roxborogh 2014: 1–18). Modeled on St. Mary's, Madras (Chennai) in India, St. George's was the first Anglican church to be built by the British east of India. Penang was one of Britain's four future "Straits Settlements," along with Melaka, control of which alternated between the Dutch and the British during the first two decades of the nineteenth century. With Penang and Melaka, the other important British territory in the region was Bencoolen, on the west coast of the island of Sumatra, in modern-day Indonesia. Noticeably absent from the list of colonial ambitions at the beginning of the nineteenth century was Singapore, which was considered insignificant.

Control of Southeast Asia was tenuous, unstable, and hotly contested, and its economic importance was critical; the need for all-embracing dominion of the region generated further official support for the religious aspect of colonization. Parliament in London increasingly framed its support for colonial ventures as a moral imperative rather than as a purely economic one, and installing the Church came to be seen as a priority for colonial government, not an add-on. It was expressly intended, in other words, that British colonization should have a religious dimension, both at the practical and philosophical levels, and this intention was soon to be enshrined in government policy. In an atmosphere of new impetus being given to colonial expansion, the Charter Act (also called the East India Company Act) of 1813 outlined, among other things, Britain's supposed sacred duty to provide Christian instruction to the non-Christian peoples who came under its control. This contrasted greatly with previous legislation, which ruled out any concerted missionary strategy and mandated official religious neutrality in colonial territories. The existing policies were not abandoned immediately and would take even longer to depart from the general consciousness, but the new legislation was affirmed the following year with the establishment of the Bishopric of Calcutta, belonging to the Church of England, covering all of South and Southeast Asia, and even as far as Australia (Glendinning 2012: 242).

Dissemination of the Christian religion now became explicit and central to the government's colonial vision, and this vision would, to a significant degree, inspire, shape, and define what came to be known as the golden age of Victorian mission. This vision was considered superior to what could be seen as fashionable and transitory philosophies of the age, touting equality and fraternity; the British Empire would deliver nothing less than actual salvation, through "Christianization" and its purported synonym, civilization. The boldness of Parliament's new direction was somewhat moderated by the caution for which the Church of England was famed, however. At a distance of three centuries since their independence from Rome, Anglicans nurtured a perception of their Church as a bridge between contrasting and opposed interpretations of Christianity, sympathetic to the reformers' zeal for the gospel while retaining ancient order and the sacraments. This understanding of Anglicanism as a middle path or "via media" that reconciles Evangelical and Catholic schools of thought was arguably designed to address the Church's nineteenth-century internal woes, rather than being a dispassionate reading of sixteenth- or seventeenth-century Church history. Even so, it was not an excessively contrived reading, and its theological rather than historical rationale has endured; Anglicans' way of emphasizing their appreciation for both scripture and historic Church order has quite effectively sustained the perception of Catholic and Evangelical as being not only compatible but inextricably connected, and not just in theory, but in essence (Ramsey 2009: 175–88).

Anglicanism established and sought to protect this reputation for reconciling different points of view. Throughout all the violent upheavals and countless disputes in the Church of England's history, it was maintained, a clear but undogmatic set of core beliefs and practices had been adhered to, while being tolerant and accommodating of difference. By the beginning of the great British colonial boom, the British government preferred to appoint moderate bishops to all dioceses of the Church of England, because they were perceived as being most capable of holding the Church's opposing wings together, and Calcutta would be no exception to this cautious preference. The desired attitude in a bishop was "mild [but] firm churchmanship," as the Bishop of Calcutta and first Metropolitan of India, Daniel Wilson, described it; "I have maintained [this position] all my life," he wrote, "in the face of High Church principles and No Church principles." Wilson considered this diplomatic balance to be "of infinite importance" in the complex colonial Church (Wilson 1863: 7). The government's tactic of choosing bishops from the Church's middle ground, as long as orthodoxy in theology, scripture, order, and personal morals were seen as non-negotiable, worked for many decades. Church disputes would increasingly spring from the stand-off between Evangelicals and Catholics, but both streams could be peacefully accommodated, and their basic orthodoxy was not in doubt (O'Donovan 2008: 4–5). By the time Wilson's career as Bishop of Calcutta began, he had more immediate cause to worry; his four predecessors had all had their tenures cut short by dying in office. The first, Thomas Fanshaw Middleton, died of sunstroke aged fifty-three; Middleton's replacement, Reginald Heber, died less than three years later, aged only forty-two; Thomas James, the third post-holder, was also aged forty-two and died after less than a year in office; John Turner died aged forty-five after less than two years in office (Wilson 1863: 6).

Despite Parliament's preference for mild Church leaders who eschewed the extremes and wisely mediated between Anglicanism's factions, the reality of colonial mission would force the landscape to change. Bishop Wilson claimed to uphold the middle-ground ideal, and although he did not openly sympathize with the forms of High Churchmanship that would eventually become dominant in Southeast Asia, he humorously disparaged the "unprincipled" Low Church position as being "No Church" at all (Wilson 1863: 7). The need for trained, dedicated missionaries for Southeast Asia, of any persuasion, would become increasingly apparent, however, and the Church's main missionary societies were allied to one or other of the Church's opposing wings, such as the Anglo-Catholic SPG and the Evangelical-oriented Church Missionary Society (CMS). The effect of this was that individual missionaries were rarely mainstream Anglicans; they were often unconventional and sometimes quite eccentric. Anglo-Catholics in general were committed to reviving rituals and practices that clashed with the Church's standardized worship; this would, ironically, make Anglo-Catholic missionaries more accepting of local nuances in worship, more open to ethnic traditional influences, and ultimately more supportive of the development of indigenous Church identity and character (Maughan 2014: 113). Their openness to local input and ethnic integration in the Church would gradually influence attitudes in wider colonial society too.

SINGAPORE: RAFFLES, RELIGION, AND A REGION TRANSFORMED

In 1818, the small but significant British colony of Bencoolen, Sumatra, was governed by a young man called Sir Thomas Stamford Bingley Raffles (1781–1826). Stamford Raffles was committed to trade (through the EIC), the advancement of the British Empire, and his own broadly Christian values. He was born on board the ship *Ann,* just off the harbor of Port Morant, Jamaica, on July 5, 1781. He was the only surviving son of Benjamin Raffles, one of the oldest captains on the West India trade route, sailing out of the port of London. Beyond this, little is known about Raffles's family. The surname appears in the oldest registers held at Beverley, East Yorkshire, both in those of the Minster church and St. Mary's; it seems that five centuries ago Raffles's ancestors resided there, and one of them died during his tenure as Mayor of the borough. From there it is believed that the family moved to Berwick upon Tweed, and then, in the days of Raffles's great-grandfather, to London. Raffles was baptized at Eaton Bishop, in Herefordshire, where his mother had taken him to visit her brother, the Reverend John Lindeman, who was the incumbent. Raffles's beginnings were not especially privileged. At the age of just fourteen his relatives paid a bond to have him taken on as a clerk at India House in London, the headquarters of the EIC (Glendinning 2012: 7–17). Raffles forever regretted that his formal education was cut short, and though he resolved to become a lifelong self-student, he felt that he never recovered from this disadvantage (Buckley 1902, vol. 1: 1). After ten years, Raffles went out to Southeast Asia for the EIC and rose to senior positions, making his name during the brief period of British rule in Java. He was knighted in 1817, and the following year he was appointed Lieutenant-Governor of Bencoolen, on the southwest coast of Sumatra (Raffles 1835, vol. 1: 1–3).

From Bencoolen, Raffles looked east toward Singapore, an island with strategic potential and almost no inhabitants; there was a small settlement of about a hundred Malays from mainland Johor to the north, and smaller clusters of indigenous people, reputedly devoted to fishing and piracy, who became completely assimilated with the Malay settlers. There were already a few dozen Chinese settlers as well, making up a grand total of about one hundred and fifty inhabitants at the time when Raffles proposed the colonization of Singapore (Saw 1969: 37). Raffles did not aspire so much to gain subjects or territory, but rather to secure a port deep enough to anchor a battleship; this, Raffles felt, would send out a message sufficient to break the Dutch monopoly of the region and expand trade for Britain. Raffles's plan received tacit (and therefore plausibly deniable) approval from his superiors; he quickly brokered a deal with the Sultan of Johor, the mainland state to the north of Singapore (Singapore had been a dependency of Johor until then) and, on Friday, January 29, 1819, the British flag was hoisted at Singapore. The date has been disputed, and it is sometimes reported as February 29, 1819, which was a non-existent date (Boulger 1897: 306–7). What is undisputed, however, is that by opening the island to free trade and free residence, Raffles launched Singapore on a trajectory to become the greatest port in the East and one of world history's greatest cities (Raffles 1835, vol. 2: 6–12). This step, Raffles wrote triumphantly to his friend William Wilberforce in September 1819, "has given us command of the [Southeast Asian] archipelago as well in peace as in war [*sic*]: our commerce will extend to every part, and British principles will be known and felt throughout" (Raffles 1835, vol. 2: [44–57] 53–54).

Long before Raffles's day, the very first colonizer of Singapore was also believed to have sailed across from Sumatra; according to tradition he was a prince from Palembang, the Sumatran capital of the Buddhist Srivijaya Empire. This may have been Rajendracota Deva I (1014–44) of the Chola dynasty, ruler of Thanjavur (Tanjore) in modern-day Tamil Nadu state, India, who almost certainly led an attack on the island at some stage. Legend has it that the prince, to honor the leonine courage of his men, gave the island the Indian name of Singapore (Lion city), but the origins of the island's name have long been disputed. Javanese inscriptions and Chinese writings up to the end of the fourteenth century, long after the time of Rajendracota Deva I, use the island's Javanese name, Temasek or Temasik, from the word tasik (sea), and meaning "Place surrounded by sea." Malay colonists in the twelfth century may also have landed at Singapore before colonizing Melaka (Buckley 1902, vol. 1: 18–19). When it came to the British arrival, the colonization of Singapore followed their preferred method in Southeast Asia; not invading militarily as such, but stealthily achieving effective control through the facilitation of trade. This was generally done patiently and peacefully, a notable exception being the violent and costly colonial war being fought for Burma during the same period.

Britain's ambitions in the region received a boost from positive negotiations with the Dutch, with whom the Anglo-Dutch Treaty would later be signed. Bencoolen would be ceded to the Dutch, after which Penang (Prince of Wales Island) would become the most prominent settlement in the region; as mentioned above, Penang was the first settlement to receive a church and an Anglican chaplain, provided by the EIC. Singapore also began to attract interest, however, especially from people based in rival settlements, such as the Dutch colonies. News of the launch of a new, free port drew a much more diverse collection of prospectors, traders, and opportunity-hunters than some histories record, and they poured in almost immediately from India, China, and the Indonesian islands (Saw 1969: 37–38). Raffles was eager to stress the all-round superiority of "his" project in Singapore, compared to Penang: "Singapore, I am happy to say" he wrote in January 1820, "continues to rise most rapidly in importance and resources" (Raffles 1835, vol. 2: 71), but he craved greater recognition; "Were the value of Singapore properly appreciated, I am confident that all England would be in its favor," he wrote to his cousin, the Reverend Doctor Thomas Raffles, a Congregational minister, on July 17, 1820, adding (with some exaggeration) that "[Singapore] gives us the command of China and Japan, with Siam and Cambodia, Cochin China etc." (Raffles 1835, vol. 2: [131–36] 134). Singapore initially remained politically subordinate to Bencoolen, before being placed under the administrative supervision of Bengal in 1823, as its importance grew (Pascoe 1901, vol. 2: 696). Raffles's intuition about Singapore's destiny was gradually proving to be correct (Buckley 1902, vol. 1: 3).

Religious belief in general interested Raffles, and his vision of colonization certainly included religion. He was troubled by what he saw as the questionable moral environment of some colonies he had experienced, but he was also generally unimpressed by the behavior of Christians in those colonies; his support for the Church would remain tinged with reservations as a result (Raffles 1835, vol. 2: 37). Romanticized and quasi-hagiographic characterizations of Raffles as a devout, reborn Christian, fulfilling a divine plan in Singapore, are not supported by evidence (Sng 1980: 32–34). Raffles himself admitted that personal religious conviction was not part of his motivation; "All that I attempt is to pave the way for better things," he wrote to Wilberforce in September 1819; "I am far from lukewarm towards higher ends," he asserted, but his priority was "the general spread of moral principles" (Raffles 1835, vol. 2: [44–57] 50). This was clearly not incompatible with Christian missionary endeavors, but, conscious that others would share his wariness of unrestrained Church involvement, Raffles wrote thus to Wilberforce; "I am far from opposing missionaries, and the more that come out the better; but let them be enlightened men, and placed in connection with the schools, and under due control" (Raffles 1835, vol. 2: [44–57] 51).

Raffles had already correctly identified schools as being the most appropriate and unobtrusive missionary activity, presaging decades of impactful work in this field by generations of missionaries. True to his word to Wilberforce, Raffles granted permission to the Extra Ganges Mission of the interdenominational London Missionary Society (LMS) to establish a college in Singapore, "for the study of the Chinese language, and the extension of Christianity," as he wrote to his friend, the future Member of Parliament Sir Robert Harry Inglis (Raffles 1835, vol. 2: [28–39] 37). News of the nonconformist Protestant LMS's arrival may not have impressed the vehemently High-Church Anglican Inglis, but Raffles was clearly not concerned with such intricacies of Church life. The LMS had been based in Melaka since 1815 (Goh 2005: 7); it was led by Robert Morrison (1782–1834) and Raffles's friend William Milne (1785–1822), founder of Melaka's Anglo-Chinese College. Milne was broad-minded and well-informed, the kind of "enlightened man" that Raffles wanted in Singapore, regardless of religion (Glendinning 2012: 243); he was saddened by Milne's untimely death (Raffles 1835, vol. 2: 255).

Raffles, it is believed, personally allocated a piece of land, in 1823, for the first Anglican church in Singapore, though it would be quite a long time before construction began (Swindell 1929: 6). The future church site was on the Esplanade, where Raffles had first raised the Union Jack; with unintended symbolic irony, a Chinese temple had been set up there in the intervening time (Buckley 1902, vol. 1: 96–97). Raffles's own Christianity may have been nominal, but his support for the early presence of missionaries in Singapore became substantial. "There is no political objection whatever to missionaries in this part of the East," he repeatedly affirmed, writing to his Congregational minister cousin, Thomas, to tell him that Baptist missionaries (bringing printing presses, as was their custom) had also offered their services, which Raffles accepted; he also proudly informed his cousin of the launch of a Bible society, more schools, and the planned LMS college (Raffles 1835, vol. 2: 67–68). The LMS enjoyed mixed results in Singapore, but their own printing presses were also very active, as were those of the Bible society, producing the gospels in Malay and Javanese (Raffles 1835, vol. 2: 209, 260–61). The proposed college, however, would not materialize in the lifetimes of Raffles or his nonconformist missionary friends.

THE ARRIVAL AND ACCLIMATIZATION OF THE ANGLICAN CHURCH

Raffles died on July 5, 1826, his forty-fifth birthday; all but one of his five infant children had predeceased him. In that same year, Singapore was formally added to the Straits Settlements of Penang and Melaka. Also in 1826, the Anglican Church's corporate presence in Singapore officially began, with the appointment, by the EIC, of the Reverend Robert Burn (often mistakenly spelled Burns) as "residency chaplain." Prior to this date, the few Church of England members on the island were usually ministered to by chaplains of the EIC's fleet of ships, whenever a ship happened to call, if indeed it was carrying a chaplain (Loh 1963: 1). Burn's arrival led to the construction of a simple Anglican chapel at the northeast corner of North Bridge Road and Bras Basah (or Brass Bassa) Road, not to be confused with an earlier LMS chapel at the same location, on land donated by the EIC (Sng 1980: 32). The earliest plan of Singapore, Jackson's of 1822, calls that section of Bras Basah Road "Church Street" in reference to this earlier chapel, but the Jackson Plan takes the form of a proposed street layout, not an actual map. Within a few years discussions began for the construction of a major church just a block away from the chapel; this would become the first incarnation of St. Andrew's cathedral (Buckley 1902, vol. 1: 123–24, 286–90; vol. 2: 572).

The whole human landscape of Singapore was also changing. Increasing trade brought more Europeans and more laborers from India, especially Tamils from the southern Indian states, with significant numbers of Christians among them. Ever-larger numbers of Chinese immigrants also arrived, especially from the southern provinces of China, as well as Javanese immigrants and others. Throughout Singapore's modern history, all manner of crises and disasters in China would propel immigrants toward Singapore (Goh 2005: 36). The first census taken by the British recorded a population of 10,683, of which 4,500 were Malays, 3,317 were Chinese, and 2,681 were Indians, which leaves just 185 "others." The early censuses were quite haphazardly executed, however, and it is probable that the Javanese and European cohorts were much larger than these figures suggest (Saw 1969: 36–38). By the time of the chaplain Burn's arrival the number of Chinese incomers appears to have exceeded the demand for port labor, and many were rounded up and taken to the hinterland to work on hacking through the jungle to allow for development of the land; no easy task, and many lives were claimed by the large tiger population inhabiting the jungle (Buckley 1902, vol. 1: 200; vol. 2: 501–2). Burn died in post in 1833 and was replaced as residency chaplain by the Reverend Frederick J. Darrah (Swindell 1929: 4). Darrah is remembered for starting the first Sunday school, based at the small chapel (Buckley 1902, vol. 1: 230). By 1830, the population had risen to 16,634, and by the end of that decade it would reach 35,389 (Saw 1969: 39). Singapore was transformed, and in 1836 it would replace Penang as the center of the Straits Settlements colonial government, in a blow to Penang's standing from which it would never recover (Roxborogh 2014: 18).

In September 1834, Bishop Wilson of Calcutta approached the Malay Peninsula by sea, in the prelude to his first visit to Singapore. "The rising sun is shedding its glories over the whole scene," he wrote, onboard ship, "but oh, the misery of man! Malay pirates, Chinese idolaters . . . Mahometans [sic], Siamese Bhoodists [sic]; all is ignorance, pollution, enmity against God and holiness. They are strangers to themselves, to Christ, to peace. The prince of this world here revels in the blindness and woes of a fallen world" (Wilson 1863: 13). Wilson's horror mutated into enthusiasm upon arrival in Singapore the following month; "The view as we approached the island was enchanting," he wrote, noting that "the mass of shipping from all nations—American, Bornese [sic], Japanese, Celebes, Chinese—formed a tout ensemble perhaps nowhere to be equaled. . . . [W]e are in the midst of the gold and silver and tortoise-shell trade, as well as nutmeg, pepper, and all the spices which render our European food fragrant." Wilson laid the foundation stone of the original St. Andrew's church and noted the significance of the event; "The visit of a Bishop is of the utmost value. I speak not of the individual, but of the office, of course. The settlement has existed fifteen years, and this is the first time a Bishop has been here" (Wilson 1863: 15).

The prospects for Singapore were good indeed; the land was apparently fertile, rich in coconuts as well as spices, with the ground full of minerals and the surrounding waters teeming with fish. Cultivating cotton, coffee, sugar, and nutmeg were tried and soon declared hopeless, but the conditions were perfect for mango, pineapple, orange, and durian, which depend more on climate type than soil quality (Buckley 1902, vol. 1: 180). Malay inhabitants in the coastal areas retained their unfortunate reputation for piracy, while the inland Malays were devoted to agriculture, with, it was said, occasional warlike interludes. Cynics asserted that only the British presence stopped the Chinese and Malays from killing each other, but in general cohabitation was considered successful (Buckley 1902, vol. 1: 76). Beyond their own communities, the Malays interacted quite freely with the various newcomer groups; mixed relationships were not uncommon, giving rise to fringe communities of mixed-ethnicity families (Thompson 1951: 403). The apparent normalcy of Muslim Malays in mixed families, from today's perspective of regional and global Muslim revival, may be surprising, but Islamic laws were not as strictly enforced as they are today (Goh et al. 2021: 7).

A third residency chaplain, the Reverend Edward White, was in Singapore by 1837, and he died in post in 1845. Chaplains' life expectancies in office resembled those of the bishops; all of the first three chaplains, Burn, Darrah, and White, died quite young, one after another, complaining of similar ailments. Sages of the time apparently opined that they all adhered too strictly to teetotalism (Buckley 1902, vol. 1: 226). During White's time, discussions began for the foundation of a sailors' home or lodging house, but this would not be realized for many more years (*Singapore Church Record Book* vol. 1, 1838–63: unnumbered page). White's replacement was the Reverend Horatio Moule, sent from Calcutta; he came from a prominent multigenerational clergy family, and in some accounts he has been mistaken for his slightly better-known brother, the Reverend Henry Moule, the inventor of the patented dry earth toilet. Moule would remain in post for six years (Buckley 1902, vol. 2: 547). As the mixed-denomination Christian community increasingly interacted, Anglicans gently asserted their Church's special role, while having to acknowledge their small number and comparatively late arrival, for which they made due concessions. The naming of St. Andrew's church, for example, was in recognition of the significant material contribution made by the Scottish community; this contribution, understandably, came with a suggestion that the building could be used jointly between Protestant denominations, including the Presbyterians of the Church of Scotland. This proposal was quickly scaled down; Presbyterian services would sometimes be accommodated, but on an occasional, permission-only basis (*Singapore Church Record Book* vol. 1, 1838–63: unnumbered page).

The cost of the new church was almost eleven thousand Spanish dollars (the near-universal currency at the time) of which about 40 percent was paid by the government. The rest of the money came from the Society for Promoting Christian Knowledge (SPCK), the Church Building Fund, the Bishop of Calcutta, and the general public. St. Andrew's was consecrated in 1838 in the presence of Bishop Wilson and other dignitaries, including the governor of the Straits Settlements. The church building was 102 feet (31 meters) long and 95 feet (29 meters) wide, with porticos 20 feet (6 meters) wide on each side. The architect was George D. Coleman, superintendent of public works and Raffles's original Singapore architect of choice, after whom Coleman Street in Singapore is named. The church stood within an ample churchyard, measuring 540 feet (165 meters) east to west, and 720 (220 meters) north to south, "to secure the said church from desecration" (Swindell 1929: 15).

Members of the Scottish community met in 1846 to discuss the possibility of bringing a Presbyterian clergyman to Singapore, while graciously taking care to stress that they meant no offense to the Anglican chaplain, Moule. Once again, the Scots hoped to receive some help from the Anglicans, but the arrival of a Church of Scotland minister would not happen until 1856 (Buckley 1902, vol. 2: 453–54, 639). There is a distinct sense in all these Scottish matters, including the question of using St. Andrew's church, that the existence of Britain's other Established Church was generally ignored in Anglican circles. The new church building itself also proved to be a disappointment; it was unpopular and disaster-prone, with a leaking roof whose noise drowned out everything, including the Bishop of Calcutta on his

1851 visit (Buckley 1902, vol. 2: 539). The church was damaged by lightning in 1845 and again in 1849, and it closed its doors a few years later. St. Andrew's troubles did not end with its closure; rumors were rampant among the populace that the church was infested by evil spirits, to such an extent that even the impious Europeans now avoided it. In reality it was in such a dangerous state that services were held at alternative locations, including the court house and assembly rooms (Buckley 1902, vol. 2: 575–77).

CONCLUSION

The two main Protestant colonizing nations in Southeast Asia, the Dutch and the British, went into the region as a commercial capitalist venture, and initial management of the colonies was either entrusted wholly to private companies or, as in Singapore, it also depended on the initiative of certain pioneering individuals. Both Dutch and British colonists encouraged Protestant religious representatives to join them, but the private administrations, whether company or individual, tended to be wary of the potential for missionary activity to interfere with trade relations, and they wanted to keep it under control. Only later, after these private entities had been replaced with a proper colonial government apparatus, would Protestant missionaries begin to make real progress. Even then, reservations about missionary work would often feed into the legislation, regulations, and treaties that underpinned the management of the colonies. The Churches were generally grateful for whatever degree of freedom to operate they could secure, even with limitations (Goh 2005: 5–6). Contrary to some impressions, the spread of Christianity in Southeast Asia was not usually based on coercion, and instances of coercive behavior were attributable to particularly zealous individual officials rather than Church or government policy. Roman Catholic missionary work was reputed to be grossly coercive, as part of a supposed ideological imposition of Christendom, and while their Protestant counterparts disapproved, they would not entirely escape similar criticism.

Some colonial missionaries blamed official restrictions for smothering the early development of the local Churches, and some blamed the fact that places like Singapore did not have their own bishops for such a long time. Others lamented that the Church could only develop in "political" stages, keeping strictly in step with stealthy British colonization. In Singapore, Raffles actually showed little regard for the EIC's restrictions, and he pushed for missionary intervention, which he himself could keep in check. In all cases, mission aims were strictly prioritized; care for the British, then consider the locals, while respecting the Malays (Loh 1963: 3–5). Missionaries had to accept the fact, still relevant two hundred years later, that evangelism among the Muslim

Malays could be fruitless or unwelcome, and evangelism among other ethnic groups must accommodate the coexistence of previously held beliefs. Beyond strictly religious beliefs, every community had a range of customs addressing many aspects of life, from medicine to marriage, from infancy to interment, which Christianity was not about to supplant completely. Missionaries had a limited toolkit to offer, though their contributions to education and printing were hugely impactful.

The inclusion of religion on a political or economic agenda, especially when it is subordinated to that agenda, can lead to that religion being politicized (Roxborogh 2014: 98). In colonial settings, the reverse was often true; pioneers like Raffles encouraged the perception that their colonial ventures were imbued with evangelistic qualities and a Christian moral basis, thereby arguably religionizing their political aims as well. Men (they were invariably men) like Raffles were not mere adventurers or fortune-hunters, according to the most laudatory interpretations, but a kind of modern apostle, and their ultimate goal was to be bringers not of subjugation but of salvation. Only a true Christian, it was said, could have achieved such a God-willed expansion of the white man's capitalist civilization (O'Connor 2000: 63). It is clear that Raffles, in reality, took a utilitarian view of the presence of missionaries, many of whom he personally liked, but he had no personal investment in religion, unlike his wife. He never referred to Christ, repentance, or redemption; like many nominal Christians of his era, Raffles talked about Providence more readily than he talked about God, and he nearly always wrote "god" lowercase. This may have been a cryptic statement or a subconscious clue, but either way, it was an unconventional habit for his time. His attachment to Christianity may have been loose, but his attitude was pragmatic; he believed in the positive and constructive influence of Christian principles, and he was aware of the social benefits that a Church presence could bring to the colony (Glendinning 2012: 241–42).

Raffles's letters insisted on the coherence and continuity of "British power and Christian principles" (Raffles 1835, vol. 2: 326) and he saw British aims as being contiguous with Christian ones. In Raffles's own "created" universe of Singapore, it was clear who the father creator was; "It is a child of my own," he wrote of the island society that he had willed into existence, and of which he was understandably proud (Buckley 1902, vol. 1: 6). Raffles did not lack a darker side, exemplified in dramatic fashion by his apparent fascination (in theory rather than practice) with cannibalism (Glendinning 2012: 230). Furthermore, while he publicly deplored slavery, Raffles's rejection of it appeared to stem from economics rather than morals; he argued that sugar cultivation in Southeast Asia, using impoverished workers, could be cheaper and more efficient than in the West Indies, using slaves; "Here, laborers may be obtained on contract," he wrote to the Duke of Somerset in 1820, "at wages not higher than necessary for their subsistence" (Raffles 1835, vol. 2: [143–52] 147–48). Raffles's amalgam of views and values was not particularly incongruous; the prevailing "Christian" mindset in Britain's Southeast Asian colonies was effectively a capitalist outlook informed by Protestantism, and, as a result, Christianity in the region was to be forever perceived, at least to some degree, as an imported, Western philosophy (Chia 2021: 128). The work of Anglican missionaries would also be mostly interpreted as an endorsement of the British Empire, which was marketed as replacing barbarism and bestowing "civilized" benefits on "idolaters and Mohametans" (Wilson 1863: 5). The missionaries' support earned them credibility, resources, and freedom to operate, and non-Anglican Western missionaries, largely indistinguishable from the Anglicans, enjoyed similar freedoms by proxy (O'Connor 2000: 72).

Churches across Southeast Asia, in general, would maintain a distinctly Western orientation for most of their history, including in their theology, worship, attitudes, and approach to missionary work, until truly local Churches could be developed (Roxborogh 2018: 288). The Church may well be perceived as an intrusion into Southeast Asia, but evidence indicates that it was also widely welcomed. Christianity in the region would show consistent growth during the later colonial era and after the end of colonialism. Conversions generally occurred in uneven clusters rather than systematic patterns or waves, suggesting spontaneity rather than orchestration. Church engagement and the emergence of local leaders tended to occur organically, driven by community commitment. All of this implies that Christianity was usually adopted willingly, albeit in a mixture of gradual and piecemeal fashion (there was rarely a "boom" of conversions), rather than being imposed (Goh 2005: 6). Coercive or not, the Church's perceived collusion with colonialism would become the almost default lens through which to view colonial mission history (Cox 2008: 7). It was long taken for granted that beyond what Andrew Porter called the "complicity paradigm" there was little to say (Porter 2004: 2–6). Gradually, however, the boundaries between colonial history, Church history, and mission studies have broken down (Cox 2008: 4–6). Even so, some regions, particularly Southeast Asia, failed to attract scholarly attention compared to the vaster topics of India and Africa (Porter 2004: 2–3). As the story of the Church in the region continues to unfold in our times and impact current developments, however, its history must not be ignored.

Raffles, though no doubt flawed, was evidently no tyrant, and if his Christian credentials were less than impeccable, he seems at least to have been aware of this, and he still stands out as far more humane than the average colonial governor. His self-sacrifice and his belief in his project were clearly genuine; having seen his own four children die in the unforgiving tropical environment, he ended his own days referring lovingly to Singapore as "my political child" (Raffles 1835, vol. 2: 240). The question arises as to who actually takes the credit for bringing Anglican Christianity to Singapore; is Raffles, the EIC, or the hierarchy of the Anglican Church to be thanked? The establishment of colonial Christianity, like its cousin, colonial capitalist commerce, would be widely regarded as having stemmed from individual initiative, and not as being primarily the work of a missionary society, such as the SPG, or the institutional Church, at all. And what kind of a Christian society resulted from all this initiative? Liaisons between colonial staff, traders, immigrants, and locals would soon produce marginalized mixed-ethnicity communities; the government, meanwhile, would soon seize control of the rackets in pawn, opium, and other drugs, while officially tolerating outrageous gambling, for the pacification of a trafficked labor force working under appalling conditions. This was all within a context of disparaging "uncivilized" local cultures, for the sake of replacing them with something supposedly advanced, and "paving the way to better things."

Chapter Two

"Desiring to Enter the Fold of Christ"

Struggling to Balance Priorities in a Missionary Church

The meanings and motivations of missionary work can be varied and debatable, but, whatever lies behind it, interface with local populations is inescapably at mission's core, with a view to witnessing and propagating religion among them. A thorough understanding of the indigenous population is agreed to be essential for mission, but this can be challenging in Singapore. The Malays' relatively recent presence in Singapore was predated by complex roots in the wider region. They are thought to have migrated to Maritime Southeast Asia (also referred to as the East Indies or the Malay Archipelago) in a long series of migrations between 2500 and 1500 BCE. The location of their first settlements in the region, possibly on Sumatra or Borneo, and their actual origins, are the subjects of long-running controversies. Malays were almost certainly not the first or aboriginal people of the Malay Peninsula, and by some interpretations they sidelined and supplanted the true indigenous population (Ferguson-Davie 1921: 12, 26–27). Malays were certainly the dominant group there by the first millennium CE, and they are argued to be the "definitive" rather than indigenous people, in the same way that Anglo-Saxons came to be seen as the definitive peoples of North America and Australasia (Chia 2021: 121–22). Singapore never had an indigenous native population in the true sense (Saw 1969: 41).

Islam arrived in the Malay Peninsula during the thirteenth century, brought by traders from the Muslim port kingdom of Pasai (Aceh in modern-day Indonesia) and then by Indian Gujarati missionaries, who introduced the Sufi form. Islam became firmly established in Melaka after the Sultanate's first ruler, Parameswara, embraced the religion in 1414, adopting the name Megat

Iskandar Shah. In 1445, When Muzaffar Shah became Sultan, he declared Islam to be the official religion. Under the patronage of successive Sultans, Islam spread throughout the Peninsula and then to the islands, including Singapore as part of the Johor sultanate, of which it remained part until the British takeover (Winstedt 1962: 18–28). Early European missionaries in the region usually concluded that religion was going to be an insurmountable barrier in their relations with the Malays. Islam shaped their disposition and temper, the missionaries felt, compelling them to seek to persuade others of their religion's truth. They noted the Malays' effortless confidence, especially when accompanied by social status and commercial success; these were presented as proof of the superiority and divine nature of Islam, missionaries perceived, while they were actually due to the power and influence of the Sultan, and enjoyed by proxy. Despite all this, some missionaries in Southeast Asia believed that there was enough common ground with the Malays to facilitate subtle, stealthy evangelization, consisting of tactfully catechizing the children in schools and cautiously challenging the adults' beliefs (McDougall 1849: 31–32; Trevor 1849: 158).

The courtesy and generosity of the Malays often surprised outsiders who had been warned to expect piracy and cannibalism. Raffles, who did not always choose his words carefully, vacillated in his opinion of the Malays. In a September 1819 letter to William Wilberforce, Raffles praised the Malays for their "absence of . . . intolerance and bigotry" (Raffles 1835, vol. 2: [44–57] 50), while in a February 1820 letter to the Duchess of Somerset he wrote as follows; "You know that I am far from wishing to paint any of the Malay race in the worst colors, but yet I must tell the truth . . . should any accident occur to us, or should we never be heard of more, you may conclude we have been eaten" (Raffles 1835, vol. 2: [75–82] 82). The treaty that established Singapore cursorily acknowledged the Malays' rights as Muslims, namely their marriage customs, inheritance rules, religious observances and worship, with the rather acidic premise that "these [customs] are to be respected where they shall not be contrary to reason, humanity, etc. [sic]" (Buckley 1902, vol. 1: 160). As mentioned above, there was no uniform viewpoint on the question of evangelization of the Malays in Southeast Asia, but it appeared unlikely to happen in Singapore. A worrying omen seemed to come from Borneo, where the modest initial success of Christian missionaries apparently spurred a Muslim revival, stoking fears of new Muslim missionary expeditions even among the non-Malay indigenous groups (McDougall 1850: 58). Bishop Wilson of Calcutta viewed the "ignorant" Malays with profound disdain (Wilson 1863: 13). Wilson's emissary, Bishop Spencer of Madras (Chennai), on an official visit to Singapore, formed a similar opinion of the "louring, sulky, dangerous" Malays, though he considered them "less actively vicious" than the Chinese. Spencer noted the presence, even among Anglican converts, of a few mixed Chinese-Malay families; Chinese men outnumbered Chinese women by about forty to one, and unions with Malay women became quite common (Spencer no. 3, 1847: 92; no. 4, 1847: 132).

Amidst increasing interaction, profound ethnic prejudice was part of everyday relationships in the Church. Practically all of the clergy's interaction with Asians, whatever their role or position, was founded on a perception of fundamentally unequal status. On December 15, 1852, Joseph Alexander Dorin, Financial Secretary to the Government of India, affirmed the provision of funds, to the clergy, for such "items" as a bearer, a sweeper, a chowkeedar (or chowkeydar; a gatekeeper or watchman) and possibly a bheesty (water carrier). These human "items" were listed along with other clergy expenses such as sacramental elements and church lighting. Dorin stated that the government would not pay for punkah-pullers (operators of hinged ceiling fans, worked by pulling on a cord) or chaprassees (general servants). These particular "items" were considered luxuries and signs of elevated status, which individual clergy were free to finance for themselves. Despite being filtered through a variety of prejudices, the frontline clergy's real knowledge of local populations inevitably increased, and this would eventually be formally encouraged. The Calcutta diocesan circular of January 25, 1855 relayed an announcement by Cecil Beadon, Secretary to the Government of India, stating that chaplains and assistant chaplains would be permitted to sit the colonial service's local language exams, just like other colonial officials, and for the same bonus payment of one thousand rupees if they passed. The official objective was, of course, more effective government of the local population rather than to foster closer relations with them, but greater language knowledge inevitably enriched everyday interaction (*Singapore Church Record Book*, vol. 1, 1838–63: unnumbered page).

VISIONS, VIEWPOINTS, THEORIES, AND REALITIES OF THE CHURCH'S PRESENCE IN SINGAPORE

The political, commercial, and evangelical objectives of Britain's colonial endeavor were separated by blurred lines; the Church's very presence in Southeast Asia was largely owed to the initiative of unconventional individuals with multiple motives. Much also depended on the ability and inclination of local administrators to balance these priorities and to challenge, if possible, the negative attitudes toward missionary work still promoted by the EIC. The balance for the Church was delicate; Parliament had legally reworded its imperial ambitions in terms of Christian moral duty, but this did not mean unbridled freedom for the Church in the colonies. Anglican clergy had to tread particularly carefully, because the Church in the colonies was the same established, institutional, home Church, a formal extension of it, and the Church's relations with the colonial authorities were in effect relations with the British state. Emissaries of the Church of England, a state entity by law, had to curate the Church-state relationship above all else (Strong 2007: 8–9).

The leading Anglican missionary society of the day, the SPG, was keenly aware of this restrictive relationship. The solution, some began to believe, was to enable the locally autonomous transmission of Christianity as soon as possible. This viewpoint gained traction especially under the influence of Bishop William Grant Broughton (1788–1853) of the new Diocese of Australia, during the period of his work with the SPG in the 1840s. Broughton's thinking was far ahead of its time; he argued for involving the laity in the foundation and governance of missionary dioceses, because the laity would be the real long-term fount of resources for future growth, not the English Church. Dioceses across the Pacific and Southeast Asia must adapt Anglican traditions to local ways, Broughton believed. He saw the future unity of worldwide Anglicans as a dialogue between local Churches and Canterbury, rather than establishing local Churches as satellites or replicas of Canterbury. The resulting Church across Asia should be a family of "patriarchates" rather than branches, Broughton felt (O'Connor 2000: 297). This ecclesiological vision was of little interest to colonial governments, predictably, and it provided no immediate comfort to the exasperated bishop of the "difficult [and] vast diocese" of Calcutta (Wilson 1863: 10). Converted to pessimism by his colonial experiences, Bishop Wilson put no faith in solutions proposed by "feeble, sinful, wretched man" that risked leaving the institutional Church "weakened, divided, and exposed" (Wilson 1863: 6).

George John Trevor Spencer (1799–1866), Bishop of Madras (today's Chennai) in India, made a tour of inspection of the Straits Settlements in May 1846. As the second-highest-ranking cleric in the colonial Church across the whole of India and Southeast Asia, Bishop Spencer visited on behalf of Bishop Wilson of Calcutta, who went on a much-needed furlough (*Singapore Church Record Book*, vol. 1, 1838–63: unnumbered pages), and he made a detailed record of his experiences. Spencer was part of an aristocratic dynasty with several prominent members, including a cousin, also called George Spencer, born just ten days after Bishop George Spencer, who later became a notable convert to Roman Catholicism and is currently on course for beatification. Bishop George Spencer was struck by the intense commercial atmosphere in Singapore, in contrast to relaxed and refined Penang. He observed the crowded port at Singapore, in which "huge misshapen Chinese junks" were particularly conspicuous. "Indeed," Spencer wrote, somewhat confusingly, "there is a Chinese look about the place, which makes you feel that you are no longer in India [*sic*], but on the confines of that vast Eastern world, the empires of Burmah [*sic*], Cochin-China [Vietnam], China and

Japan, and the great islands of Sumatra and Borneo, to which Singapore is, as it were, the entrance-gate from Europe" (Spencer no. 3, 1847: 92). Spencer's sense of geography may sound conflated to modern ears, recalling an old British assumption that Singapore must be somewhere in the middle of India (Buckley 1902, vol. 1: 5); in fact, as implied by the name of the EIC, Singapore and the other Straits Settlements were indeed politically part of India at that time (Legislative Council 1869: 50). Aside from this, Spencer's perception of Singapore as the new gateway to the East was insightful.

Spencer noted a fairly healthy number of congregants during his tour of the churches; about one hundred and forty worshippers, on average, at Singapore's services, compared to about two hundred each, on average, in longer-established Penang and Melaka. He was disappointed, however, that the respective proportion of those congregants receiving Holy Communion was only about a third. Spencer was quite furious to learn about unethical sources of public revenue in Singapore; the colonial government held monopolies on the lucrative trades in opium, betel, arrack (coconut or sugar-cane moonshine) and pawnbroking; "pandering to, and fattening upon, the lowest vices of the Chinese and Malays," Spencer wrote (Spencer no. 4, 1847: 133–35). He expressed ironic surprise that the government did not also control gambling, which was rampant and had led to tragic deaths (Buckley 1902, vol. 1: 317). Spencer learned that there were a hundred and ninety-one gambling dens in Singapore. "It is a shocking system, and such as must, sooner or later, bring down a curse from God," he wrote, horrified that these rackets of drugs and desperation were "deliberately legalized and practiced by religious and moral England!" Part of the defense for the government running these monopolies was, predictably perhaps, that they could not otherwise find funds to cover their considerable expenditure; Spencer questioned whether such a defense would cut much ice when it came to the Day of Judgment (Spencer no. 3, 1847: 95; no. 4, 1847: 133–35). The clergy were essentially powerless in these areas; the same government, in the form of the EIC, appointed the chaplains for Singapore and the other Straits Settlements, but the EIC's interference and regulations meant that they tended not to remain for very long, so any ambitions that they may have nurtured about having a lasting positive impact on society could hardly be satisfied. There was no point in a chaplain complaining to his superiors, because they were similarly beholden, though the chaplains had "every right to look [to their superiors] for brotherly support" (Spencer no. 4, 1847: 132–33).

The work of Roman Catholic missionaries, who already had their own bishop and various colleges and schools in the Straits Settlements, seemed to be flourishing. The first Catholic settlers in Singapore did not come from far away; they were Portuguese and French settlers relocating from Melaka (Sng 1980: 22–23). As early as 1821, they secured a plot of land from Raffles (before he had even allocated land for the Anglicans, in fact), but a Catholic church was not built until 1833 (Buckley 1902, vol. 1: 242–45). The inspecting Bishop Spencer, despite having a prominent Catholic convert cousin, held Catholicism in disdain; only begrudgingly did he acknowledge the significant progress of "popery," as he called it, in Singapore. Being unimpressed with St. Andrew's church, he admitted that the rival Catholic place of worship was "larger and handsomer [than] the shapeless, tasteless mass" built by the Anglicans. He broodingly surmised that the Catholic institution itself, if it deserved to be called a Church at all, was "far more like a Church than ours." The root of Spencer's irritation was the lack of missionary work being done by the Anglicans, especially in contrast to the Catholics, and he feared stagnation and complacency. He warned against trying to replicate the English parish system ("the system bequeathed to us by Christ and his Apostles") in the Straits Settlements, stating that such an attempt would be doomed; an outgoing, evangelizing, missionary Church was required, Spencer believed. In the absence, at that moment, of Anglican missionary societies, it was, in Spencer's view, "the obvious duty of every Christian congregation to labor to impart spiritual things to those who as yet know not Christ." Spencer's appraisal, with its flaws, showed considerable understanding and foresight (Spencer no. 3, 1847: 93–95; no. 4, 1847: 131–34).

A BISHOP OF THEIR OWN: THE ANALOGOUS CHALLENGES OF SINGAPORE AND BORNEO

Bishop Wilson's tenure in Calcutta had begun in wonderment; he was struck, as so many Europeans were, by the complexity and enormity of India, and he reveled in the splendor and excitement of his mission. After a few years, however, some of those same features wore him down; "The effects of climate are more depressing and visible than at first. The novelty and surprise and distraction are gone," he wrote. Calling the diocese "vast" and "awful," Wilson retracted his own prior rejoicing, reflecting on the price in health paid by his predecessors; "Surely the tombs of four bishops in nine years are heaped up on purpose [so] that human glorying may be buried under the mound of death . . . The hour of temptation and darkness and penetrating sorrow is coming on like a tide" (Wilson 1863: 6–10). The responsibility he bore, like the diocese itself, which originally stretched from the Cape of Good Hope to Australia, including Singapore, Malaya, and Borneo as well as India and Burma, was indeed vast, and in 1835 Wilson resolved to subdivide it, with the formation of the See of Madras (Chennai), assigned to Bishop Spencer. This was followed by the creation of the Diocese of Australia, mentioned above, in 1836, assigned to Bishop Broughton, and Bombay in 1837, assigned to

Bishop Thomas Carr. The idea of increasing the number of colonial bishops was supported at the highest levels of the Anglican Church, leading to the creation of an endowment fund for that purpose in 1841. The SPG and the SPCK contributed 7,500 pounds and ten thousand pounds respectively (0.87 million and 1.15 million pounds in today's figures). These were important and influential steps toward the conceptualization of a worldwide Anglican Church, and they prepared the ground for what would begin to be understood as an international Anglican Communion twenty-five years later (Pascoe 1901, vol. 2: 752–53). The Diocese of Colombo, Ceylon (now Sri Lanka) was created shortly afterward, followed by many more. The precedent now existed for the fledgling Churches of Southeast Asia to acquire bishops of their own (Swindell 1929: 2).

The development of the Church in Singapore was destined, somewhat incongruously, considering the geographical differences and distances, to be tied to the development of the Church on the island of Borneo (Swindell 1929: 21–23). This remarkable island is the third-largest in the world and the largest in Asia, sitting at the center of Maritime Southeast Asia. It is divided almost exactly in half by the equator, and it is home to one of the oldest rainforests in the world. North Borneo, the modern-day Malaysian state of Sabah, was brought into the EIC fold in the 1760s, though control of it was uncertain until further colonial expansion secured its flanks. This colonial expansion, with the accompanying intervention of the Anglican Church, was largely owed to James Brooke (1803–68), later Sir James Brooke, known as Rajah Brooke or the "White Rajah." Between 1838 and 1842 Brooke assisted the Sultan of Brunei in fighting pirates, for which the Sultan awarded him the title of Rajah and allowed him to take control, in a broadly peaceful and humane way, of a large northern stretch of the island of Borneo called Sarawak. He was soon lauded as "a Christian, a philosopher, and a patriot" for doing so, and hailed as "the apostle of civilization to the Malayan Archipelago" no less, which echoed the praise previously heaped upon Raffles in Singapore (Mission to the Island of Borneo 1847: 26). Like Raffles, Rajah Brooke was only superficially attached to Christianity at a personal level, but he too was firm in his ambition to bring missionaries to Borneo. This required a lot more persuasion than Raffles had to employ to bring missionaries to Singapore, but in December 1847 the first two Anglican missionaries set sail for Borneo. They arrived in June 1848, at the same time that the small island of Labuan, sitting just off Borneo's northern coast, became Britain's only official territorial possession in the region, at that time (McDougall 1848: 5). The takeover of this little-known island would provide a route toward stabilizing the Anglican Church in the region; it was now British, not leased under treaty, and it could legally become an episcopal see of the Church of England, the first in Southeast Asia, as long as a suitable bishop could be found.

The senior of the two missionaries in Borneo was the Reverend Doctor Francis Thomas McDougall (1817–86) who was a surgeon. Modern medicine, McDougall discovered, made a strong impression upon the Malays, and he felt that this might provide a gateway to evangelization (McDougall 1848: 9). In 1851, Bishop Wilson traveled to Borneo to consecrate the new St Thomas's church, in a clear endorsement of McDougall's leadership and of Brooke's administration (Buckley 1902, vol. 2: 660–61). For the Church in Singapore, as well as the Church in Borneo, this was a significant step towards having a regional bishop of their own, but huge difficulties lay in the way. The soon-to-be Bishop McDougall's personal life began to mirror Raffles's experience in Singapore thirty years earlier. Both Raffles and McDougall, and their wives, were repeatedly ill, and just as Raffles had mourned four of his five children, all deceased in infancy (his fifth, remaining child had also subsequently died before the age of twenty), the McDougalls lost all five of their children during their first six years in Borneo; four died shortly after birth, and the fifth died of diphtheria in Singapore, when the McDougalls were finally heading home to England on furlough (Taylor 1998: 463).

Amidst the immensity of this tragedy, the identification of McDougall as a future bishop for Southeast Asia raised manifold legal questions, but eventually the British crown approved the creation of the episcopal see of the island of Labuan. Parliament authorized the Archbishop of Canterbury to permit, in turn, Bishop Wilson and his suffragans to consecrate McDougall in India, while he was en route back to Borneo from furlough; it was the first ever Church of England consecration to take place outside of the British Isles. 1855 saw the McDougalls arrive back in Sarawak, with Francis now Bishop of Labuan. Rajah Brooke then added "and Sarawak" to the new bishop's title, as he was entitled to do. Later, after McDougall's tenure, the designation "and Singapore" would also be added to the bishop's title (Thompson 1951: 396). McDougall, though not yet even unofficially Singapore's bishop, did carry out episcopal duties there; he felt, as others did, that Singapore was destined to be the region's primatial Church, though there would be further obstacles to achieving this (Pascoe 1901, vol. 2: 661–62). McDougall's interpretation of events in the region was understandably influential, and with uprisings in several parts of Asia, not least the so-called Indian Mutiny, McDougall perceived a generalized surge in anti-Christian violence (McDougall 1857: 137). Following a traumatic Chinese workers' insurrection in Borneo, there was unrest among the Dayak ethnic group the following year, accompanied by rumors of an impending Malay revolt as well. Borneo often acted as a cautionary tale of what could be round the corner for Singapore, both in encouraging and worrying potential developments (McDougall 1858: 168).

BREAKING THE MISSIONARY IMPASSE AND DEFYING THE EIC

Singapore had grown consistently since the 1830s, and by the middle of the century the population rapidly approached eighty thousand, comprising both immigrant and native-born residents; more than half of that number were ethnic Chinese, with seven to eight thousand ethnic Indians (Saw 1969: 39–41). The original, lightning-damaged and "shapeless" St. Andrew's church was closed in 1852 and marked for demolition in 1855, to eventually be replaced by the fine cathedral building visible today. Shapeless too, in a sense, was the whole Anglican project on the island; often regarded with indifference (or worse) by the civil authorities, and officially restricted in its ability to minister among the locals, the colonial Church inhabited a vague no-man's-land between the colonizer and the colonized (Cox 2008: 6–7). This, Raffles had contended, was deliberate; the EIC, he believed, was actually averse to real, lasting colonization, which would be characterized by the presence of institutions such as the Church, preferring instead to maintain a loose chain of noncommittal trading stations, because this was the more immediately profitable model (Raffles 1835, vol. 2: 149). The goal of discouraging permanence was apparently demonstrated by the EIC's continued policy of moving its chaplains around at intervals of one to three years and being slow to replace them when they quit in exasperation (Pascoe 1901, vol. 2: 695). A circular of the Diocese of Calcutta dated January 25, 1856 was especially critical of this policy, calling these long and frequent interregnums "evils . . . resulting from the [EIC's] system of appointing chaplains" (*Singapore Church Record Book*, vol. 1, 1838–63: unnumbered page).

In contrast to the demographic development of Singapore, the Anglican Church's numerical growth was modest. The Diocese of Calcutta's concern for Singapore was evident; on June 4, 1855, Bishop Wilson wrote from Calcutta in preparation for his seventh triennial visitation of Singapore, demanding to know how many Europeans, East Indians, and native-born residents were affiliated with the Church. The new (seventh) residency chaplain in Singapore at the time was the Reverend William Topley Humphrey. Humphrey's reply to Wilson, dated July 17, 1855, stated that the total Protestant population on the island was six hundred and fifteen: 240 adult Europeans, 170 adult East Indians, 20 adult natives of Singapore, and 185 children. The old St. Andrew's church had been demolished about six months earlier, and a large dwelling had now been fitted out for use as a temporary St. Andrew's chapel. Answering Wilson's queries about Holy Communion and attendance, Humphrey wrote that a Communion service was held monthly, with an average of fifty-one communicants; the collection was around twenty (Spanish) dollars and forty-five Indian rupees. The average Sunday attendance, comprising communicants and non-communicants, was 166, with around thirty of them being military personnel and their families. These figures of attendance and Communion were almost identical to Bishop Spencer's findings of nine years earlier, despite the considerable population growth. There were, on average, twenty-six Baptisms a year, ten to fifteen marriages, and around forty-five burials in the dedicated and consecrated burial ground (*Singapore Church Record Book*, vol. 1, 1838–63: unnumbered pages).

It was an unimpressive prospectus, to be sure, but change was on the horizon. Britain's foreign policy faced an overhaul prompted by the war against Russia (1853–56) and major unrest in India (1856–58), amidst which the inadequacies and mismanagement of the EIC were exposed; Parliament began to consider dissolving the 250-year-old company and taking direct control of India. Humphrey, the chaplain in Singapore, decided that the time was right to unilaterally break free from the restrictive policies of the weakened EIC. On Whit Sunday of 1856 he challenged the St. Andrew's congregation to join him in launching a new missionary project aimed at the Chinese and Tamil communities and the local population in general. His appeal gave rise to the establishment of St. Andrew's Church Mission (SACM) on June 25, 1856. This mission would consolidate and complement a few existing initiatives, but Humphrey's entreaty was that it was the duty of the congregation to start a mission of their own. St. Andrew's must, in spite of its limitations and conventional parish character, become a missionary congregation, especially for sections of society not yet reached (Gomes 1888: 2–5). This was precisely what Bishop Spencer and others had appealed for, and it is a role that St. Andrew's has sustained to this day. SACM was launched partly in response to (and in order to take advantage of) the loosening grip of the EIC, but there were other contributory factors. Most of Singapore's original Raffles-era missionary efforts had ceased by then, leaving only the official chaplains; changes in the political situation in China had created new opportunities for the London Missionary Society in their preferred land of operations, leading to their withdrawal from Singapore. Benjamin Keasberry, in charge of the LMS's Mission Press, decided to stay on in Singapore as an independent missionary, but apart from him and the Chinese Female Education Society, no other organized missionary work was going on by 1856 (Goh 2005: 7–8).

SACM was no immediate success, and it would be plagued by debts and other problems for some time (Loh 1963: 2–3). Humphrey originally aimed to collect a dollar a month from each congregant, towards the mission; whether he underestimated the costs, or whether not all the congregants would pay, or a combination of the two, is not clear. Humphrey's fundraising priority was to secure the services of a Chinese Christian to work as a catechist among recently-arrived Chinese immigrants, and to find a Christian from

Madras for the same duties among the recently-arrived Tamils. Humphrey approached the Church Missionary Society (CMS) in London, of which he was an associate, asking them about the possibility of sending a missionary to supervise this work, but it was not deemed possible for the foreseeable future. Humphrey and his committee decided not to turn immediately to the rival SPG, and vowed to run SACM for themselves, meaning that the catechists would have to manage their large workloads quite independently. The Reverend Thomas C. Smyth succeeded Humphrey as the eighth residency chaplain in 1858, the year in which the British government finally took control of the colonies away from the EIC. There were by then not one but three catechists working among the ethnic-Chinese community (Ah See, Sim Kam Tong, and Phoah Sin Soe) and one Tamil catechist (Peter Tychicus). A substantial non-European congregation had been built up, but the most successful mission in terms of bringing new people into church continued to be the previous venture, the Chinese Female Education Society, aimed at young Chinese women (Gomes 1888: 1–5).

Alongside all of this was the ongoing construction of the new St Andrew's church building. Smyth, it seems, had neither the time not the language skills to drive the missionary work forward, so in 1859 he wrote to Bishop George Edward Lynch Cotton (1813–66), the new Bishop of Calcutta and second Metropolitan of India, asking him to convince the SPG to do what the CMS apparently could not do before, and send a missionary to oversee SACM. The SPG agreed, but it would be two years before a suitable missionary, the Reverend Edward Sherman Venn, could be sent (Pascoe 1901, vol. 2: 695). With Venn's arrival, a major Anglican missionary society, the SPG, had formally committed personnel to the field in Singapore for the first time. An SPG Mission House was established on Government Hill (later renamed Fort Canning Hill) on plots donated by the government; the later Stamford Road chapel, the missionary's house, and school house would all sit on the edges of Fort Canning Hill. There were suggestions that the new church should have been located there too, but these were rejected (Buckley 1902, vol. 1: 300; vol. 2: 621). The end of the eventful decade of the 1850s saw small increases in the Church's numbers; there were then approximately 260 European, 150 East Indian, 30 Chinese, and 35 Tamil Anglicans. There were smaller numbers of non-Anglican Protestants; approximately 100 Europeans and 65 Asians. Smyth, the chaplain, reported that there were about 180 European Roman Catholics but, astonishingly, around two thousand Asian Roman Catholics (*Singapore Church Record Book*, vol. 1, 1838–63: unnumbered page).

VALUES AND PERSPECTIVES, CLASHES AND CONTROVERSIES, IN THE COLONIAL CHURCH

The commanding position of the future St. Andrew's cathedral was a source of great pride, considered unequaled among the cathedrals and churches of the East, standing on an open seafront and surrounded by an ample churchyard. The style chosen was early English, thirteenth century, the building consisting of a nave with north and south aisles, crossed by a transept, with side porches. The north porch was later converted into the chapter house. An apse of semi-diagonal form was attached to the chancel, containing three stained glass windows with memorials, funded by public subscription, to Raffles and other prominent figures. The main entrance was placed in the west doorway, beneath the groined vaults of the tower, which was divided into organ and bell lofts, and the whole surmounted by a simple spire without lights. The moldings throughout the building were plain but carefully wrought. The organ gallery, erected subsequently to the rest of the building, by private subscription, featured the only element of real ornamentation in the molding, the arches being crocheted and the pillar capitols foliated. A projection in the form of a triforium surmounted the gallery. Ironically, perhaps, the cost of construction, 120,000 rupees (about 2.5 million US dollars in 2023) had been covered by the now-defunct EIC (Swindell 1929: 6–7).

The Reverend Alexander Dunbar Nicolson replaced Smyth as the ninth residency chaplain on May 29, 1860. Nicolson oversaw the final preparations for inaugurating the new church, which was substantially ready for use by December 1860, except that the stained glass windows and the lamps were yet to arrive from England. The temporary chapel was by then having to hold two services one after another, due to the growing congregation. In the run-up to the inauguration, questions persisted over the future use of the church by non-Anglican denominations, especially the Presbyterians of the Church of Scotland, whose earlier requests to use the church had effectively been rebuffed. Nicolson was firmly in favor of accommodating the Presbyterians, as he wrote in a letter to Bishop Cotton of Calcutta on December 24, 1860 (some of Nicolson's letters are preserved within the bound volumes of miscellany latterly called the Church Record Books, held at the National Archives in Singapore). Cotton replied on February 2, 1861, confiding to Nicolson that "The application of the Presbyterian congregation of Singapore has placed me in a real embarrassment. I am most desirous to oblige them, and your strong recommendation makes me still more reluctant to refuse their request." The problem for Cotton was one of consistency; he had already refused a similar request from the American (rather than Scottish) Presbyterians at Murree, in modern-day Pakistan. As there was apparently conflict between these two branches of the Presbyterians, it would not be wise, Cotton believed, for the Church of England to be seen as favoring one branch over another. Within Singapore, Cotton also felt, conceding the Presbyterians' request might lead to similar requests from other groups, such as the Unitarians. Cotton's argument here may sound vaguely unconvincing, and it seems to have once again evaded an important point; the Church of Scotland was and is an established Church of the United Kingdom exactly like the Church of England, not just another rival Protestant group, and the British monarchs, when in Scotland, worship as Presbyterians, not as Anglicans. The decision was unchanged; only very limited permission would be given for non-Anglican use of the new church (*Singapore Church Record Book*, vol. 1, 1838–63: unnumbered pages). St. Andrew's was officially opened on October 1, 1861, and would be consecrated on the Feast of the Conversion of St Paul, January 25, 1862, by Bishop Cotton.

Nicolson's preparations for the inauguration of the new church included, in September 1861, appointing a new organist for a three-year term. Mr. Edward R. Terry, a very accomplished musician, was brought specially from England, travelling alongside the new organ, built by John James Walker (of Joseph W. W. Walker, his father's firm) of London (Buckley 1902, vol. 1: 295–96). The previous organist was given less than a month's notice and a gratuity. Over the subsequent two years, the relationship with Mr. Terry also soured. In July 1864, a meeting was called to discuss two matters relating to Terry. This case, through Nicolson's papers, offers an insight into the Church's handling of moral concerns in the already cosmopolitan and permissive context of Singapore. The first matter regarding Terry was fairly trivial, an unexplained absence, but the second matter concerned reports, including from church trustees, that Terry was living "an immoral life [with] a profligate woman." Nicolson described these reports as being absolutely irrefutable, and he warned Terry that in all likelihood the trustees would elect to remove him in order to avoid "constant scandal." Nicolson implored Terry to come to him for guidance, and to abandon his "profligate life . . . which, if continued in, will ruin both your temporal and eternal prospects." In perhaps not quite the response that Nicolson and the trustees expected, Terry showed no fear for his eternal prospects, replying "I do not deny [the accusation] . . . in fact I confirm it, but does this interfere with my duties as an organist?" The trustees voted unanimously to dismiss him at once. Terry demanded that they pay him the remainder of his salary for the three-year contract and a ship's passage to Shanghai or England, as he chose, reminding them that he had always fulfilled his duties. He had no luck. Terry also wanted to tune and service the organ one last time and thus leave it in a reasonable state for his successor, as a professional courtesy. Nicolson replied: "I must refuse your request and hereby forbid your touching the organ again." A temporary organist was found, and

Edward R. Terry's immediate fate is not recorded (*Singapore Church Record Book*, vol. 2, 1859–70: unnumbered pages). Some fifty-something years later, Terry was reportedly manager of a prominent music shop in Bond Street, London, probably Chappell's, with whom he also published a number of popular piano arrangements (Buckley 1902, vol. 1: 296).

The unusual pressures and opportunities of colonial society, combined with the environmental conditions and hazards of the Tropics, seemed to create numerous challenges for the conventions of relationships and marriage. Young lives could be cut tragically short, as already discussed, and this left widows and widowers, often with children, in search of a second spouse, usually from within the closed community of fellow expatriates. Bishop Cotton approached the Advocate-General of Bengal (Calcutta), Thomas Hardwicke Cowie, QC (Queen's Counsel), asking him to clarify the legal position regarding widowed persons who seek marriage with their deceased spouse's sibling; in practice, such cases usually involved a widower wanting to marry his late wife's sister. Apart from causing a degree of scandal, such marriages were forbidden at the time under English law, which considered them illicit and improper; this was because the original marriage bond was believed to make the sister-in-law a true, if not consanguineous, sister. Cowie drew up a memorandum affirming that English law applied throughout the British Empire, lest there be any assumption that it did not, or that certain laws may be relaxed in contexts where it was more common to lose a wife in young age. The law itself drew directly upon the Table of Kindred and Affinity in the Anglican Book of Common Prayer; therefore, while arguably being archaic the law was hardly arcane, especially for the clergy (*Singapore Church Record Book*, vol. 1, 1838–63: unnumbered pages).

The 1835 Marriage Act had solidified this potentially contentious law into an absolute prohibition in England and the colonies, while in Scotland such marriages were already prohibited by the Scottish Marriage Act of 1567. Reassured by the Advocate-General's confirmation, Bishop Cotton emphasized that it was illegal for a clergyman to officiate a marriage of a man with his deceased wife's sister, regardless of couples' needs due to the tropical death rate. It is not clear how many such marriages had already been conducted in order to prompt Cotton's forceful intervention, which was signed "G. E. L. [George Edward Lynch] Calcutta" and dated June 2, 1862, also enclosing Cowie's memorandum. Cotton stated that, henceforth, offending clergy would have their license withdrawn and face suspension or censure (*Singapore Church Record Book*, vol. 1, 1838–63: unnumbered pages). The law in question would later be effectively overturned by the very specifically named Deceased Wife's Sister's Marriage Act 1907, though individual clergy were allowed to opt out in favor of the old rules.

THE ENDLESS AND EXPANDING CHALLENGE OF MULTICULTURAL, MULTILINGUAL MISSION

A human challenge with less capacity to cause scandal than the "Terry affair" or the irregular marriages was the ever-present language barrier. The Malay language provided a lingua franca of sorts, but it was often substituted with a Malay-based creole known as Bazaar Malay (Melayu Pasar) or another version called Baba Malay or Baba Patois, which was based on Chinese (Hokkien) grammar with Malay vocabulary. Missionaries faced a variety of linguistic challenges among the Chinese immigrant community, some of whom were short-term residents, some of whom were settlers, and many of whom were en route to other places, and who spoke many different dialects (Thompson 1951: 394). Despite this, for Church purposes, Chinese speakers were initially split into just two congregations, each with its own catechist. The Tamil and Malay groups also had their own catechists, who faced a less complex linguistic challenge than their Chinese counterparts, but there were plenty of other challenges. The commitment of the Malay congregation was generally doubted, and their reasons for attending church, when they did, were considered a mystery. Ensuring good attendance from all of the local groups was difficult, reported Venn, the SPG missionary in charge of SACM. He speculated that, on the positive side, if the Malays, for example, were not physically present in church, they were perhaps out spreading the word among their community, a view that confirmed Venn's credentials as a great optimist (*Singapore Church Record Book*, vol. 1, 1838–63: unnumbered pages).

Venn's most enduring achievements included the foundation, along with catechist Chok Loi Fat, of St. Andrew's school for boys in 1862, and of a smaller school for girls, both of which boosted attendance at church services as well. St. Andrew's provided only primary education for its first fifty years. The girls' school, which would eventually be known as St. Margaret's, was placed in the hands of the Church of England Zenana Missionary Society (CEZMS) (Sng 1980: 151). One year later, in 1863, SACM was officially affiliated to the SPG. A resident Mission to Seamen chaplain, the Reverend John C. Ince, also arrived in Singapore at that time (*Straits Times* no. 1, 1863: 1). New Chinese catechists (Tye Kim, Eng See, and the aforementioned Chok Loi Fat) were employed under Venn, and Peter Tychicus continued to work as catechist to the Tamils. Tychicus was implicated in a minor controversy, as recorded by an unidentified Anglican commentator in the *Straits Times* in 1863. The outline of the story was that Peter Tychicus, Anglican catechist among the Tamils, a Hindu-majority ethnic group, proudly announced the successful conversion of a Tamil family from Roman Catholicism to

Anglicanism. "We cannot conceive what necessity there is," the unnamed journalist wrote, "for Mr. Peter Tychicus to extend the sphere of his usefulness from the broad field of heathenism and positive unbelief existing in this place, to the narrow and well cared-for preserves of the Roman Catholic Church." If the Catholics were challenged to do battle for converts, the *Straits Times* feared, the Anglicans would find it hard to compete; "the Romish Religion [sic] . . . has many attractions in its outward worship which our own religion has not." The writer then shamelessly attacked the sincerity of the converts in question, calling it "absurd" that "uneducated Tamils" might appreciate "the fine points of difference between the two religions" (*Straits Times* no. 1, 1863: 1). Venn responded laconically in the following week's edition; "[We] never invite Roman Catholics to leave their communion. . . . We simply instruct all who come to us" (*Straits Times* no. 2, 1863: 1).

Conflicts and controversies aside, the first phase of real missionary work in Singapore surpassed expectations. Within the three decades since the island had been established as the chief city of the Straits Settlements and the major port in the East, both chaplains and missionaries had defied the bans and cast off the old prohibitions on reaching out to locals, and they had provoked neither censure, nor rebuke, nor loss of trade as a result (Gomes 1888: 5–7). These developments coincided with the onset of institution-wide shifts in Anglican attitudes towards mission. As Victorian imperialism entered its heyday, the Anglican Church's long-evolving approach to global expansion would look a lot more concrete after 1867, the year commonly linked to the beginning of an international Anglican Communion, and, incidentally, the year in which Singapore and the other Straits Settlements came under the direct control of the British Colonial Office. Ever since Britain's former American colonies achieved independence, and an Episcopal Church was reconstituted in Scotland, the Anglican Church had already been, de facto, an international communion of Churches, and the increasing autonomy of Church of England dioceses in the African and Asian colonies accelerated this perception. The beginning of the Anglican Communion, therefore, was more a case of gradual acknowledgment of reality than the launch of a new organization. As the Anglican Communion idea gained currency, the obvious paradox of an autocephalous national Church, the English Church, becoming global by replanting itself around the world was finally being addressed. Back when the English Church's colonial expeditions were still largely exploratory there was no such paradox, as the Church did little more than provide chaplaincy for groups of British pioneers overseas, but several decades on it was clearly incongruous that the fully-fledged dioceses of Calcutta, Madras, Honolulu, Wellington, and many others were actually dioceses of the national Church of England. The accepted model of colonial chaplaincy, furthermore, clearly could not easily be converted to a true missionary role; far-sighted observers argued that the Churches' future effectiveness would depend on authentic and autonomous local growth, not continued subordination to England (Cox 2008: 4–7, 13–14; O'Connor 2000: 99–100).

The beginning of the Anglican Communion (AC) is tied, with hindsight, to the first of the ten-yearly Lambeth Conferences, in which optimists saw the potential for maintaining unity in theological and ecclesiological essentials between Anglican Churches worldwide, while allowing great diversity in all of the practical, location-specific and culture-specific aspects of the Churches' work. Advocates envisaged the AC as being non-hierarchical and collegial, with a non-executive president, the Archbishop of Canterbury, as "first among equals" and its figurehead. The AC, it was hoped, would exemplify the Anglican ethos of reconciling potentially contradictory tendencies and drawing members of the global Church community towards their common ground (Goodhew 2017: 3–5, 23–24). Reconciliation, with the sacrifices it entails, was affirmed as being the essence of Anglicanism, supposedly reflecting the ideal of the English Church, which, in the nineteenth-century retelling at least, had managed to embrace the Protestant Reformation without sacrificing its ancient Catholic patrimony. Two powerful influences, coming from a foreign, alien continent, had thus been successfully reconciled, according to this arguably idealized interpretation, and the result was not a compromise between the two, neither an impoverished Catholicism nor a lukewarm Protestantism, but rather a balance of the two forces in an autonomous Church that already had its own culture and identity (Ramsey 2009: 175–88). The same core principle of reconciliation was apparently now ready to be exported around the globe.

CONCLUSION

"How comforting it is to carry the Church with us wherever we go" (Spencer no. 3, 1847: 89); so wrote Bishop George Spencer, in what could be read as an unintentionally ironic appraisal of the "unholy alliance" between colonialism and Christianity. Cultural domination in the colonies relied in part on the successful introduction of Western religion, or at least the dissemination and normalization of its values, but it was not such a comforting experience for the clergy on the ground. Anglican clergy had to cope with hostility or indifference from the authorities, half-heartedness from some fellow Anglicans, draconian restrictions on their activities, hot competition from other denominations, and a shortened life expectancy for them and their families, all of which would have to be accepted as ongoing issues. The Anglican Church had a "special" responsibility to know its place in the colonial order, with missionary initiative quashed by the almighty priority of commerce;

colonialism and Church was not a happy relationship. The colonial clergy's role was to be interpreted narrowly; they were chaplains, not missionaries. Church leaders sympathized with the clergy's sense of being restrained and restricted while potential for real missionary work surrounded them, and in theory the law was not against them (Spencer no. 4, 1847: 132). In practice, during the first three decades of the Church's presence in Southeast Asia, the East India Company's limitations on doing ministry beyond the strict bounds of colonial society showed few signs of loosening, and it was the initiative of individual clergy to defy the rules that eventually forced a change. This contradicts perceptions of an Anglican Church wholly complicit in colonial expansion, privileged and facilitated by the authorities (Pieris 2004: 256; Evers 2014: 68).

So much for the supposed "unholy alliance" between Church and empire; the Church should, still in theory, have been able to rely on the civil and political administration for support, as Parliament explicitly willed that colonial expansion be framed in terms of Christian duty. Individual colonial pioneers were often lauded for their high Christian values, which they put into practice through trade and governance, though this usually reflected aspiration rather than reality, and most of them were only nominal Christians. All sides were obliged to view the colonial project in religious terms; not only had the Church's teaching been molded, once again, to conform to the values and vision that the rulers wanted to impart, but the underpinning Christian-inspired rationale for colonialism had actually been enshrined in law as well. It was perhaps, in many cases, not only the law that required colonialism to be understood in Christian moral terms, but also the individual conscience. Doubts about the justness and fairness of colonialism were, thanks to the Church, a little easier to push aside, publicly, especially when these doubts were placed alongside the real, tangible benefits to a community of a school or a printing press.

While the situation could be deeply discouraging for the clergy, it did at least nurture a strong (though suppressed) desire to do real missionary work. They contemplated a vast challenge, reaching out to a mixed, complex, and ever-changing population of immigrants, imported laborers, and residents. Many of the individual ethnic communities had well-established and well-functioning intra- and interrelationships, networks, and cultures of leadership, with firm spiritual bases, which they were generally not inclined to relinquish. Even among the significant numbers of Christian arrivals, from China and India, there were already intricate sociocultural frameworks in place, which were alien to the Anglicans' very English, churchy way of doing things. Anglican Christianity would not find any easy inroads. In all their "target" groups they faced a resilient combination of cultural hegemony and pervasive religion, which, ironically, is what British colonialists and their missionaries would forever be accused of attempting to install themselves. The Church should have been more at ease ministering to the expatriate cohort, for whom the Church's presence was primarily intended, but there too, in increasingly cosmopolitan Singapore, the values, mores, and morals of young Europeans were evolving, as the Church looked on helplessly. The rules, laws, and expectations surrounding relationships and marriage, life and death were being questioned and challenged; this would only accelerate as the great Victorian age of empire drew to a close. Wherever the Church turned, then, it faced an unfamiliar and rapidly changing culture.

Singapore in the middle decades of the nineteenth century presented a different challenge to the rest of Southeast Asia, but it was no less daunting. No one religious community or ethnic group in Singapore was truly dominant over any other; the demographics of the island were in flux, with continual new arrivals and departures. This was an obstacle to evangelization, because in situations of instability people can cling even harder to pre-held cultural and creedal norms, while receptiveness to new ideas is, as a generalization, a feature of confidence, settledness, and stability. These unpromising circumstances did produce some genuinely remarkable, industrious, and crusading characters, both within and outside of the clergy, but prejudicial attitudes towards certain groups were also widespread. The supposed negative qualities of the Malays and Chinese formed a familiar litany, labeling them as inherently dishonest, dangerous, and debauched; the Chinese were seen as a wild and "very profligate race" with predilections for opium, gambling, and vice (Spencer no. 4, 1847: 131). Many Malay servants and, especially, Chinese servants did earn a high degree of trust, being considered an important part of the domestic arrangement, but often only in the same sense as other, inanimate "items" impinging upon the household expenditure. Prejudice remained rife, but the question of caste, especially regarding ethnic Indians, generally mattered less in the diaspora than it did in India. The British found the Indian caste question distasteful and embarrassing, but it clearly did not stop them from imposing their own condemnatory hierarchy upon the locals (Wilson 1863: 9).

Some of the clergy, fired up by their zeal for the Anglican Church, reserved their disdain for the Roman Catholics, and a distinct rivalry ensued. Anglicans need not have worried about losing their distinctiveness; Catholic missionaries may have been more confident and better-established in the region, but the Anglicans, even in the 1840s, struck people as more relaxed and approachable, being "[of] simple dress and simple manners" compared to the Catholics (Spencer no. 5, 1847: 170). Rivalry seemed unavoidable, however, and it was both fueled and exemplified by the "poaching" of converts between denominations. These age-old conflicts and prejudices ran counter to the progressive achievements of chaplains like Humphrey, missionaries like Venn, and administrators like Raffles, who all demonstrated that Christian advancement in Southeast Asia depended on innovation and breaking with conventions. In their vision, evangelizing and "civilizing" people, in the paternalistic wording of the time, were complementary. Church schools, which started slowly but surely in Singapore, had the potential to showcase the great benefits of European civilization and generate interest in the religion that had inspired that civilization. It is easy to reject these good works as being transactional, a cunning imperial plot to win converts, but the evidence does not support the idea of a contrived or devious strategy; Church growth would eventually happen thanks to the conviction and commitment of ethnic-Chinese and ethnic-Tamil workers on the ground rather than British planning at senior levels (Ward 2006: 268–69).

For the global Anglican Church, a vision was forming that may be called progressive. Bishop Broughton of the SPG had foreseen a future Anglican Communion as a family of autonomous and equal patriarchates, anticipating a day when the colonial dynamic of mother Church (which was white and Western) and daughter Churches (which were black and Asian) could be consigned to the past. Even so, the steps toward this were slow and difficult. In terms of Anglican ecclesiology, polity, and practice, a Church needs a bishop, but there were many and varied hurdles to Southeast Asia obtaining one of its own. Perhaps most daunting among the hurdles was the question of who on earth would do such a job. The health risks involved in tropical colonial life were multiple and staggering; the apparent normalcy of young widowhood, usually a man losing a young wife, forced the Church to remind its clergy that siblings of deceased spouses were legally out of bounds. The great Raffles himself had died terribly young, predeceased by all but one of his children, who died a few years later. Southeast Asia's first bishop, as it turned out, lived to nearly seventy, but he too had buried all of his poor infant children in mission lands. Such fates could have awaited any one of the clergy and missionaries who ventured out to the Southeast Asian colonies; it is difficult not to admire their courage and conviction, whatever attitudes or prejudices they may or may not have taken with them.

Chapter Three

"Wherever the Sun Shines"

From the Victorian Mission Boom to the End of Empire's Golden Era

With an increasing number of Christian denominations, large and small, at work in growing colonies like Singapore, competition would become a persistent issue. Roman Catholics, Anglicans, Presbyterians, and, later, Methodists, often agreed to refrain from missionary work in neighborhoods that were historically linked to another main denomination, and this appears to have limited conflict, but all denominations suffered defections to other Churches, whether by clergy or laypeople, at some point (Buckley 1902, vol. 2: 640). There were also social entities outside of the Christian denominations that competed for people's adherence, but this was apparently not a cause of great concern. Freemasonry, for example, was quite well-established in Singapore by the mid-1840s, and lodge membership was not considered incompatible with Church membership; the Reverend Thomas C. Smyth, the eighth residency chaplain, was a high-ranking Freemason who frequently chaired meetings (Buckley 1902, vol. 2: 496–97, 673). The real fear was of losing hard-won local converts to other denominations, especially through deliberate "poaching" of members, as illustrated by the story of Peter Tychicus. This may indicate that the colonial Anglican Church and its competitors were slow to grasp the priorities and sensibilities of new Asian Christians. They strove to establish and transmit their distinct identity, particular values, and denominational worldview, and, for the most part, they respected the boundaries between themselves and other denominations, little realizing that denominational differences were not particularly decisive or important factors for Asian Christians (Roxborogh 2014: 63–65).

Anglican chaplains and missionaries generally believed in their brand of Christianity's potency as a "civilizing" force, and the tasks of Christianizing and civilizing were so closely related in the European mindset as to be almost synonymous (Cox 2008: 13). Gentlemanliness, refinement, and good manners, which were considered prerequisites for churchmen, were considered by extension to be the hallmarks of a successful convert as well, demonstrating that the missionary had transmitted these qualities effectively. This thinking expanded into a belief that Christianization on a grand scale could be achieved by nurturing a new social elite made up of converts; this was felt to honor the all-important example of English society, in which evangelization of the "lower orders" had always started from the upper class downwards (Cox 2002: 4). Once again, this seems to betray a failure to understand the Asian spiritual experience, in which the lived reality of faith is more important than concepts and principles, has no concern for airs and graces, and within which faith is nourished by experiences of disenfranchisement and conflict, rather than by rising socially above the lowly and mundane. Some missionaries may have assumed that becoming Anglican signified, for Asians, a demonstration of appreciation for the colonial social order, or a declaration of allegiance to Britain; neither assumption was correct. For the ethnic and immigrant collectives of Singapore, becoming Anglican was, and would remain, about following Jesus's teachings in ways that made sense to their lives and spoke to their experiences; it was not about identifying with British colonialism, the English class system, or a prescriptive confessional identity (Roxborogh 2018: 288–96).

Some clergy were perhaps too deeply invested in colonialism to ever doubt that England and Empire were God-given ideals to be universally disseminated, but while most of them were broadly supportive of colonial expansion, they generally advocated for it to be done humanely, with the provision of social services (Cox 2008: 13–14). The Anglican understanding of mission stood on three legs; the church, the hospital, and the school, and the Church in Singapore's gradual successes in these fields were emboldening for a small organization (Hayter and Bennitt nd: 29). The Church's encroachment into the secular and political domains of healthcare and education was potentially objectionable to enlightened Western minds, but the maxim that religion and politics do not mix has no resonance in Asia; there is no Asian equivalent of the Western philosophical dividing line between the worldly and the sacred (Bell 2004: 430). Unhindered, therefore, by binary conceptual divisions of sacred and profane, and free of slavish impulses to honor preset denominational demarcations, Southeast Asians' engagement with Christianity developed organically with local characteristics, reflecting their values and customs. Inspired by forward-thinkers of previous decades, some Anglican missionaries in the late nineteenth and early twentieth centuries increasingly accepted, accommodated, and encouraged local religious expressions. They opposed the idea of recreating the English Church in the tropics and foisting it on people who already had their own religious and spiritual traditions, which they recognized as noble and valid. They acknowledged the flaws in colonial Christianity and promoted the idea of autonomous local Churches to replace it. These missionaries became known as the "atheists of empire" due to their loss of faith in the British imperial ideal (O'Connor 2000: 99–100).

Rivalry between denominations gradually lost its potency, and, as the century progressed, changing denomination, even after Confirmation, and mixed-denomination marriages, would become quite common in Singapore (*Singapore Church Record Book* vol. 8, 1917–28: 35–37). Increasing local participation in the Churches and loosening boundaries between the denominations would prompt the first discussions about a possible "united" Christian Church. Some rivalries persisted more than others, notably between Anglicans and Roman Catholics. Anglican perceptions of Catholicism were often confused, with feelings vacillating between resentment and respect. Back in the 1840s, Bishop Spencer noted that believers of "that persuasion" already had a "so-called Bishop of the Straits" long before a local Anglican bishop was appointed; the "legitimate catholic [sic] prelate" of the land was the Anglican Bishop of Calcutta, he asserted. Furthermore, Catholics already had major schools by the early 1850s, ten years before the Anglican equivalents opened their doors (Goh 2005: 38). Spencer blamed his own Church for not spreading "the real Catholic and Apostolic faith" quickly enough (Spencer no. 3, 1847: 93; no. 4, 1847: 134). Begrudging respect and self-flagellation was a popular combination, and many agreed with Spencer that the Roman Catholics seemed to have greater institutional commitment than the Anglicans (Buckley 1902, vol. 2: 660–61). The British authorities, for their part, showed no particular interest in seeing Protestantism "triumph" over Catholicism, though simple national pride occasionally led to them taking sides in the battle to win converts (Chia 2021: 124).

There were also Catholic-leaning Anglicans who admired the Roman Catholics' intrepid missionary societies and resolved to emulate them. Through the suppression of religious orders in the British Isles, the English Church had been deprived of its most mission-oriented branches, but the missionary urge resurfaced during the age of imperial expansion, and the conditions were viewed as right to nurture it (Cox 2008: 9–23). Missionary work in Asia, consequently, tended to attract Anglicans from the wing of the Church that was sympathetic to Catholic theology and ecclesiology, emphasizing sacraments, liturgy, apostolic succession, and Church order. This "Anglo-Catholic" tendency developed as an expression of the High Church tradition (which also has Evangelical expressions) and organizations such as the SPG and the SPCK were flagships of it (O'Connor 2000: 6–8). The colonial boom was seen as an opportune moment for Anglo-Catholics. It coincided with a period in which Roman Catholic missions were being rolled back due to an internal crisis in their Church, inadvertently creating openings for their rivals (Cox 2008: 9). In parts of Southeast Asia, the influence of High Church Anglo-Catholicism is still visible in today's Anglican churchmanship, but it is usually intertwined with both local traditional influences and more recent worship styles. Anglo-Catholic missionaries' main contribution to the development of Southeast Asian Churches, however, was not about churchmanship as such. They saw the overseas mission field as a laboratory for experimenting with the Catholic liturgical and theological inheritance that they were in the process of rediscovering; their Church tradition, in fact, was still a developing one, much like Christianity in Southeast Asia. Anglo-Catholics were essentially advocating for greater diversity, which in turn made them tolerant of diversity coming from the local context, and this acceptance of local expression and experimentation directly translated into support for greater local Church autonomy (Maughan 2014: 113).

THE EXPANDING VISION AND SCOPE OF MISSIONARY WORK IN SINGAPORE

Missionaries could find themselves in difficult positions, and the expectations placed upon them were not always clear. The missionary societies' presences in overseas territories, the first Lambeth Conferences affirmed, were not supposed to mutate into a permanent structural basis for future local Churches; they were intended to lead the initial missions, develop the local Church up to a certain point, and then step back. Missionary clergy, meanwhile, at whatever stage they were in their mission, should always be strictly subject to a bishop, however far away he may be based, Lambeth asserted (Davidson 1920: 238–39). Authentic supervision may not have been possible, but colonial missionaries were reminded that they were not free agents; nor did they enjoy the same benefits as colonial chaplains, such as government service pensions, which were first equivalent to those of an army major and then raised, in the 1860s, to the level of a lieutenant-colonel (*Singapore Church Record Book* vol. 1, 1838–63: unnumbered pages). This all contributed to a feeling of insecurity in the missions. At SACM, the initial momentum had not endured; the lead missionary Venn's career was cut short by his sudden death in 1866, and the difficult quest to find the right person to lead the mission recommenced. When the new (eleventh) chaplain of Singapore, the Reverend John Alleyne Beckles, arrived in 1868, he found the SACM finances in a poor state. The Tamil catechist, Peter Tychicus, took an unscheduled leave in India, which gave Beckles a premise for temporarily halting the Tamil mission; Tychicus was given notice and six months' pay, with gratitude for his decade of service. The remaining Chinese catechist, Chok Loi Fat, was also dismissed. Thus began a period of hiatus combined with strenuous fundraising efforts, led by devoted laypeople, while the search for the right missionary leader continued (Gomes 1888: 8–10).

Beckles was Singapore's eleventh chaplain, but he was the first to bear the title of colonial chaplain rather than residency chaplain (Swindell 1929: 5). The political administration of the Straits Settlements (the island of Singapore, Prince of Wales Island [Penang], the town and fort of Malacca [Melaka] and their dependencies) passed from the Government of India to the direct rule of the Colonial Office in London in 1867, following an Act of Parliament of the previous year. The combined Straits Settlements became a single Crown Colony, and the old EIC chaplaincies in the settlements became permanent incumbencies, with the chaplains directly employed by the government. In terms of ecclesiastical administration, there were corresponding developments. There had been talk of assigning the old EIC chaplaincies to the ecclesiastical jurisdiction of the Diocese of Labuan and Sarawak since the late 1850s, and in 1869 this proposal passed into law; the old limitations on missionary work imposed by the EIC thereby passed definitively into history (Thompson 1951: 398–400).

The Straits Settlements were now permanently detached from the see of far-off Calcutta and placed under the second Bishop of Labuan, Walter Chambers (Legislative Council 1869: 50). Singapore had its own bishop at last, though not yet in name (Pascoe 1901, vol. 2: 695–97). Walter Chambers (1824–93) had become bishop the year before, in 1869, replacing Bishop McDougall, who had retired. Chambers was considered an obvious choice for bishop; he was an experienced missionary who had served for many years in Borneo and had mastered several local languages (Taylor 1983: 83). On his way to formally take up his post in Labuan, the newly consecrated bishop paused in Singapore to make arrangements for managing the new jurisdiction. Borneo would claim the largest share of the new bishop's attention, but his presence was needed everywhere, as health and personal problems continued to cut missionary and clergy careers short; this would eventually be Chambers's own fate as well. While he was able, Chambers's ambition was to overhaul the training of catechists and clergy, but the ongoing plagues of ill health and despondency, coupled with Chambers's own full schedule and eventual health problems, would ultimately make this unachievable (Thompson 1951: 398–401).

St. Andrew's church was formally designated as Bishop Chambers's cathedral on December 20, 1870; it was duly consecrated by the newly-collated Canon Beckles, who was also appointed first Archdeacon of Singapore, as well as being colonial chaplain (Swindell 1929: 4–5). As Chambers's tenure as bishop began, there was another important arrival from Borneo in 1872, when SACM finally acquired a new leader; the Reverend William Henry Gomes (1827–1902) was a Ceylonese (Sri Lankan) Eurasian of part-Portuguese descent, and a highly skilled linguist and translator who he had been working in Borneo since 1852. The SPG-sponsored SACM's work could now be revived after a break of several years. The Chinese catechist, Chok, and the Tamil catechist, Tychicus, were contacted and reinstated, but more personnel would be needed (Swindell 1929: 10–11). Gomes made plans to train new staff, enlarge the boys' school, and build a new chapel for it; he later also opened a hostel for the boys of many ethnicities and backgrounds who came to attend government schools in Singapore (Pascoe 1901, vol. 2: 697). Gomes faced SACM's perennial linguistic challenges head-on, translating texts into Malay and Hokkien (Chinese), which eventually led to the publication of the Hokkien Prayer Book in 1901. By the 1870s, the Church's non-English-language audience consisted of Straits-born ethnic Chinese who spoke Malay, more recent immigrants from China who spoke only their own dialect, assorted Eurasians, and Indians, who mostly, but certainly not all, spoke Tamil. In response to this demographic breakdown, the Anglican churches of Singapore increasingly aimed to provide three sets of services; in Malay, Tamil, and Chinese (Gomes 1888: 11).

Significant new mission opportunities presented themselves. From among the Chinese-dominated gambier and pepper plantations in the Jurong district, a request came to open a mission station, under quite unusual circumstances. A planter of gambier and pepper, who had resided at Jurong for twelve years, came to see Gomes one day, asking to receive religious instruction and requesting that a catechist be sent to instruct his plantation workers as well. This individual had apparently been a great opponent of Christianity prior to this moment; he had gone to tyrannical lengths to dissuade his workers, mostly Chinese like himself, from engaging with the Church, and he had been vindictive toward those who had converted. Now, after a Road-to-Damascus-type conversion of his own, he was remorseful over his past behavior and eager to make amends. God, he believed, forgiving his prior conduct, had blessed his plantation with great success. The planter had built a chapel on his estate at his own expense, in order to help spread the gospel among all of the local plantation workers, scattered across several plantations, not just his own. This chapel was later replaced by a permanent church, St. John's, which was built with various donations and entrusted to the diocese (Pascoe 1895: 697).

As the Church's work expanded and developed, driven by especially industrious individuals like Gomes, the first examples of "hybrid" chaplain-missionaries began to appear, as an initiative of the SPG. The SPG was in favor of the continued practice that when chaplains were officially appointed for a British colonial community, the colonial government should provide for their needs, as indeed they did, supplemented with donations from the expatriate congregation. This allowed SPG resources to be devoted to purely missionary work, which was increasing. However, the situation in the Straits Settlements was unusual; British people were comparatively few, and the government used this as an excuse to pay only small grants to chaplains, thereby making the support of a chaplain often untenable. In response, the SPG developed a practice of appointing priests as joint or "hybrid" chaplain and missionary. The SPG would provide one-third of the hybrid priest's stipend, and government funds and public contributions would make up the other two-thirds. Both aspects of the chaplain-missionary's work, the government chaplaincy aimed at expatriates and the missionary work aimed at everyone, were thus provided for, though the number of priests was actually still too small. These adaptations, both in the government's way of working and in the policies of the SPG, are indicative of how evolving needs demand flexibility and creativity from institutions. It had taken several decades, but models of missionary work were finally emerging that were better suited to the geographical, political, and demographic reality. In 1874, the Reverend George Frederick Hose (1838–1922), until then chaplain at Melaka, took over from Beckles as both archdeacon and colonial chaplain; he would remain in post until 1881, when he became bishop. Beckles returned home to Dorset and died four years later, aged only thirty-seven (Swindell 1929: 4–5).

ADAPTING TO THE EVOLVING POLITICS AND PRIORITIES OF CHURCH AND EMPIRE

British involvement in Southeast Asia was intensifying in all sectors, and, inspired by success in Singapore, the basis upon which Britain engaged with the states of the Malay Peninsula was transformed in the years following the demise of the EIC. The British government now acted directly in Malay affairs, and this was soon to be regulated by the landmark Treaty of Pangkor, which was signed on January 20, 1874. From the Anglican, Christian point of view, the treaty is mostly remembered for regulating the relationship between the Church and the Muslim Malay rulers, and by extension between Christianity and Islam. Its main purpose, however, was to establish the extent of and conditions for British control of the Malay states, laying the foundations for an entity called British Malaya, which included Singapore. By the early 1870s, disputes and conflicts around trade, particularly the tin trade, had created a crisis of authority and order in the Malay states. The situation deteriorated into violence, initially between Chinese tin-mining gangs, but what started as a mining dispute escalated to such a degree that at one point thousands of mercenaries were imported to fight, and the violence spiraled. The Sultan of Perak finally appealed for intervention by the British, who saw the crisis as an opportunity to extend their influence and increase their commercial dominion. They cunningly resolved to emphasize, however, the rights and privileges being secured for and conceded to the sultan, rather than those being grabbed by the British. The resulting document would provide the blueprint for future agreements with the other sultans as well (Khoo 1974: 1–4).

Pangkor was the godsend that the British had been praying for, and it did actually instill order and provide genuine safeguards for the Malay states, as promised. The British highlighted the moral righteousness of Pangkor in freeing the masses from economic uncertainty, and the crucial issue of inter-religious relations took second place to commercial matters, not for the first time (Khoo 1974: 4). The Church perspective differed, viewing the treaty as being, in effect, a British pledge of non-interference in local religious affairs, from which could be extrapolated that missionary outreach to the Malays was now forbidden. Though this was not explicitly stated, it would become received wisdom that "a tacit understanding" or "gentleman's agreement" had been reached on the matter (TNA FCO 141/7399 Sheet 2: November 20, 1948; January 7, 1949). While there was indeed nothing in the treaty to expressly restrict the work of Christian missionaries, the line separating everyday Christian witness from encroachment upon Islam was not defined, and such definitions would be left to future generations to wrestle with (Ferguson-Davie 1921: 11–12). The more cautious, tacit interpretation would be reaffirmed over time, and the Pangkor principle has guided religious affairs in the region ever since (Ponniah 2000: 31). For Singapore, the treaty highlighted a divergence in social and political destinies between itself and its neighbor states. Following the success of Pangkor, the British went on to formalize their involvement in other Malay states, eventually creating, in 1896, the Federated Malay States. This was, arguably, a first step toward the future unification of the mainland states; it provided a glimpse, for the first time, of what a modern, federal, united states of Malaysia might look like. Meanwhile, the differences in Singapore's composition, identity, and status were becoming increasingly obvious (Khoo 1974: 1–8).

Political reorganizations were shaping the destiny of Singapore and its Church, while at a global level too, the way that the Anglican Church engaged with the world continued to evolve, but unevenly. As discussed previously, the decennial Lambeth Conferences were intended to gather Bishops from around the world and by extrapolation an international Anglican Communion (AC) had come into being. Lambeth was both a response to the increasing internationalization of the Church and a way for the dominant English Church to generate interest in, and support for, the international aspects of its work. There were concerns that Anglicans in "remote" places, especially colonies, were in danger of exclusion, and it was hoped that the Lambeth Conferences would facilitate their participation in the developments and deliberations of the worldwide Church. A less open concern, however, may have been that increasingly self-sufficient Churches might go their own way, and the language initially used by Lambeth sounded more like a process of centralization than devolution; the stated aim was "[to] bind the Colonial Church, which is certainly in a most unsatisfactory state, more closely to the Mother Church" (Davidson 1920: 3–5). Indicative of this dissonance, Archbishop Campbell Tait (1811–82) opened the second Lambeth Conference in 1878 with a suitably internationally oriented welcome; "My brothers, representatives of the Church throughout the world, engaged in spreading the Gospel of Jesus Christ wherever the sun shines," before cleverly asserting the Church of England's effective primacy; "[I] welcome you here today, to the cradle of Anglo-Saxon Christianity" (Davidson 1920: 20). The 1878 conference would nevertheless make resolutions that were harmonious with the increasingly popular idea of an Anglican Communion; they promoted parity between member Churches, encouraged better relations between bishops and missionaries who were active in the same territories, and pledged to review the status of chaplaincies and chaplains, which, as explained previously, often enjoyed significant privileges denied to missionaries. These resolutions seemed designed to discourage the perception of hierarchical divisions between "home" Churches and "local" Churches, between chaplains and missionaries, and between bishops and clergy. These resolutions may have better reflected Lambeth's original aspirations, but, curiously, they would not reappear at the third Lambeth Conference in 1888 (Davidson 1920: 18–20).

Bishop Chambers, though not universally loved, led an intense and committed missionary life in Southeast Asia for thirty years, including ten years as bishop, and it took a heavy toll on his health. Nevertheless, his resignation, in 1879, due to illness and exhaustion, came unexpectedly, and this time there was no obvious successor (Thompson 1951: 401). Chambers was finally succeeded, in 1881, by the until-then Archdeacon of Singapore and colonial chaplain, George Frederick Hose (1838–1922) (St. Andrew's Church Mission 1881: 3). The Reverend Thomas Meredith took over Hose's roles of archdeacon and colonial chaplain (Swindell 1929: 4–5). The name of the diocese was altered, at long last, to include Singapore, though Singapore was not yet an official see; it would be referred to in full as the Diocese of Singapore, Labuan and Sarawak, because Labuan was still the only official Church of England episcopal see in the region. Hose was experienced in both Chinese- and Tamil-language mission by that stage, and language was less of an obstacle for him than for others; he was one of the foremost Malay scholars of his time, and he translated the prayer book into Malay. Malay mission may have been largely ruled out, but the Malay language was a useful lingua franca. Hose resolved to divide his time between Borneo and the Straits Settlements, much as Bishop Chambers had attempted to do, but it was still too much. Neither part of the vast diocese, it was felt, made as much progress as they would have done under two separate bishops. Much of the strain was borne by the ordinary (or rather extraordinary) clergy, whose careers always seemed to either span several decades or end tragically, and sometimes both.

Missionary work based out of St. Andrew's cathedral continued to expand under Gomes, assisted by a Tamil priest. With a shifting population like Singapore's, it was, and still is, difficult to evaluate SACM's work. It is recorded that up to 1890 there had been 356 baptisms, most of them adults, and that the Chinese missionary work was generally the most successful feature of SACM (Pascoe 1901, vol. 2: 698). The so-called Chinese-language congregations were in fact made up of speakers of many different dialects, rather than being single-language congregations. Many of the immigrants at that time hailed from Xiamen and Shantou, on the southeastern coast of China, but the total linguistic collective included Cantonese, Fuzhou (alternative spellings Foo Chow or Foochow), Hailam (Hylam), Hakka, Hinghwa, Hockchia, Hokkien, Kheh (Kay), Macao, Shanghai, Teochiu (Tehchew) and others (Ferguson-Davie 1921: 39–45). The dilemma was whether to employ one very busy ethnic-Chinese catechist who could communicate in several Chinese dialects, or to employ several part-time catechists who could each speak one dialect perfectly; this question was moot to a degree, as it was very difficult to find the right candidates to be catechists anyway. Nevertheless, by 1890 the SACM team had grown to five ethnic-Chinese catechists, each working mainly among their respective language group, catering for the Hailam (Hylam), Hakka, Hokkien, Macao, and Teochiu (Tehchew) dialects. At church services, one solution was to deliver the sermon in Hokkien, while a congregant simultaneously translated into Cantonese, so that at least two of the most widely understood languages were covered. Ironically, Gomes pointed out, none of this would have been an issue in China itself, as missionaries there always worked with one single-language community, whereas the Chinese diaspora was mixed, multiethnic, and multilingual (St. Andrew's Cathedral 1876: 26). There was no ideal solution, and the situation was compounded by the fact that the population was mobile anyway; congregants were constantly coming and going in search of work (Gomes 1888: 20–22). Gomes died in 1902, aged seventy-five (Buckley 1902, vol. 1: 300); his successor at SACM, the Reverend Richard Richards, would remain in his post for an impressive thirty-two years.

DYSFUNCTION, DISCRIMINATION, AND PREJUDICE IN CHURCH RELATIONSHIPS

By the close of the nineteenth century and the dawn of the twentieth, British society's blind faith in the wonders of empire had begun to deteriorate. Larger-scale colonial wars, especially in South Africa, consumed ever-greater quantities of men and materials and increasingly impacted British families, for whom the supposed riches of empire never seemed to be reflected in their living conditions. The effects of this dwindling enthusiasm for empire were felt in the colonial Church; Bishop Hose bewailed the shortage of missionaries, and the SPG agreed that never in its history had there been "such a dearth of clergymen offering themselves for missionary work" (Thompson 1951: 402). It did not help, possibly, that Hose was quite demanding in the outline he promoted of the ideal cleric for mission lands. He suggested, as minimum qualifications, in this order: ardent faith, physical fitness, theological learning, and useful practical skills of some kind; the candidate should preferably be an abstainer, he added, and he should have "[the] character and manners of a gentleman." It is necessary to point out that the term "gentleman" conveyed a much narrower meaning, in 1900 British parlance, compared to today; it meant, unequivocally, high social class by birth and upbringing, rather than simply being virtuous, courteous, and refined. Hose stipulated that the potential cleric for the missions should have "the character and manners" of a gentleman, rather than actually "being" a gentleman by breeding, but he was not going to accept working-class or lower-middle-class pretenders just because his diocese was desperate; "It is only a very exceptional man," he wrote, "whom distinct social inferiority will not deprive of influence." The expatriate community would quickly see through a chaplain or missionary from the "wrong" social class, according to Hose, and the locals would not be fooled either; "[they] have had much to do with English gentlemen and they instantly observe and resent any lack of good manners" he warned (Hose quoted in Taylor 1983: unnumbered pages).

Clergy faced several forms of discrimination in return for their commitment to serving in the colonies, the fourth Lambeth Conference (1897) reported. Clergy ordained in England for service in a colonial diocese or mission usually had great difficulty getting licensed in England after their return; this was despite the fact that they had been ordained by English bishops, had passed the standard examination for Holy Orders, and had been trained in the normal way. After their approved service overseas, and returning to England with the sanction of their bishop, they were regarded as wholly inferior to clergy who had been ministering in England all along. Colonial clergy who were ordained in the colonies experienced an analogous difficulty; having served faithfully, and often with distinction, for ten to fifteen years, they struggled to obtain a license to serve in England on the same terms as clergy who had been ordained by English bishops. The same difficulty applied to clergy traveling from the colonies to England simply for a rest, without plans for permanent resettlement; they experienced great obstacles to being granted permission to officiate in England during their leave of absence, even with the endorsement of their respective bishops. The victims of these double standards were, in theory, all equal members of the same Church of England (Davidson 1920: 282).

The discrimination faced by colonial clergy was mostly ignored, and they were not the only cases of discrimination. In the commentary of the time, and in most subsequent mission history, women of the colonial Church have been largely invisible. In most accounts, the missionary, almost by definition, was a masculine, heroic, and rather solitary figure; the missionary's wife, if mentioned at all, was usually a dutiful, unremarkable, and silent appendage. Contrary to this "masculine hero" myth, however, most missionaries by far were women, and most of them died in obscurity (Cox 2008: 14–17). Local women in the missions, on the other hand, were not just excluded from the Church's vision but were frequently seen in terms of a nuisance. Evidence of gender equality in some of the indigenous communities of Southeast Asia, and even female leadership roles, perturbed the male Victorian mind. Received wisdom taught that local male converts to Christianity would lapse if they were unable to find a female Christian to partner up with, and the shortage of these was blamed on the notoriously independent female spirit (Koepping 2006: 62). In male-dominated urban areas, the presence of women, especially European, Christian women, was sometimes lauded as a positive influence on men's behavior and at other times deplored as an incitement to immorality; either way, accountability rested with the women. Some progressive attitudes did also manifest themselves; mixed long-term relationships, responsibly entered into by foreign men with local women, broke taboos and gradually achieved acceptability. It is worth noting, also, that successful mission schools for girls were often deliberately oriented toward improving women's position in society (Goh 2005: 38). Nevertheless, the praise lavished on prominent male missionaries very rarely extended to the women who worked alongside them, often but not always as their wives; European missionary wives were at least considered useful, though peripheral, while those who were non-European as well as being women were doubly excluded from the history books (Cox 2008: 16–17).

Outside of masculine hero myths, it need hardly be said, few male missionaries were truly hailed as heroes either, but women missionaries struggled even to be recognized as missionaries. Women's contribution to fledgling colonial societies in general went largely unacknowledged, though their efforts and sacrifices were often enormous. This was starkly illustrated in the case of Harriette McDougall, married to Bishop McDougall, who mourned their five infant children in Borneo, and Sophia Raffles in Singapore, who also lost all five of her children, as well as her brother and her husband. By the early twentieth century, the work of many women, especially in medicine and education, had become specialized, and their profile was, at last, appropriately raised. The physician Charlotte Elizabeth Ferguson-Davie, OBE, MD, BS, sometimes simply called "Mrs. Ferguson-Davie" because she was married to Bishop Ferguson-Davie (*Singapore Diocesan Magazine*, vol. II, no. 7, May 1912: 1), revolutionized healthcare in Singapore. Ferguson-Davie received belated recognition when she was inducted into the Singapore Women's Hall of Fame in recent years, and her colleague, Dr. Ruth Patricia Elliot, has a street named after her in Singapore. In the vast majority of cases, however, the true contribution of women is largely lost to history. As the wives of missionaries did not usually appear on any official lists of missionary societies or Church bodies, they tended not to receive so much as an obituary notice in the sponsoring organization's newsletter. The writings and letters, where available, of the women of the missions, and their remarkable contributions, clearly merit closer scrutiny. In terms of women's roles within the leadership structures of the Church itself, change would begin much sooner than many people expected but more slowly than many hoped (Taylor 1998: 461–65; O'Connor 2000: 315–28).

Successive decennial Lambeth Conferences had emphasized, since 1867, both the growth and the growing international character of the Anglican Communion; resolutions of the early conferences show, on the whole, eagerness to understand the colonial missionary Church and its challenges. Attitudes to other world faiths present across the British Empire demonstrated a degree of sensitivity; "The Mohammedans [*sic*]," the fourth conference resolved, in 1897, "must be approached with the greatest care to do them justice. What is good in their belief must be acknowledged to the full and used as a foundation on which to build the structure of Christian truth" (Davidson 1920: 196). As tactfully proactive as this may sound, it is difficult to square it with the "gentleman's agreement" to abstain from Malay missionary work in Southeast Asia, after the Pangkor treaty. The Lambeth bishops also began to echo the more radical voices in the colonial Church, agreeing that "the establishment of completely autonomous native Churches" must be the goal. With impressive foresight and forewarning, they declared their determination to maintain international communion at all costs, though great cultural differences would surely increase as the local Churches attained and developed their autonomy and as identities of their own evolved (Davidson 1920: 232–37).

The subsequent Lambeth Conference, in 1908, was similarly ambitious, resolving that so-called racial problems, "the despair of statesmen," could be tackled by the Church "with the old true message of the gospel; 'Ye are all one in Christ Jesus'" (Davidson 1920: 306). In theory, however, the primary focus of the colonial Church's work was still supposed to be the British and wider white expatriate population; after all, Lambeth stated, "[t]he colonists are our own kin, and we cannot leave them to drift away from the Church of their fathers." The conference did acknowledge the broader task of evangelizing the whole human race, but dealing with the "natives" was always treated as a separate challenge, framed in terms of saving and civilizing. "It is an imperative duty," the conference resolved, "to give all possible assistance to the bishops and clergy of the colonies in their endeavors to protect the native races from the introduction among them of demoralizing influences, especially the mischief of the trade in intoxicating liquors and noxious drugs" (Davidson 1920: 192–93). Most of the vices and illicit trades in colonial society had either been introduced, encouraged, appropriated, or monopolized by the colonial authorities, but the irony here was presumably unintended.

THE STATE OF THE CHURCH APPROACHING THE CREATION OF A SEPARATE DIOCESE OF SINGAPORE

As the nineteenth century, the Victorian era, and the golden age of empire drew to a close, the Church in Singapore took stock. The ethnic breakdown of Singapore was fascinating; there were 122,000 ethnic Chinese (including immigrants and the locally born) residents, 36,000 Malays, and only 5,250 Europeans, with ethnic Indians, Eurasians, Javanese, and other residents (whether immigrants or locally born) making up the remaining 22,000. Chinese immigrants alone numbered around 125,000 a year, though, as the numbers suggest, most of these passed through to other countries. With 184,500 inhabitants in total, Singapore, though chief of the Straits Settlements, was not the most populous of them; Penang's population was 231,500, but the once-great Melaka had a much smaller population of just 91,000. Of the new Federated Malay States on the mainland, prosperous Perak was by far the most populous, with 214,000 registered inhabitants, followed by Selangor, home to Kuala Lumpur, with just 81,000. All of these areas fell within the diocese. Anglicans' links to government, business, and the military remained strong, and these links came with responsibilities and expectations. New arrivals from Britain often expected to find a parish church at the end of the road, just like at home, though with the vicar surely dressed in white linen rather than black worsted, ably assisted by his doting wife. It was not a realistic expectation to place on the pioneering missionary Church in the tropics, which would never succeed in pleasing everyone; after all, the British cohort was actually only a small part of the Church's audience (Church of England 1894: 302–3).

With the dawn of the Edwardian era, Singapore's rise to global prominence began. Its still-growing population was overwhelmingly Chinese, with approximately four ethnic-Chinese people to every Malay, and the Malays outnumbered the Europeans by about five or six to one. With the exceptions of the Eurasians and the Malays, there was a large preponderance of males over females in each ethnic group. As the population topped two hundred thousand, Singapore was still not the most populous component of British Malaya, but it had grown from being the pipe dream of a pioneer to a burgeoning commercial island-city. The potentially misleading term "British Malaya" was the unofficial name commonly used for the combined entities of the Straits Settlements (Melaka, Penang, Province Wellesley [today Seberang Perai], and Singapore, with the Dindings, Christmas, and Cocos islands added in 1886), the Federated Malay States, and the non-federated or "Unfederated" Malay States. British Malaya would form the bulk of the future separate Diocese of Singapore. The Straits Settlements, forming a single Crown Colony under the Colonial Office in London, were administered by a Governor who simultaneously served as High Commissioner of the Federated Malay States. Since 1896, the Federated Malay States had been four in number; Negri Sembilan, Pahang, Perak, and Selangor, with Pahang being the largest but also the least developed. Government of these four states, from the British point of view, consisted of the High Commissioner, his Federal Executive and Legislative Councils, and a delegate (called the British Resident, later renamed British Advisor), a man on the ground who was attached to each state council. Each of these states, it is important to remember, was ruled by its own sultan, who was of course Malay and Muslim. The remainder of British Malaya consisted of the non-federated states of Johor (Singapore's neighbor to the north), Kedah, Kelantan, Trengganu, and Perlis, whose collective designation as Unfederated Malay States was intended to suggest parity with the Federated Malay States (Ferguson-Davie 1921: 11–12).

The total population of British Malaya, according to the 1911 census, was 2,659,262. The Straits Settlements were the least populous component of British Malaya, with around seven hundred thousand inhabitants combined in 1911, while the rest were fairly evenly divided between the two groups of Federated and Unfederated Malay States. With new immigrants further swelling the existing ethnic-Chinese and ethnic-Indian communities, however, the combined population of the Straits Settlements would increase to nearly one million by the end of the First World War, and the population of British Malaya would rise to three point three million by the subsequent census. The total number of Europeans, mostly British, in whose hands day-to-day control was concentrated, was just 10,500, with a similar number of Eurasians. The number of Asian Christians exceeded the combined number of Europeans and Eurasians, being around 29,000 (Ferguson-Davie 1921: 20–21). At the end of the nineteenth century, the then-Diocese of Singapore, Labuan, and Sarawak covered a vast and diverse territory with just seventeen European clergy, twelve of whom were from the SPG. The old diocese included not only Singapore, mainland Malaya, and the Borneo territories of Sarawak, Labuan, and British North Borneo; it also had responsibility for individual British or other Anglican residents in independent Siam (Thailand), Java, Sumatra, and all the adjacent islands, the latter of which were Dutch, not British, colonies. This need to work across colonial administrations burdened the Church with extra work, for example when marriages solemnized under British law had to be validated according to Dutch law as well (*Singapore Church Record Book* vol. 8, 1917–28: 10).

Clearly, an assortment of responsibilities faced the clergy, whose main task was still to minister to the English-speaking community, but the word "main" was somewhat moot, because in reality all the clergy were involved to some degree in ministering to local communities, whether English-speaking or not, locally born or not. The distinction between privileged chaplain and sacrificial missionary had once been painfully clear, but the boundaries between chaplaincy, parish, and mission had become increasingly blurred in practice. The SPG's innovation of hybrid chaplain-missionaries recognized and addressed the inadequacy of existing models of ministry, but regardless of how much flexibility and freedom could be worked into the role, the number of priests at the diocese's disposal remained small (Ferguson-Davie 1921: 21). One upside was that experience as a chaplain-missionary often provided a route to senior positions; the Reverend William Herbert Cecil Dunkerley (1860–1922), Archdeacon of Singapore from 1902 to 1904, had served in both Melaka and Penang prior to his arrival in Singapore. Dunkerley took over from the Reverend John Perham (1844–1928), who was archdeacon from 1891 to 1901, after missionary service in remote areas of Borneo (Swindell 1929: 4–5).

The Church of England reported three and a half thousand Church members in the diocese at the turn of the century, but there were problems with this figure: firstly, it was unclear whether these were apart from the 2,300 members concurrently reported in Singapore alone, though this probably was indeed the case; secondly, it was unclear whether all physical persons present in a church congregation (children, the unbaptized, catechumens, casual attendees, for example) were counted. It was never clear, in fact, to what extent any colonial Church membership reports were reliable. Church growth had at least been encouraging enough that the talented linguists Bishop Hose and the Reverend William Henry Gomes had begun translating the New Testament into the lingua franca of Malay, a project supported by the British and Foreign Bible Society (Church of England 1894: 304–5). The Anglican Church was an important reference point for Christian Europeans, regardless of denomination; it would be an exaggeration to call it the center of colonial community and social life, but its role and influence certainly extended beyond the boundaries of the small, strictly Anglican cohort. The Anglican Church consistently took third place among the Christian Churches, after the Roman Catholics and Methodists, in that order, or after the Roman Catholics and Presbyterians in some locations. The Anglicans' third place was not a very distant third place, numerically, and in some locations the number of Christians was fairly evenly split between three denominations. There were also other factors that made the three-way "ranking" of denominations quite complicated. Members of other Christian denominations benefited from Anglicans' connections to power; it may be crude to call them Anglicans by proxy, but they shared in the freedom to operate and umbrella of protection that were primarily provided for the official colonial Church.

Hose's closing years as bishop were devoted to preparations for finally dividing the diocese into two. It was by then unanimously agreed that Singapore and the Malay Peninsula (British Malaya), on the one hand, and Borneo on the other, each needed their own bishop. Hose resigned in 1908, before this goal was reached, after forty years in the region and an impressive twenty-seven of them as bishop (Thompson 1951: 402–406). Despite the colonial Church's ongoing limitations, the Church of England leadership was eager to promote the principle of material independence to match increasing ecclesial autonomy. This was clearly going to be difficult; "[Colonial] Church people [have] been accustomed to the assistance of endowments at home, and [they are] slow to recognize the combined privilege and duty of self-support" (Davidson 1920: 277). The message was rather blunt; being a diocese on your own means just that, but Lambeth was not about to cut its ecclesiastical progeny off overnight; "[T]hey are the children of the Church of England [and] it becomes her duty to care for them until they have been aroused to a sense of their responsibility and are able to provide for themselves." Thus, the mother Church confidently assured "a supply of men and means commensurate with the needs of the [local Church]" (Davidson 1920: 277). It was a huge promise, and a difficult one to keep.

CONCLUSION

In today's world so dependent on oil, gas, technology, and air transport, it can be difficult to appreciate the extraordinary formula for economic success that was British Malaya, with its rich sources of rubber, tin, coal, and a strategic maritime location. Return on investment in British Malaya was substantially higher than in any other part of the world, and, while the assumption has been that exploitative labor practices were a main factor in this success, return on investments actually increased after the most oppressive period of colonialism had passed, when working conditions and standards of living significantly improved. The economy of British Malaya was not very diversified, mostly consisting of rubber and tin, and it was also immature; these characteristics combined to create a high-risk environment with a corresponding potential for high return. World market prices for tin and rubber could be high but also volatile, as rising demand came from industrializing economies, and particularly for military purposes (Rönnbäck et al. 2021: 150). British Malaya had become the real jewel in Britain's crown, and its economic success continued to be safeguarded by the principles of the Pangkor treaty, a "gentleman's agreement" of non-interference in religious affairs. This was widely seen as an unspoken continuation of the old EIC's much-regretted restrictions on missionary work, which prioritized good trading relations at all costs, and, in the process, permanently disadvantaged the Anglican Church (Ponniah 2000: 31).

By absolutely prioritizing economic interests, Britain expanded its control across the region. This control was then progressively formalized and consolidated by treaties, establishing the three neighboring entities making up British Malaya; the Federated Malay States, the Unfederated Malay States, and the Straits Settlements, which included Singapore. What was missing was a unifying vision or a common feeling of belonging to this partway unified entity. In the early twentieth century there was very little, if any, sense of national identity as such among the various peoples inhabiting British Malaya, their allegiance either being to their state of residence, their ethnic group, or their country of origin. British Malaya was a manufactured political entity without a shared vocation for national development. If reasons for a sense of unity were lacking, however, reasons for a sense of division were not. British Malaya's guiding Pangkor principles, with their resulting tensions and dynamics, were viewed very differently from the vantage point of Singapore, which had no sultan as such, no Malay majority to appease, and a more diversified economy than the mainland. In other words, Singapore and Malaya, despite having much in common, were beginning to contemplate very different destinies, and it was not just about ethnic majorities, which did not necessarily translate into power and influence. Simplistic assessments may conclude that the big difference between Singapore and Malaya was that one was "Chinese" and the other was "Malay," but these generalizations are circumstantial; economics, and the underlying politics, shaped British Malaya's diverse futures, with ethnicity and religion as collateral dimensions.

The Anglican Church in Singapore had spent decades probing and experimenting, negotiating and discovering the limits of their evangelization efforts. By the time of the creation of the new Diocese of Singapore in 1909, Anglicans accepted that Christianity's appeal would be confined to some of the quarter million-or-so ethnic Chinese and some of the fifty-thousand-or-so ethnic Indians. Serious ambitions with regard to converting significant numbers of Malays had evaporated. These clear demarcations of where their target audience began and ended were in some ways convenient for the Church, in terms of allocating resources and planning operations, and having boundaries sent out the right message for maintaining good relations with other religious groups. The Church's challenge on the Malayan mainland and in Borneo was, in contrast, to be increasingly marked by the convergence of civil, military, and ecclesiastical efforts to keep the peace with the respective Malay Muslim majorities at all costs (Taylor 1983: 5–6). This interethnic tension became one of the defining features of regional Church life, but it was a tension that the Church in Singapore was largely spared. Diverging demographics would bring forward separate challenges, of course, as well as the challenge of how Singapore and Malaya would resolve to engage with each other, acknowledging their growing differences, while still being joined in the same diocese for many decades to come. The enduring challenge of competition between denominations paled in comparison to these bigger issues, and competition was not entirely negative anyway; it produced a surge in charitable and social work (amidst a proliferation of independent missions and churches) as denominations vied to outdo each other, which sometimes led to greater cooperation between them (Goh 2005: 13–14).

The Church in Singapore could operate with considerable self-confidence. In 1881, when the island's government moved to disestablish and disendow the Anglican Church in the Straits Settlements, the measure was unanimously repudiated by the Legislative Council of Singapore. The council's four Nonconformist members and the Roman Catholic governor were among the most vehement objectors, and the decree was revoked (Pascoe 1895: 696). The Church's presence, clearly, was still widely appreciated; many colonial administrators liked the old idea of spiritual and temporal powers being in alignment, but in reality the Church was becoming less vital to the late Victorian vision of empire, and the pretense that the Church's priorities were the same as the state's had worn thin (O'Connor 2000: 8). Both Church and colonialism had moved on from their former interdependent, dysfunctional relationship, and this could have left the Church vulnerable, but international support was increasing. The first Lambeth Conferences coincided with a timely shift in the Anglican global vision, whereby support for local Church autonomy went from being a minority, eccentric position to being a mainstream Anglican viewpoint. There were still reservations, but the vision of diversity favored by the "atheists of empire" and indirectly promoted by Anglo-Catholics was set to become reality. Lambeth Conference resolutions, though generally more effusive than effectual, formally provided basis and rationale for the further development of the Church in Singapore. The Church had earned its place in Singaporean society, and it had adapted effectively to new conceptions of mission, country, and economy, in preparation for becoming a separate diocese, equipped to face the challenges of the nascent twentieth century. Having secured its place, it looked toward developing much-needed social services accessible by all sections of society, but this would have to be done sensitively; different as it may have been, the wider Malayan experience taught that a busy, proactive missionary Church would always be more likely to upset non-Christians than an insular or sectarian one.

Chapter Four

"Between What Is Christian and What Is Western"

Evolving Outlooks in an Age of Change

Bishop Hose had masterminded the division of the old, overly large diocese into two; the Diocese of Singapore and the Diocese of Labuan and Sarawak, but he resigned before this was effectuated in 1909. The first bishop of the new, separate Diocese of Singapore was Charles James Ferguson-Davie (1872–1963) who, like most of the clergy at this stage of the story, was an SPG missionary, fresh from service in India. He arrived with his wife, Dr. Charlotte Elizabeth Ferguson-Davie, MD, BS, and later OBE (1880–1943), a distinguished physician and medical missionary. Bishop Ferguson-Davie toured and took stock of his new diocese, which was rapidly growing in importance. With ships thronging Singapore harbor at a rate of eight hundred a month, British officials and businesspeople arrived in an ever-increasing torrent, and Indian, Chinese, and Javanese laborers (referred to, in those days, as "coolies") disembarked in droves, as the demand for labor exploded. In addition to the long-established tin mines, rubber plantations were developing everywhere, and railways were being built to serve them. This latter development had all the usual knock-on effects of better infrastructure, from stimulating the growth of new urban and suburban areas to becoming a catalyst for Church expansion as well. In terms of clergy, the new bishop counted only twelve European or Australasian priests and three ethnic-Indian (Tamil) priests, aided by a few ethnic-Chinese and ethnic-Indian (Tamil) catechists. The New Zealand-born Reverend Herbert Crawford Izard (1869–1934) was appointed archdeacon; he had been colonial chaplain since 1905 (Swindell 1929: 4–5). No serious medical missionary work was being done at that time in Singapore, but Dr. Charlotte Elizabeth Ferguson-Davie would soon transform this aspect of Church activity.

The creation of the new diocese was a significant step forward for the Church in the wider region, and a clear indication of Southeast Asia's unrelenting rise to prominence. The new husband and wife team of bishop and physician was a highly industrious and talented partnership, but the diocese faced an ongoing problem; the thinly spread-out clergy were few, isolated, and quite lonely, being "scattered" around the long and complicated diocesan territory (*Singapore Diocesan Magazine* [*SDM*], vol. IV, no. 14, February 1914: 1–2). Bishop Ferguson-Davie declared from the outset that it was important for the clergy of Singapore to tour the diocese and appreciate its expanse and diversity for themselves (*SDM*, vol. I, no. 1, November 1910: 13). The bishop himself, meanwhile, resolved to travel to England to appeal for missionaries, and, while he was there, he founded the Singapore Diocesan Association (SDA) to rally support both at home and in Singapore. The first meeting of the SDA was held in London in the small hall at Church House, Westminster, during the bishop's visit (*SDM*, vol. I, no. 4, August 1911: 4). The SDA, in coordination with the SPG, devoted its attention to Europeans, whether resident in or somehow connected to the diocese, while the SPG concerned itself with work among non-Europeans. The SDA would also sponsor its own chaplains or chaplain-missionaries, in the style of the SPG, and the diocese would soon start to gain significant reinforcements.

The inauguration of the new diocese and the foundation of the SDA called for the launch of a diocesan magazine. The *Singapore Diocesan Magazine* (*SDM*) first appeared in November 1910, offering an overview of the diocese and highlighting its diversity. Most of the diocese's thirteen official lay readers were described as "English" (meaning English speakers), with four being Tamil speakers, while most catechists were "Chinese" (meaning Chinese speakers). Four of the Chinese-speaking catechists spoke "Hokien" (Hokkien), while "Foo-Chow" (Fuzhou) and Cantonese were also represented; there were three Tamil-speaking catechists, making nine in total, some of them being multilingual. Aside from the SDA, the list of diocesan institutions was comprehensive; the Church Workers Association, the Ministering Children's League, the Clerical Central Society of Sacred Scriptures, the Diocesan Intercessory Union, the Diocesan Clerical Library, St. Andrew's House for Schoolboys, St. Andrew's Church Mission School, St. Mary's Home for Schoolgirls, and the Chinese Girls' School (later renamed St. Margaret's) under the direction of the Church of England Zenana Missionary Society (CEZMS) (*SDM*, vol. I, no 1, November 1910: introduction). At a distance of one year since the enthronement of Bishop Ferguson-Davie, the same list was augmented by the Navvy Missionary Society, the Central Church Reading Union, the Mothers Union, the Girls' Friendly Society, the Scripture Union, Church of England Men's Society, and the Cathedral Glee Society (*SDM*, vol. I, no. 2, February 1911: 15–25; no. 4, August 1911: 7).

MANAGING INCREASING DIVERSITY

The Church's diversity was set to increase further. Soon, only half of the diocese's official lay readers would be primarily English speakers, with seven out of seventeen being Tamil speakers plus two Malay speakers, and the mix of catechists was similar to this (*SDM*, vol. I, no. 4, August 1911: introduction, ii). The absence of Chinese speakers from this picture may be due to several factors; the linguistic make-up of the Chinese community was changeable, so providing catechetical materials and even ascertaining basic literacy presented compound challenges. The use of the Tamil language, meanwhile, was clearly increasing, indicative of the large number of laborers arriving from India during those years of growing prosperity. In November 1911, the diocese's annual clergy conference and quiet day, conducted by the Reverend Charles E. Garrad of the SPG in Burma, included the "novel feature" of prayers in Tamil (*SDM*, vol. II, no. 6, February 1912: 6, 10). Ethnic Indians, more than 80 percent of them Tamils, would soon make up almost 15 percent of the population of British Malaya, and they made up an even greater proportion of the labor force, especially in rural areas. Along with the consistent growth of the ethnic-Chinese community, who were generally concentrated in urban areas, this led to the ethnic-Malay population becoming a minority in British Malaya after 1911 (Guilmoto 1993: 114).

The early years of Ferguson-Davie's tenure were perceptibly a time of change; some key members of the "old guard" of the diocese died, including the Reverend William Greenstock, the diocese's emissary in Siam (Thailand), who died in Bangkok, aged eighty-two, on March 3, 1912 (*SDM*, vol. II, no. 7, May 1912: 17). The Reverend Cecil Ross Simmons took Greenstock's old post in Bangkok in 1914, and in partnership with his wife they expanded St. Mary's girls' school there and added a small school for boys, St. Peter's. The SPG gave grants for filling vacant chaplaincy posts, usually with the proviso that they focused on Tamil or Chinese work; significantly, these posts were preferably entrusted to clergy or catechists from the respective ethnic community (Thompson 1951: 649). There were signs of growth in general as well as growing diversity; the first quarter of 1912 saw more weddings and fewer funerals, unusually for that time in Singapore (*SDM*, vol. II, no. 7, May 1912: 57–58). There were typically fairly equal numbers of marriages, baptisms, and burials at St. Andrew's cathedral, between fifteen and twenty-five of each, per quarter, and similar proportions of marriages, baptisms, and burials at the other churches but in single figures per quarter (*SDM*, vol. II, no. 6, February 1912: 46–47). New teaching missionaries, most of them women, arrived in Singapore and other parts of the diocese, as new schools were founded and existing schools expanded (*SDM*, vol. II, no. 8, August 1912: 2; no. 6, February 1912: introduction vii; vol. III, no. 9, November 1912: 3). Bishop Ferguson-Davie would eventually succeed in vastly improving clergy numbers as well, bringing five new priests to Singapore island itself, while six worked in the Federated Malay States, one each in Melaka, Penang, Bangkok (Simmons), Java, and Sumatra, with one roving chaplain, making a total of seventeen, plus one port chaplain and one chaplain to the forces (Ferguson-Davie 1921: 21). A key arrival in 1912 was the Reverend John Romanis Lee, who was placed in charge of St. Andrew's school; he transformed it, expanding it into a high school for six hundred boys. Between 1862 and 1912 it had provided only primary schooling (Sng 1980: 151).

A look at the service schedules of the new diocese's five churches in Singapore reveals the cultural and linguistic complexity being faced. St. Andrew's cathedral offered English-language Holy Communion every day and twice on Sundays, while St. Peter's (on Stamford Road, then next to St. Andrew's school and now the site of the National Library) alternated the language of Holy Communion from Sunday to Sunday, between Malay, Tamil, Hokkien, and Tamil again, with further occasional saints' days' services in Hokkien and a regular midweek service in English. St. Matthew's at Sepoy Lines, near the General Hospital, launched under the patronage of St. Peter's in 1902, offered Holy Communion just twice per month and was mainly Cantonese and English speaking. St. Peter's itself had begun as the Reverend William Henry Gomes's new chapel in 1875 and was consecrated as a church in 1907 (*SDM*, vol. I, no. 2, February 1911: 9). The Reverend Richard Richards oversaw the Chinese-language work (in several dialects) and Malay-language work there, the Reverend John Romanis Lee of St. Andrew's school was acting priest in charge, and A. R. Thavasiapan took care of the Tamil-language work (*SDM*, vol. II, no. 6, February 1912: introduction, i). St. John's, the Jurong neighborhood plantation church, also started by Gomes and consecrated in 1884 [*SDM*, vol. I, no. 2, February 1911: 9], held one Hokkien service per month, and the Garrison Church (better known as St. George's) at Tanglin Barracks had no fixed public service schedule at that time (*SDM*, vol. VIII, no. 29, November 1917: iii). The predominance of Hokkien among the Chinese dialects is evident, but the Fuzhou (or Foo Chow, Foochow) ethnolinguistic community had been growing since the turn of the century; 1916 would see the first Fuzhou deacon ordained, in a service with ordination prayers, candidate's responses, and scripture readings each in different languages (*SDM*, vol. VI, no. 23, May 1916: 39). Most parishes started life as offshoots of St. Andrew's; church plants, in today's parlance, and "missions" in the terminology of a century ago. This aspect of St. Andrew's ministry, launched almost as soon as it became Singapore's cathedral, continues up to the present day.

The presentation of colonial history in various media has tended to uphold an image of Western expatriates, relatively few as they were, as being at the center of all aspects of colonial life. Most of Singapore's residents, in fact, had little or no direct contact with Westerners, whether through their work, school, or religious life, and the majority remained largely oblivious to and unconcerned with Westerners' thought, values, and day-to-day activities. British and European expatriates, by the same token, mostly came into contact with locals within a dynamic of master and servant, not as teacher and pupil or priest and parishioner. Christians' primary interface with Singapore's diversity was therefore not about constructive gestures such as providing language-specific church services; how to introduce a Christian, evangelistic dimension into hierarchical daily relationships was the subject of some debate, exemplified by a 1913 *SDM* article titled "A Servant Question." Servants were considered a necessity for most Western expatriates, and attaching at least one or two servants to the household was within the budget of even modestly paid colonial employees. This situation was, a correspondent of the *SDM* argued, a missed opportunity for evangelism: "If everyone at all interested in Missions [sic] would start at once on the practical work of beginning a Christian household, evangelizing the world would not present half the difficulties that it does," the anonymous author, signing off as E. C. S., boldly suggested. "A Scotch lady attended her cook's Confirmation lately at St. Peter's church and spoke afterwards with amazement of the apathy displayed towards the question of Christian servants." This question was presented as being twofold; why do Christian households not make a point of exclusively employing Christian servants, or why should the household not be a context for converting those servants who are not already Christian; "If all our European Christians helped their servants . . . they would learn and be converted, as I know from experience." The author claimed that members of the Chinese congregations were mystified by the fact that British families would gladly employ Chinese servants, but not give preference to Chinese Christian ones; "Personally my husband and I have had none but Christian servants . . . with excellent results" (*SDM*, vol. III, no. 10, February 1913: 50).

WAR, WEALTH, AND CHANGING VIEWS OF EMPIRE AND CHURCH

Singapore, already successful, was about to experience an economic boom, triggered by the First World War, which would see global demand for rubber and tin skyrocket. The hunt for raw materials had always been central to the colonial ambitions of the imperial powers in Southeast Asia, though this was not, initially, the main motive behind the colonization of Singapore. The island originally appealed because of its strategic maritime location, and the potential for exploiting Malaya's vast resources was identified subsequently; with good reason, the modest nature of Britain's initial expectations led to the colonization of Singapore being characterized as "stumbling upon a treasure chest" (White 1999: 176). As the financial and commercial hub of British Malaya, Singapore's economy presented interesting paradoxes, however; it was focused on a comparatively narrow range of exports, which drew high prices and generated high returns, while also suffering from fluctuating demand and requiring large capital investment to begin with. Global demand for rubber and tin hinged upon highly unpredictable local and international factors, making it very unstable. Rubber and tin were increasingly essential for the world's developing societies, but developing markets are immature markets, and these factors combined to make Singapore both a very high-risk and a very high-potential-return economic environment. According to conventional economic analysis, colonial economies were usually characterized by high returns, largely due to the exploitation of labor; this has been shown to be less the case in British Malaya, where returns actually increased as labor relations and working conditions steadily improved (Rönnbäck et al. 2021: 150–53).

The increased wartime demand for British Malaya's exports was good news for Singapore economically, but the Church had nothing to celebrate, as the war prevented new clergy from arriving to replace the steadily disappearing old guard (*SDM*, vol. VI, no. 22, February 1916: 2). Clergy who might otherwise have been able and willing to venture out to Southeast Asia could not easily make the trip (Ferguson-Davie 1921: 21). The flow of men was reversed, in fact, as some Singapore residents resolved to return to Europe to join the armed forces, and others joined local volunteer units as a patriotic gesture. Around two hundred men from the diocesan area departed to enlist in Europe, including a French contingent; the published list of enlistees would grow from one page of names to five pages by February 1915. Initial war panic quickly subsided, especially as the overall economic impact proved to be positive, but imports were inevitably affected. The biggest strictly military impact of the war on Singapore, arguably, was the mutiny of Indian Sepoys in February 1915, which claimed more than thirty lives in addition to those of forty-seven mutineers, who were publicly executed. The mutiny, in wartime no less, laid bare the extent of latent discontent in the British Empire, confirming that its golden age was well and truly over (*SDM*, vol. V, no. 17, November 1914: 1–3, 50; no. 18, February 1915: 1, 7–11; no. 19, May 1915: 1–5).

Events like the 1915 mutiny prompted important questions in Church circles about how the empire was to be understood going forward, and this is evident from the sometimes surprisingly frank editorials in the *Singapore*

Diocesan Magazine (*SDM*). The war in course was supposedly being fought in defense of the "ideal of empire," but empire, the *SDM* asserted, is not an intrinsically good or bad thing; the British Empire was only barely excusable, the magazine said, through achievements such as the eradications of slavery, cannibalism, and suttee (the self-immolation of a widow on the funeral pyre of her husband) in India. If this argument was not enough to distance Singapore's Christians from the war hysteria gripping England, the *SDM* pointed out that while imperial citizens were rightly shaken by the war, not all of the area of the Diocese of Singapore was technically part of the British Empire; the bulk of "British" Malaya was only tied to Britain by treaty rather than actually being a British possession. Hundreds of Christians belonging to the diocese, furthermore, whether British citizens or not, actually lived and worked under the Dutch or Thai flag, not the British one (*SDM*, vol. V, no. 17, November 1914: 1–3; no. 20, August 1915: 37–44).

With its distinctly less than jingoistic response to the war, the Church was gratified to find that staffing problems began to ease from 1918 onwards. New clergy arrivals coincided with renewed Church growth and a quarterly rise in baptisms, weddings, and funerals, though overall numbers were still modest. According to the postwar census, British Malaya's population stood at three-point-three million, but only around seventy thousand of these were listed as Christians. Of these, fifteen thousand were Europeans, twelve and a half thousand were Eurasians, more than twenty thousand were ethnic Chinese and twenty-four thousand were ethnic Indian. To offer a pew-based Anglican Church perspective, on Christmas Day 1922, this boiled down to 499 communicants at St. Andrew's cathedral and 250 communicants elsewhere in Singapore (*SDM*, vol. X, no. 38 [printed document misnumbered, actually no. 39], April 1920: 2; vol. XI, no. 41, February 1921: 5–6; vol. XII, no. 48, November 1922: 5; vol. XIII, no. 49, February 1923: 3). The economic boom sparked by the war gave way to a postwar slump, which saw demands placed upon the Church's fledgling social assistance programs multiply (*SDM*, vol. XI, no. 43, August 1921: 1). Demand for both rubber and tin began to pick up again after a few years, but perhaps the biggest economic news of the period was also a clue to Singapore's future; the collapse of the German fleet had focused naval pundits' attention on maritime expansion in the Pacific, and Singapore was to be developed as a major naval military base (*SDM*, vol. XIII, no. 49, February 1923: 3; no. 51, August 1923: 5).

From every perspective, it seemed, an age of transformation was underway. The first postwar Lambeth Conference opened up a vast and consequential area of discussion, namely the role and participation of women in the Church; the *SDM* described it as the most debatable and controversial matter at Lambeth 1920. A key outcome of the conference was that women would be permitted to conduct morning and evening prayer and to exhort the congregation in intercessory prayer, though this milestone ruling was only passed by a slim and contested vote. The *SDM*'s anonymous and very conservative correspondent dismissed the conference's "concession" and warned that the move "would not satisfy a tiny but active minority of women [who] only wish to occupy the reading desk or the pulpit on their way to the altar" (*SDM*, vol. X, no. 40, November 1920: 25). The women's ordination lobby, in other words, had just received a significant boost, and they were not about to stop there. This "revolutionary" possibility was "fraught with untold dangers," the SDM warned, admitting "a genuine feeling of alarm" over women's ordination; the SDM's own proposed compromise was to allow an order of deaconesses to be established (*SDM*, vol. XI, 43, August 1921: 28). It is not clear, at the distance of one hundred years, to what extent the *SDM* spoke for the clergy and people of the diocese on these issues, but it would later become clear that there were a few vehement supporters of women's ordination in their ranks.

Bishop Ferguson-Davie, firmly SPG-Anglo-Catholic in his theological outlook, was in practice committed to reconciling differing visions; his ecclesiology, by his own description, was that of "Ecclesia Anglicana," the reformed but continuing Catholic Church in England, combining Catholic and Protestant elements in harmony (*SDM*, vol. III, no. 10, February 1913: 24). However, the old "tightrope" policy favored by the British government, of maintaining harmony between the Church's opposing wings by appointing "liberal" bishops, would prove inadequate to deal with the challenges of the twentieth century. As Lambeth 1920 demonstrated, the Church's internal disputes were becoming more frequent and more complex; even the much-anticipated revision of the prayer book in 1928, for example, ended up disappointing both Evangelicals and Catholics (*SDM*, vol. XVIII, no. 71, August 1928: 1–2). There were further paradoxes at the Singapore clergy conference that year, when the clergy voted to refuse other denominations' requests to use Anglican buildings, to share buildings, or even to invite Anglicans to preach in their buildings, while also expressing support for the idea of a cross-denominational "united Church" (*SDM*, vol. XVIII, no. 72, November 1928: 28). The latter idea promoted the organizational amalgamation of different denominations (typically Anglicans, Methodists, Presbyterians, and some others), building on their similarities and working round their differences. This proposal was already gaining traction in India, where potential postcolonial models of Church were already being explored. As an intermediate step, the Church of India, Burma, and Ceylon (CIBC) was formed in 1930, as a province in communion with Canterbury, while the united Church idea remained on the discussion table. Enthusiasm for a united Church grew among Singapore's Anglicans, notwithstanding the potential obstacles of theology, polity, and ecclesiology, while similar discussions were taking place among the missionary Churches in China. The Anglican clergy of Singapore admitted, at the following year's clergy conference, that their actual day-to-day cooperation with other denominations was poor, but they nevertheless asserted that the united Church was a model to aspire to (*SDM*, vol. XVIII, no. 72, November 1928: 41–42, 88–97; vol. XIX, no. 76, November 1929: 56).

CLERGY'S INSTABILITY AND ETHNIC MISSION CHALLENGES

Bishop Ferguson-Davie retired in 1927, and he was succeeded by Basil Coleby Roberts (1887–1957), until then chaplain-missionary in Selangor on the Malayan mainland, who had also served as a forces chaplain during the First World War (*SDM*, vol. VII, no. 26, February 1917: 16). Like his predecessor, Roberts was married to a physician (Wardle 1984: 22). Clergy numbers in the diocese hovered around twenty priests during the interwar years, comprising ethnic-community-specific Cantonese-, Fuzhou-, and Tamil-speaking priests, multilingual Chinese-speaking priests, and a mix of SPG- or SDA-sponsored chaplains and missionaries, in addition to diocesan priests (*Singapore Church Record Book*, vol. 8, 1917–28: 174). Meanwhile, in Bangkok, Mr. and Mrs. Simmons were joined, in 1927, by the Reverend Clarence William Norwood from Perth, Australia, who arrived at the same time as two new teachers for the growing schools. The new bishop sought the SPG's support to increase the number of mission-chaplaincies in the diocese, but this was made unlikely by the worldwide depression, which was being felt in Singapore. The Church experienced a drop in financial help from overseas, also due to the emerging needs of newer Church configurations around the world, including the large new CIBC (*SDM*, vol. XX, no. 77, February 1930: 37–38; no. 80, November 1930: 6). The Church's demographics were also affected, as rubber planters and others responded to plummeting exports by reducing production, cutting wages, and ultimately demanding that their immigrant estate workers be sent home. Between 1930 and 1932 more than one hundred and fifty thousand Indians were repatriated, and assisted immigration programs were cancelled (Guilmoto 1993: 114).

A crucial role in the diocese became vacant in 1930, with the resignation of Archdeacon Frank Guthrie Swindell (1874–1975), who had been in that role since 1916, and had been colonial chaplain since 1914. It would be well over a year before a suitable successor was found, in the person of the Reverend Graham White (1884–1945). The announcement sadly coincided with the death of a revered Tamil-language priest, the Reverend David S. Ponniah, aged sixty-six (*SDM*, vol. XX, no. 77, February 1930: 45; vol.

XXIII, no. 83, August 1931: 1; no. 84, November 1931: 9). White arrived in Singapore the following year, 1931 (*Singapore Church Record Book*, vol. 9, 1928–41: 66–67). The few other new arrivals around this time included the twenty-six year old Reverend Thomas Reginald Dean, as assistant chaplain at the cathedral (*Singapore Church Record Book* vol. 9, 1928–41: unnumbered page). Dean's brief tenure ended in "unhappy circumstances" with his "totally unexpected" resignation at the start of 1932; this was accepted immediately, and "Mr. Dean . . . sailed for England on 2nd February, having been married to Miss Adeline Shaw on the same day" (*SDM*, vol. XXIV, no. 85, February 1932: 3). More than eight decades later, Dean (1902–2013) would be feted as the oldest man in the United Kingdom. Also in 1932, in Bangkok, Mr. and Mrs. Simmons retired, and after a couple of years the Reverend Cecil George Eagling would arrive to take charge of the mission. Norwood continued as chaplain, while a bequest of real estate provided much-needed funds for the two schools there (*Singapore Free Press* 1933: 4).

In terms of evangelization, the focus continued to be the ethnic-Chinese and ethnic-Indian communities, while significant engagement with the Malays generally remained elusive. In 1933, Canon Stacy Waddy (1875–1937), General Secretary of the SPG, visited the diocese during a tour of the Pacific. He was impressed, he told the *Malaya Tribune,* by Singapore's pioneering diversity, exemplified in the multiethnic Eucharistic service at St. Andrew's cathedral, which was not the global norm at that time. Waddy saw Singapore as a beacon of future Christian influence in Asia, shining towards the lands further east (*Malaya Tribune* 1933: 9). This was optimistic language, given that Japan had already invaded China. Bishop Roberts certainly intended to build on regional and international connections; he favored sending candidates to train for ordination in Rangoon, Burma, as well as in Kuching, Sarawak, and the SPG offered some financial support to make this possible. The hub of missionary work in Singapore was still St. Andrew's, with its multitude of offshoots in several neighborhoods. The Reverend Richard Richards, who had mastered several Chinese dialects, led the St. Andrew's staff of ethnic-Chinese clergy and catechists, and one ethnic-Tamil priest. The SPG supported this and the work of ethnic-Tamil priests in other locations of the diocese, such as Penang. Richards often pointed out how much more effective the Chinese work might have been, had there been just one or two more missionaries with knowledge of one or more Chinese dialects, and a few more Chinese staff to work under them. The right combination of people was never quite achieved, and the great variety of dialects in use made a single training center for such staff impractical. There was no realistic alternative to importing staff from China, and this was not always popular or feasible. Richards retired in 1934, after an astonishing forty-eight years devoted mainly to ethnic-Chinese missionary work, and thirty-two years in Singapore (*SDM*, vol. XXVI, no. 93, February 1934: 1).

At the time of his retirement, Richards had three churches and a mission hall under his care. A successor was not found until 1938, when the Reverend Albert John "Jack" Bennitt took up the task of superintending, by then, thirteen congregations, speaking, between them, eight Chinese dialects, as well as Tamil, English, and Malay, in many and varied combinations. Having survived the global depression, however, Singapore now faced a new international crisis. Japan had effectively been at war with China since 1931, and this brought a new wave of Chinese arrivals to Southeast Asia, with many seeking refuge in the perceived safety of Singapore. Wealthy merchants generously provided assistance for the refugees, but the strain on the island community as a whole was considerable. Time would reveal, of course, that Singapore was no long-term refuge from the Japanese. One man with particular insights into the developing international situation would be the Reverend Albert Victor Wardle, known as Victor or Vic, who was appointed Chaplain of the Mission to Seamen (today renamed the Mission to Seafarers) in 1934 (*Singapore Church Record Book* vol. 9, 1928–41: 128). Wardle loved the sea and seafaring and had served on deck in the Royal Navy as an ordinary sailor during the First World War; he never shared this fact with the mariners he ministered to, refusing to capitalize on this shared experience, but he was able to relate to them with confidence. Under Wardle, the Mission, based at the Marine Hostel, strategically placed between the docks and the city, at the fork of Anson and Robinson Roads, became a vibrant and highly valued ministry (Wardle 1984: 18–31).

EVOLVING UNDERSTANDINGS OF EDUCATION AND HEALTHCARE AS MISSIONARY WORK

All of the main Christian denominations considered it a priority to establish educational institutions across Southeast Asia. They aspired to span the whole spectrum from preschool to university, from one-room village schools to well-equipped high schools and colleges. But if Church leaders thought that this would lead to large numbers of conversions, they could think again; while conversions to Christianity did occur, they were no more likely to happen in a school setting than anywhere else (Goh 2005: 9–10). This had been a source of disappointment for early missionaries in Southeast Asia, with some concluding bitterly that education missions amounted to "casting pearls before swine" (McDougall 1851: 77), but the Church had persisted in its efforts. The Reverend Reginald Keith Sorby Adams (1901–76) was an Australian priest who was appointed principal of St. Andrew's school in

Singapore in 1934, the same year in which the diocese also took over a private school in Katong that would become St. Hilda's school (Sng 1980: 151). In 1938, the government requisitioned the sites occupied by St. Andrew's school and the adjacent St. Peter's church on Stamford Road, which was then home to four ethnic-Chinese congregations and two ethnic-Indian congregations. The Reverend Jack Bennitt, only recently arrived, made hurried plans to build two new replacement churches; these became Holy Trinity, for the Fuzhou and Hokkien congregations, and Christ Church, for the Tamil congregations, which would be opened in 1940–41 (Thompson 1951: 651). St. Andrew's school, under Sorby Adams, relocated to a spacious new building in Woodsville, off Serangoon Road (Wardle 1984: 57). The Church's girls' school, meanwhile, had remained in the hands of the Church of England Zenana Missionary Society until 1900, when the diocese took it over. It would become a government-aided school in 1939 and would later be named St. Margaret's, in 1949 (Sng 1980: 151).

Sorby Adams, like so many of his predecessors, lamented that the relationship between attendance of the Church's schools and attendance of the Church's services was not stronger, complaining of "leakage" between one ministry and the other (*SDM*, vol. XXVI, no. 96, November 1934: 4). The Church, however, had always been conscious of some parents' fears that Christian education would mean indoctrination, or that it would erode ethnic identity; Church schools did not and could not, realistically, oblige pupils to convert, but they did aim to impart a Christian moral understanding (Goh 2005: 38–40). Despite concerns, the Church's education provision was actually widely appreciated, as well as being officially welcomed by the authorities. Colonial governments were not usually prepared to invest in local education for its own sake, but they realized that encouraging the Church's schools was in their interest. Control of Southeast Asia was regarded as nothing less than vital for the continuation of Western civilization; this was no longer a Boys' Own adventure by sailing ship to vanquish pirates, this was actually a matter of economic life and death. Britain's navy, Britain's industry, and Britain's money all depended, in some way, on Southeast Asia, and influence had to be maintained at all levels of society; in case Britain was not convinced of this, other empires were waiting in the wings and ready to take over. As much as possible, local populations had to be positively engaged with the administration's vision, with all their skills and abilities, working for the ongoing development of the territory and the economy. Some argued that by educating ordinary Singaporeans and Malayans, schools were equipping foreign competition to take away European jobs, but they were quickly reminded that the supply of willing European workers alone had never been adequate to meet the needs of flourishing colonies like British Malaya (Ferguson-Davie 1921: 73–75).

Anglican schools provided a modern English-language education that prepared the student for a career in government service, the professions, or commerce, while inculcating an unmistakably Western and European outlook. Alumni could be found working in every government department, often reaching prominent positions in society, which further enhanced the schools' reputations and encouraged greater official support (Goh 2005: 10). Anglican schooling was seen as a gateway to local and international opportunities and social advancement; it instilled confidence, transcended interethnic boundaries, and facilitated interaction with the European community (Nagata 2005: 125). It gave access not just to employment, but, crucially, employment in positions of leadership and responsibility. Church schools across the empire thereby helped, usually inadvertently, no doubt, to prepare the ground for the end of colonialism, ironically while preaching Western values, though in fact colonial personnel were increasingly frank about their loss of confidence in the imperial ideal. The West had encroached upon the East in countless ways, but, by the interwar years, few Europeans were brazen enough to pretend that the West was perfect. Notions that "West is best" or that "Western" equates to "Christian" did not go unchallenged, with Dr. Ferguson-Davie pointing out "the evils against which [the Church] has had to struggle, and still has to struggle in the West" and asserting "the vast distinction between what is Christian and what is Western" (Ferguson-Davie 1921: 75–76).

Multiethnic integration was promoted by default in Church schools; different ethnic groups were generally obliged to study side by side, for convenience and for order, and objections arising from caste and color differences were usually swept aside. The issue of caste had been allowed to interfere with education delivery in the past and this was no longer tolerated (Pascoe 1901, vol. 2: 618). Whites were still considered superior, but hierarchy among non-whites was disallowed (Burgess 2012: 389). This was not the only contradiction on display; some Anglican schools focused on less-advantaged groups in society, such as girls and orphans, while the exclusive St Andrew's school, with its privileged cohort of more than eight hundred boys by the 1930s, was recognized as one of Asia's elite institutions. Most Anglican schools were supported well enough to enable them to enlarge and improve their premises, even in the context of the interwar slump. As Canon Waddy of the SPG had observed, the multiethnic character of schooling was mirrored in church worship by the 1930s. Ethnic interaction in Singapore's prewar Church never reached the level it would achieve fifty years later, but discrimination within church activities was being successfully eliminated (Hayter 1991: 20–21).

Dr. Ferguson-Davie began to address Singapore's healthcare needs in the early 1910s, within a few years of her arrival. St. Andrew's Medical Mission was launched in 1913, with the opening of a dispensary on Bencoolen Street; the following year a small hospital opened in a former school on Upper Cross

Street, and a third dispensary opened in Pasir Panjang in 1915. In 1922, St. Andrew's Hospital was built, situated on Erskine Road in the crowded Chinese quarter; it was especially dedicated to the needs of women and children, with an additional dispensary devoted to Malays (Ferguson-Davie 1921: 68–70). Donations came from the cathedral, the SDA, the SPCK, and an anonymous Chinese donor. Gradually, medical missions were established in most of the Diocese of Singapore's locations, on the island of Singapore itself and beyond, during the 1920s, but one of the biggest challenges was keeping up with the rapacious growth of the population; Singapore island alone had gained a quarter of a million inhabitants inside of two decades (Thompson 1951: 408–16, 649–50). Dr. Patricia Ruth Elliot (later MBE) (some sources spell her surname "Elliott" and some sources reverse the first names to "Ruth Patricia") took over at St. Andrew's Hospital in 1927 and oversaw a modernizing revolution in young persons' care. Pioneering educational activities were arranged, including woodwork and music, and some children became Scouts and Guides while in hospital, which all contributed to recovery (Thompson 1951: 651–52). Further developments were made possible due to multiple acts of generosity by William Morris, Lord Nuffield (1877–1963). In 1935, on one of many visits to Singapore and Malaya, Nuffield was greatly impressed by the work of St. Andrew's Hospital; he donated 1,250 British pounds (about 95,000 pounds or 128,000 US dollars today) each to St. Andrew's in Singapore and St. Nicholas's home for the blind in Penang, and the same amount split between three other charities (*Malaya Tribune* 1936: 12). With this and further fundraising, St. Andrew's was able to expand considerably, onto a government-donated site in the Siglap seaside neighborhood, by 1939 (*Singapore Church Record Book*, vol. 9, 1928–41: 198–99).

THE STATE OF THE CHURCH IN SINGAPORE AFTER ITS FIRST CENTENARY

Bishop Basil Coleby Roberts (1887–1957) resigned at the end of 1940, and John Leonard Wilson (1897–1970), until then Dean of Hong Kong, was nominated to replace him. This wartime appointment, fraught with delays, seemed to be universally unpopular; a better choice may have been Archdeacon Graham White, some felt, including White himself, and the announcement of the outsider Wilson's nomination caused disappointment and confusion (Hayter 1991: 21). Since at least the 1860s, Singapore had nurtured a clear High Church and Anglo-Catholic identity, while Wilson, a former CMS missionary, was considered to be distinctly Low Church (McKay 1974: 15). The fact that he often dressed casually in shorts, or in slacks, shirt, and a necktie in the colors of the Durham Light Infantry (his First World War regiment) did not endear him to some (McKay 1974: 55). Wilson himself did not consider Singapore a "congenial" appointment either, and he sensed that the clergy were "spiky" about his arrival, even noting that there was talk of resignations in protest (McKay 1974: 15). The highest Church leadership had managed to make a bishop's appointment that pleased no-one, but the world was already at war, after all; options, resources, and logistics were subject to limitations, and much bigger problems loomed. In a letter of congratulations to Wilson, dated March 31, 1941, Bishop George West of Rangoon focused on the historic timing of the appointment; Singapore was "very strategic in more ways than one" and the task facing Wilson was a historic meeting of the spiritual and the patriotic; "Bring Singapore under God's direction," West wrote, "and you will certainly strike a blow for the Empire and the world at large" (Wilson, papers: JLW4).

In the one hundred years since it had achieved primacy of the Straits Settlements in 1836, Singapore had been transformed from a sparsely populated trading post into a key international commercial, logistic, and military hub. Joined to the Malayan mainland by the half-mile- (eight hundred meter-) long concrete Causeway, Singapore island was roughly the same size as New York City, and roughly the same size and shape as the Isle of Wight. Its substantial naval base sat to the north of the island, and the city, with its charming and bustling downtown, occupied the southernmost tip. Newcomers perceived Singapore as "utterly cosmopolitan" with "no color bar" (Wardle 1984: 21). The population of the island was three quarters of a million (it would reach one million after the war) and this was a substantial proportion (about 15 percent) of only about five million inhabitants for the whole of British Malaya. The Anglican clergy resident on the island, besides the bishop, were just six European priests, four ethnic-Chinese priests, three ethnic-Indian priests, and the Mission to Seamen chaplain. Two of the European clergy were solely occupied as schoolmasters, rather than as pastors of a church, as was one of the ethnic-Indian priests. One ethnic-Chinese priest and one ethnic-Indian priest were listed as honorary members of the diocese, with limited duties (Hayter and Bennitt nd: 4).

Singapore in 1940 could give the impression of being a very Christian city. St. Andrew's cathedral occupied the most prominent south-central site in the town at that time, the site originally allocated by Stamford Raffles; today, the cathedral is dwarfed by other buildings, most noticeably the Swissôtel Stamford next-door, nearly four times its height. Near to St. Andrew's were churches of the American Methodists, the Presbyterians, the Roman Catholics, the Plymouth Brethren, and the Armenian Apostolic Church; the Roman Catholic cathedral was not much farther away, and the newish Salvation Army HQ was just the other side of Fort Canning Hill. There were around fifteen Anglican places of worship on the island (the number fluctuating because some were in various stages of construction, repair, or temporary accommodation) with similar numbers for the other main denominations. The majority of Singapore's churches at that time were still primarily intended for Europeans, though they all had some English-speaking Asian attendees by 1940, while most of the general population of the island continued to speak little or no English. Anglican missionary outreach, demanding as it was to carry out, was not as extensive as that of the Roman Catholics or the American Methodists, and in some areas that of the Presbyterians or the Plymouth Brethren. It remained true, however, that all of these Churches benefited from the Anglicans' solid links to civil power, which assured certain freedoms, privileges, protections, and status for all Christian groups in principle (Goh 2005: 7). The established presence of the Western Churches could not detract from the character of prewar downtown Singapore, upon closer inspection, as being thoroughly Chinese. The overwhelming majority of downtown residents were ethnic Chinese, and, since 1921, they had been Singapore's largest ethnic group (Goh 2005: 36). The Malays were still mainly a rural people who lived on the outskirts of the city, and the Europeans, including the large number of rubber planters, generally resided in the suburbs. It was, of course, among the ethnic Chinese that most of the Churches' work was being done (Ferguson-Davie 1921: 35).

In population and area, the Diocese of Singapore was one of the largest in the world, despite its small cohort of clergy. The diocese comprised Singapore and the whole of British Malaya, the whole of independent Siam (Thailand), the islands of Java and Sumatra (politically part of the Dutch East Indies) as well as a number of smaller islands including the Dinding, Cocos and Christmas Islands as part of the Straits Settlements. Mainland Malaya was, in size and shape, comparable to Britain without the southwestern tip formed by the counties of Devon and Cornwall. The journey from the Thai border in the north to Singapore in the south was about six hundred miles (nearly one thousand kilometers) by road or rail, the main trunk road and railway line running the whole length of the Peninsula, fairly near to the west coast. Bishop Roberts, in a letter to his newly appointed successor of January 18, 1941, told Bishop Wilson that he himself had "fairly successfully" covered the diocese with a visitation over the course of each year, traveling by land, sea, and air, using a special travel allowance from diocesan funds. He would spend three to four months away from Singapore each year, on trips of up to six weeks at a time. As far as getting around Singapore on normal daily business, Roberts informed Wilson that a car was definitely needed, but not provided. Roberts also offered some strange linguistic advice to his successor. He wrote that six languages were routinely used across the diocese; Malay, five different Indian languages, and Thai in the northernmost states, which actually adds up to seven, with no mention of any Chinese languages. Roberts advised Wilson not to attempt to learn any of these languages, because it would consume so much time, and if the bishop were seen to favor one language it would risk offending the other language groups (Wilson, papers: JLW4). Wilson disagreed, and he would eventually exhort all active clergy to learn Malay as the most useful lingua franca and as the emerging national language of most of the diocesan territory (Wilson, papers: JLW2). Malay had always been spoken to domestic employees, usually picked up from the employees themselves, and it was often the "Mem" or lady of the house who acquired the better command of the language (Wardle 1984: 27).

Despite its size and growing population, Singapore was one of the smallest dioceses in the world in terms of clergy numbers. The average, including missionaries, rose to around thirty-three during the later prewar period, with all but two or three of these working in Singapore or Malaya, and this number did not include the growing cohort of armed forces chaplains stationed in the diocese. At the time of Bishop Roberts's departure there were twenty-eight clergy in total, including missionaries; eight were ethnic-Indian and seven were ethnic-Chinese. Forces chaplains numbered seven and were set to increase rapidly (Wilson, papers: JLW4). Just as Singapore and Malaya's tin mining and rubber planting industries were securely in the hands of European (usually British) expatriates, often assisted by ethnic-Indian managers and served by ethnic-Chinese staff, the European priests dotted around the diocese were typically assisted by an ethnic-Indian or ethnic-Chinese priest and one or two ethnic-Chinese staff (Hayter and Bennitt nd: 3–4). In Bangkok, the Reverend Clarence Norwood decided to return to Australia, leaving the Reverend Cecil Eagling as chaplain (*Singapore Church Record Book* vol. 9, 1928–41: 226). Costs in Bangkok rose and St. Peter's school had to close, so in 1940 that mission was reluctantly brought to an end, though the chaplaincy would remain. It had never been quite possible to staff or equip the Bangkok mission on an adequate scale to make any real impact on the majority Buddhist country. Eagling stayed on as chaplain with his wife, even as war loomed (Thompson 1951: 650–51).

Since the Japanese invasion and annexation of Manchuria in 1931, the predictions of those who foresaw a disastrous future for Southeast Asia seemed to be justified. Japanese military and economic ambitions were no secret, and these ambitions became consolidated in the policy of expansionism. War in the Pacific was now a reality, and the prospect of another global conflict was not ignored by the people of Singapore. The diocesan magazine expressed hope in the League of Nations, but noted with alarm that Christian organizations in Germany, such as the YMCA and Evangelical Youth Movement, had been absorbed into the Hitler Youth (*SDM*, vol. XXVI, no. 93, February 1934: 13, 19); no-one could have imagined that Singapore's own YMCA building would become the interrogation and torture center for the Japanese secret police. With Japan's entry into all-out war with China on July 7, 1937, the eight-year-long Pacific War had begun. Less than twenty years had passed since the 1918 Armistice, but for Southeast Asia, references to The War began to mean the new one already in progress, rather than the Great War. Southeast Asia had been left substantially unaffected by the First World War, and colonial residents had carried on with their lives largely as normal, which was regarded as the patriotic thing to do. It was all going to be very different after 1939, but the nature and full extent of the disruption to come were not foreseen (Jarvis 2021: 85). At Singapore's Marine Hostel of the Mission to Seamen, the leader of a visiting party of German sailors sadly announced that they would no longer be allowed to visit the British mission, but they vowed to come back, someday; meanwhile, the Mission chaplain also noted the arrival of a few Jewish refugees in Singapore (Wardle 1984: 35). The outbreak of war in Europe did not prevent new arrivals in the diocese; the Reverend John Hayter joined the clergy of St. Andrew's cathedral as assistant chaplain just before Easter 1941. Hayter experienced pangs of guilt for having left Britain behind at the height of the blitz, but others in Singapore considered themselves "well out of it" for being so safely distanced from war worries (Hayter 1991: 21).

CONCLUSION

Considerable peace and prosperity had been achieved across the territory known as British Malaya, and as the official colonial Church, the Anglican Church enjoyed status in disproportion to its modest presence in the country. After the creation of the Diocese of Singapore, the Church's work diversified, with a wide range of organizations, clubs, societies, and even hospitals, in addition to well-established schools, missions, and chaplaincies. The human diversity of the new diocese also increased, and Ferguson-Davie, the first bishop, considered it vital for his clergy to go out and fully understand the lived reality of the diocese. Ferguson-Davie himself was part of a tradition of bishops in Southeast Asia who passionately affirmed Anglo-Catholic churchmanship, even within contexts of widespread disdain for Roman Catholicism. Behind this arguable contradiction sat the knowledge that Roman Catholic missionary societies were generally more successful, but the Anglican Church certainly had resilient and intrepid missionaries of its own, many of them displaying a great capacity for learning about local cultures and languages. The First World War cut off the supply of new clergy, and this was not helped by the slump that followed the war, but this was apparently not enough to challenge the existing dependency on expatriates or to inspire significantly greater empowerment of local clergy. The accepted leadership model still consisted of a British or Australasian priest supervising one or two Chinese or Tamil assistant priests, thereby catering to the three main language groups. Resistance to changing this British-led model may have been rooted in an appreciation for stability and practicality, but it contrasted with the broader ethos of Churches across the empire, which were already making strides towards local leadership (Cox 2008: 15–16).

The Church in Singapore was, in fact, becoming more local and more affirming of ethnic identity, while also drawing different communities into ever-greater cooperation for a common good. There was, however, disparity between Church leaders who proactively promoted and facilitated these developments and those who continued, more or less inert, in the old models. Some may have been influenced by concerns from outside the Church, reflecting the reservations of the civil authorities, who feared the growth of local influence on all institutions of colonial society. Reasons for such fears are not hard to divine; British colonialism was entering its final phase, and local leaders of all kinds would soon come into their own. Some aspects of the Church's work actually served to challenge or subvert colonial conventions, creating unprecedented environments for interethnic cooperation. Modern schooling nourished ambitions of opportunity, equality, and self-determination, which would eventually converge in the pursuit of national independence. There were worrying previews of what an anticolonial revolt might look like, such as the Sepoys' mutiny of 1915, but there were also more subtle indications that the demise of empire might actually go forward peacefully, such as the *Singapore Diocesan Magazine* admitting that empire is neither intrinsically good nor intrinsically bad. The Church, not least through its provision of ever-more comprehensive social services, fostered expectations of a frank and amicable end to colonial rule, and these aspirations would eventually find expression in a theological shift as well. Southeast Asian Christianity would move from a theology of domination, imported by colonial masters, to a theology of liberation, developed on the ground. This would finally abolish the old "unholy alliance" between Church and colonialism, which was less a theology than a strategy for inculcating a Christian moral worldview to underpin a Western economic one (Pieris 2004: 256).

Few people, in the interwar years, imagined that every aspect of the Anglican Church in Singapore would one day be entirely managed by locals, but few, likewise, could ignore that the colonial vision, and the Church's role within it, were now open to legitimate challenge (Cox 2008: 9–20). Among the specifics being openly challenged and debated were the ethical basis of imparting Western values through education, and the received wisdom that Western values were synonymous with Christian values; this assumption, until recently, had been widely seen as the whole point of the Church's colonial presence, and it was even supported by law. Even more importantly for Singapore's future, perhaps, was the emerging consensus on society's values, exemplified by access to education and healthcare; the Church's legacy of shared values, ironically, contrasted with the increasing divergence of opinions within the Church itself. At the 1920 Lambeth Conference, the Church voted to take its first formal steps towards expanding women's roles, but only by a narrow margin; this was followed by the launch of a widely unpopular new prayer book, and then decades of controversy over the "united Church" idea. These disputes demonstrated that anything resembling centralized decision-making in the international communion would most likely face challenges as local Churches discerned their paths.

The Church in Singapore looked back with pride on over a hundred years of work, but many wondered why the Church had not achieved more; this question could cause some consternation (Ferguson-Davie 1921: 81). It was easy to lay the blame with the old EIC and subsequent administrations, but it was also easy to forget that for most of that time the mother Church's real missionary priority in Asia was China, which was seen as potentially yielding a far larger number of converts (Goh 2005: 9). The number of Malay converts in Southeast Asia was considered pitifully small compared to similarly daunting yet relatively successful missions in East Asia, but missionaries in Singapore accused their critics of minimizing the challenge and underestimating Islam (Ferguson-Davie 1921: 15–16). The ethnic limits of the Church's appeal were accepted as immovable, not just because of culture and convention but according to politics and treaty as well. The Church also had to accept that small Singapore, compared to other places, did not present opportunities for diversification in ministry; relieving abject poverty was not incumbent on the Church, thanks to a generally good employment situation and highly organized community associations, especially Chinese ones; disaster relief was likewise not really needed, and there was little scope for rural ministry in Singapore itself. The Church's education provision, by contrast, addressed a widely shared priority and was extremely welcome (Goh 2005: 40).

Wherever the blame for the Church's arguably underwhelming performance may have lain, the Church did experience considerable privileges under the colonial powers as well as limitations. Missionaries were enabled by a sociopolitical order in which they could operate with confidence and security, and this, in turn, enabled an admittedly limited range of social works that nevertheless benefited all sectors of society. These works may fairly be described as positive by-products of colonialism, and their impact has been enduring and far-reaching (Goh 2005: 6–9). Acknowledgment of colonialism's flaws and those of the colonial Church was not unforthcoming, including from within the institution itself. Women missionaries, previously largely ignored, began to achieve recognition in the first half of the twentieth century, and progress in education and healthcare is overwhelmingly credited to them. The Church was certainly entitled to feel that it was part of the economic and, increasingly, social success of Singapore, in disproportion to its size (Goh 2005: 15). Cohesion and cooperation were among the strong emerging values of society, and while interethnic tensions were, understandably, not absent, Anglican schools and Anglican churches were loci of interethnic cooperation, whether by design, definition, or default.

Chapter Five

"The Church in Times of Suffering and Persecution"

The Second World War, the Japanese Occupation, and the Aftermath

The Second World War first touched down on Southeast Asian soil on September 22, 1940, when the Japanese initiated an undeclared four-day war with the purpose of annexing Vietnam. Vietnam's strategic location and natural resources did not compare to those of Singapore, Malaya, or Burma, but it was considered vital to block China from using Vietnam's ports. Neighboring Siam (Thailand) was also quickly annexed by the Japanese, giving them a wide range of options for further attacks on Malaya and Burma. The Japanese objectives were clear and uncompromising; achieve complete dominion over Southeast Asia, divest the Allies of all their Asian colonial possessions, and secure full control of the entire Pacific region. Blockading Singapore would not be enough, it had to be captured. For the moment, however, day-to-day life in Singapore was still largely unaffected. Britain's Southeast Asian colonies, including Singapore, appeared to be gripped by apathy, and colonial life was cynically summarized as consisting of tennis matches and dinner parties, with thoughts and prayers for poor old blitzed England. Bishop George West of Rangoon called it "the complacency of the selfish, the mentality of 'it can't happen here'" (West 1945: 46).

The Japanese threat was considered genuine by some and a bluff by others, but the vast majority of people in Singapore and Malaya did not expect a serious attack any time soon, and many in positions of authority believed the Japanese to be incapable of mounting one (Hayter and Bennitt nd: 8). It was true that Vietnam and Siam had already fallen, but these were considered "walkovers" without real resistance. The defense of British Malaya, on the other hand, was thought to be well-organized, and the atmosphere in Singapore provided a comforting sense of security. There was a vastly heightened military presence, with aircraft droning incessantly overhead. Fifteen-inch caliber guns reassuringly carried out artillery practice by day as well as by night, when the sky was streaked with the pale beams of searchlights. Captain (later Colonel) Freddie Spencer Chapman of the British special forces recalled: "From the press and from conversation with people who should have known, one gathered that Japan was economically incapable of declaring war, but that, if she did, the British and American Pacific fleets would prevent her reaching Malaya, and in any case the defense of the Peninsula, especially of Singapore, was impregnable" (Spencer Chapman 1977: 15). Nearly a century earlier, by contrast, Bishop Spencer of Chennai (Madras) had intuited the strategic vulnerability of Malaya, calling it "quite defenseless" in case of war (Spencer no. 3, 1847: 95).

The extent of Singapore's complacency and unpreparedness, however, was exaggerated, according to Spencer Chapman; "The 'whisky-swilling [rubber] planter' is a myth," he wrote; "the planters were all in the Volunteers, whose eight battalions had not been mobilized, as their officers were considered to be far more valuable where they were; on the [rubber] estates and [in the tin] mines." The real problem was not the complacency but the myth that gave rise to it, and the supposed British invincibility was not backed up with substantial military hardware. The army had neither tanks nor anti-tank guns, because the generals believed that tanks were unusable in Malaya and Singapore; there were not enough aircraft, and most of the aircraft they did have were out of date; above all, there were just not enough well-trained soldiers (Spencer Chapman 1977: 15). The editor of the *Straits Echo* from 1931 to 1941, and managing editor of North Malayan Newspapers, was an Anglican journalist called Manicasothy Saravanamuttu, who came from a distinguished Ceylonese (Sri Lankan) family. Years later, he described the prevalent attitude of war denial as "wishful thinking," but at the time he himself wrote that the Japanese would be committing "national hara kiri" if they dared to attack British Malaya. In his memoirs, Saravanamuttu observed that, in retrospect, and in the long term, the Japanese had probably done just that (Saravanamuttu 2010: 103).

THE BATTLE OF MALAYA AND SINGAPORE

Bishop Wilson was in Bangkok concluding his first tour of the diocese when the news from Pearl Harbor broke, and he flew back to Singapore on the last available plane. The severity and brazenness of the attack was a rude awakening for the entire Pacific region, but there would be no time to pause and reflect before the next installment came. On Monday, December 8, 1941, the first Japanese planes attacked Singapore, while an invasion force landed at Kota Bharu in northeastern Malaya. Even then, people could not help feeling justifiably confident, or so they thought, but the sinking, a few days later, of the British Navy's two great ships, the *Prince of Wales* and the *Repulse,* left everyone feeling exposed and vulnerable (Wardle 1984: 56). The island of Penang was ordered to be abandoned, and was then bombed senselessly for days. On Sunday, December 16, British women and children throughout the Malay Peninsula were told to evacuate south, toward the supposed safety of Singapore (Hayter and Bennitt nd: 8–9). Rubber planters paid off their staffs, buried or destroyed their possessions, and shot their beloved pets, rather than let them end up as rations for the advancing army. They then drove south all night long, hoping to ship out as much rubber as they could from Singapore, with the Japanese hot on their heels (Wardle 1984: 62–63).

At All Saints' church, Taiping, in Perak, the Reverend Geoffrey Stere Clarke's preparations to flee turned into a narrow escape; he was getting ready to drive away from the front of his vicarage when two bombs blew away the rear half of the house. All he had managed to load into the car were a few pillows and the church's hymn books, but off he went. The Japanese advanced through Perak toward Kuala Lumpur, Seremban, and Melaka. The Reverend Bernard Eales decided not to flee and stayed behind in Melaka, and the Reverend Eric Scott did the same in Penang; both were immediately jailed by the arriving Japanese, and Eales was interned in Singapore several months later. When he was first jailed, Eales somehow managed to persuade the guards to allow the local ethnic-Tamil priest to bring Holy Communion in, and on one occasion, with inmates looking out for the guards, he baptized a Chinese prisoner who had been sentenced to death. This man was taken away a few hours later to be executed. A constant and confusing stream of pedestrians, trains, cars, carts, and bicycles, all loaded with belongings, flowed south. Many of the evacuated women and children had left loved ones behind, serving in the voluntary defense forces and facing dangers unknown. During all this, a "pall of false security" still hung over Singapore, which the clergy found "heartbreaking" (Hayter 1991: 27–28). The danger was still widely underestimated; the steward of the Marine Hostel, Mr. Willis, was on leave in Australia when the Japanese attacked and had to be dissuaded from returning. Vic Wardle carried on alone with the rest of the Seamen's Mission staff; in any case, few ships now risked docking in Singapore (Wardle 1984: 61).

When the evacuees began to arrive in Singapore, their sheer numbers stunned everyone, but a formidable and improvised collective effort succeeded in managing the truly chaotic situation. The ethnic-Chinese clergy at Holy Trinity church, under the Reverend John Lee Bang Hang, immediately fed and housed a large number of evacuees in the hall below the church. The illusion of Singapore as a safe haven soon vanished, as air raids on the downtown areas resumed. With only a few hours' notice, Sorby Adams and his wife Eunice prepared to feed and house about a hundred and fifty people at St. Andrew's school, which was thankfully some distance out of the city center. Volunteers flocked there to help, as well as rallying to the hospital and blood donor service (Wardle 1984: 61–64). Hotels, barracks, and private homes also housed evacuees (Hayter 1991: 25–29). The bishop and his family opened the doors of Bishopsbourne to accommodate as many as they could, before the pregnant Mrs. Wilson and her children sailed for Australia on January 16, 1942 (McKay 1974: 16–17). As the outlook worsened, all of the clergy were assigned jobs by Bishop Wilson, whether housing evacuees, assisting in hospitals, or doing a variety of rescue duties and other frontline jobs. Some served as emergency chaplains to the local forces, such as the Reverend Alfred C. Parr, senior assistant master of St. Andrew's school. Wilson himself sought an appointment as a forces chaplain, but it was considered too dangerous for him to be found wearing uniform if or when the Japanese invaded; he was partly granted his wish, however, with a nominal appointment as a chaplain second class, which allowed him to remain in civilian clothes (McKay 1974: 17).

From January 20, the bombing of Singapore became heavier and more frequent (Wardle 1984: 64). Telephone lines were repeatedly cut, but Bishop Wilson's was usually repaired because of the crucial role being played by the clergy in the city's defense (Wilson, papers: JLW1). A few ships were still managing to leave Singapore with spaces for women and children on board, but locating the evacuee families who had been assigned these places was a challenge in the blacked-out and bombed city; this job, too, was done by the clergy. The Reverend John Hayter, who had only been in Singapore since the previous April 4 (*Singapore Church Record Book* vol. 9, 1928–41: 246), scoured the darkened city by car, desperately trying to get the families to the ships, but he soon realized that order was breaking down. One night, he was stopped by two soldiers asking for a ride to the naval base; he had to refuse their request, at which one soldier said to the other "shall we take the car?" Hayter sped off, but he saw in the rearview mirror that one soldier was raising his rifle to fire; "Far more angry than alarmed," Hayter recalled, "I slammed on the brakes, got out and walked back. I told them who I was and what I was doing and that, if they took the car, an untold number of women and children would not get onto a boat to leave Singapore in the morning. I walked back to the car and drove away" (Hayter 1991: 29–30). Some families, including the family of Vic Wardle of the Seamen's Mission, eschewed the idea of getting out of Singapore; after all, Sir Shenton Thomas, Governor of the Straits Settlements, had remained, regularly touring the bombed city and encouraging everyone. Then, the chilling news broke that the Royal Navy and Royal Air Force has been ordered to quit, with no "scorched earth" policy; the

Japanese would find the port and other facilities intact. Many people still pledged to hold on, "[waiting] in vain for a strong determined lead which never came" (Wardle 1984: 64–65).

Winston Churchill's exhortation to the people of Singapore to "hold on, help is coming" rang increasingly hollow in people's ears. Night bombing raids switched to day raids, and many realized that this was the beginning of the end. Corpses and body parts, including those of children, lay in the streets, hurriedly covered with movie posters stripped from billboards, while the wounded, having been dug out of the rubble, were carried away on doors or sheets of corrugated iron. Smoke, debris, and the smell of death filled Singapore (Hayter 1991: 31–40). Fifty years later, Hayter reflected on the fact that he had mostly been occupied in dealing with the dead rather than comforting the living; "Emotionally I [too] was dead," he recalled, describing a sadness "too deep for words" as he remembered "the father who mourned the loss of his young children; one boy had been blown by the explosion onto an outhouse roof twenty-foot [sic] high; another tiny baby had been shattered. . . . [Our] sadness for the boy as we carried him down from the roof was so great that it made a numbness and a blank [sic]; it was too deep for anything but cold, revolted bitterness" (Hayter 1991: 40). The arrival of British and Australian troops from the mainland momentarily raised morale, but the renewed optimism did not last; these newly arrived defenders were there because they were retreating, and the siege of Singapore was beginning. "We seemed to be living in some sort of vacuum," recalled Vic Wardle's wife, Betty, in her *Family Journal*, "where nothing seemed real and everything had a queer, floating, iridescent quality" (Wardle 1984: 61). With Japanese air raids now at two-hourly intervals, at the end of January Sir Shenton ordered the compulsory evacuation of expatriate women and children, and Bishop Wilson quickly echoed this order for the Church's families (Wardle 1984: 67–75).

The Japanese broke through onto the island on February 9, 1942, and the following days saw incessant barrages by the artillery of both sides; there were also intensified aerial attacks, with each "all clear" siren being followed quickly by the siren for a new raid (Hayter 1991: 48–52). Resulting oil fires at the naval base caused a heavy pall of black smoke to hang over the island, where it would remain for several weeks. Military hospitals in northern parts of the island were either overrun or untenable, so wounded soldiers and civilians filled all available and undamaged church premises, including the cathedral. Vic Wardle, finding himself jobless and homeless since his staff had been dismissed and the Marine Hostel taken over by the army, now sought a place on a departing ship. After many problems and delays, ships were set to depart again, mainly with women and children, on February 11 and 12; the *Mata Hari,* the *Kuala,* the *Vyner Brooke,* and the *Giang Bee.* In some cases the boiling hot furnaces and deafening engine rooms had to be manned by civilian volunteers. The latter three of these four ships would not make it very far before being sunk, but Japanese propaganda reported all departing ships as having been sunk, in order to terrorize the husbands and fathers (Wardle 1984: 76–77). Sunday, February 15, began with a scaled-down service in the chancel of St. Andrew's cathedral, accompanied by another intense artillery bombardment. By three o'clock there were rumors of surrender, and there was a lull in the fighting at four o'clock; shortly after that, Bishop Wilson was informed that the British surrender was confirmed, and he immediately held an impromptu service. He said afterward that it was one of the most moving services he had ever experienced. By six o'clock "a complete and ghastly silence" had swept across the island; so ended the short and utterly overwhelming siege of Singapore and the battle for British Malaya (Hayter 1991: 64; Hayter and Bennitt nd: 10–12).

The onslaught of Japanese expansionism was total, rapid, and destabilizing, and it signaled the beginning of the end for the old European rulers of Southeast Asia. All of the nations of the region, with the single exception of Siam (Thailand), had been under foreign colonial domination for generations, whether by the British, French, Dutch, Portuguese, or Americans. For some of Asia's people, the Japanese pretense of Asian solidarity had a disarming and potent appeal, feeding long-standing and latent desires to oppose European colonialism by any means. The Japanese undeniably provided a different perspective on foreign occupation; unlike the European colonizers, these new invaders, or liberators, were recognizably fellow Asians, neither towering in stature, for the most part, nor particularly alien in appearance, customs, and behavior. Remarkably, furthermore, these fellow Asians had quickly driven away the mighty Europeans, demolishing white myths of invincibility and superiority, and exposing before the world's eyes that British imperialism was not so timeless or untouchable after all. The Japanese conquests of 1941–42, therefore, would be seen in some light as part of the longer-term decolonizing struggle. Hitler, during the same period, pursued his invasion of the Baltic, Russia, Southeastern Europe, and the Caucasus as an ideological war of aggression; he refused to frame these campaigns as a war of liberation from Stalinist oppression, even though he could have won local support by doing so. In contrast, the Japanese encouraged defeated local populations to view the occupiers as heralds of forthcoming independence, though in reality both the Nazis and the Japanese officially considered the respective conquered peoples to be subhuman (Chia 2021: 126).

In India and Burma, the Japanese had fostered nationalist movements for several years before the war, to agitate for independence from the British. Now, with the creation of the anti-British Indian National Army (INA), the Japanese switched from promising liberation to preying on desperation, recruiting volunteers for the INA from among the many demoralized, scared, and hungry Indian troops captured in Singapore. Under such circumstances, the Japanese talk of pan-Asian brotherhood and the supposedly imminent "Greater East Asia Co-prosperity Sphere" could sound convincing, but the prosperity would never materialize, and the reality of pan-Asian brotherhood would be revealed when senior citizens were forced to bow reverently before teenage Japanese conscripts (Roxborogh 2014: 69). Many Asians, however, not least in the Chinese diaspora, were under no illusions from the start about the reality of Japanese imperial freedom-bringing after seeing how it had played out in China. Regardless of how events were interpreted, throughout 1942–43, most citizens of Singapore and Malaya had little reason to believe that Japanese control would not become permanent. Some took to the hills and resolved to fight on, including a clandestine resistance movement that was supported and armed by the British special forces; they were called the Malayan People's Anti-Japanese Army (MPAJA), and its ranks were dominated by members of the Communist Party of Malaya (CPM). From every perspective, nothing would ever be the same across Southeast Asia, and, following this experience, foreign rule based on innate superiority would not easily be foisted upon its people again (Hayter 1991: 42).

THE CHURCH UNDER JAPANESE OCCUPATION

In the immediate fallout of the surrender, the clergy's work did not pause. Some, including the bishop and the Reverend John Hayter, were busy transferring patients to the rather spartan mental hospital and leaving the main hospital empty, having been warned that the Japanese intended to vacate it by force. Many patients could not be accommodated and had to be prematurely discharged or just left to their own devices. The Japanese ordered the staff and clergy not to take any equipment, but through a variety of ploys this order was disobeyed; additionally, Bishop Wilson became especially industrious and creative in scavenging and looting medical supplies from various places (Hayter 1991: 69–70). This was all happening on borrowed time, however; most of the Asian clergy would remained ostensibly at liberty, but the foreign clergy and missionaries of Singapore, along with all other "enemy" civilians, faced internment, with few exceptions. Bishop Wilson planned to ask the Japanese officials installed at the town hall for three exemptions from internment; these permits would allow him and two clergy to live at Bishopsbourne and operate with relative freedom. One week after the surrender, the bishop finally went to the town hall, was cordially received, and was granted the permits, valid for Singapore but not Malaya; they even gave him permits to run two cars, though he had only asked for one. Even more fortuitously, this was the last day that free-movement permits would be issued; all previous permits were immediately canceled, and the foreigners holding them were interned. With permits in hand, Bishop Wilson, the Reverend John Hayter, and the Reverend Reginald Keith Sorby Adams moved into Bishopsbourne (Hayter 1991: 70–71).

For most of 1942, Wilson, Hayter, and Sorby Adams moved around almost without restrictions, until curfews were introduced. Friends and congregants kept them supplied with food and money, as they received no rations or pay from other sources. Hardly a day went by when a visitor, whether ethnic-Chinese, ethnic-Indian, or Eurasian, did not bring them something; fruit, eggs, or money, Hayter recalled. The bishop was allowed to visit the internment camps and give Confirmation, but ultimately all aspects of the Church's work were disrupted in some way. In a memorandum of April 10, 1942, Bishop Wilson noted that church buildings had been designated "Public or / therefore Enemy property," even though they were mostly owned by international missionary organizations, not foreign governments (Wilson, papers: JLW1). Mission schools were taken over by the Japanese, who were keen to keep schools open but purged them of all religious content. The objective was to create good subjects of the new imperial order, and many parents, to their credit, responded by refusing to send their children to school. Hospitals, meanwhile, were not just neglected under the Japanese but were actually starved of drugs, equipment, food, and other supplies. The local doctors and nurses did their best to keep things running, but they were fighting a losing battle. Tragically, few of the sick children at St. Andrew's Hospital would survive (Hayter and Bennitt nd: 13–16). The war would witness a significant rise in mortality due to disease; beriberi, dysentery, and malaria were rampant due to poor diet and living conditions (Saw 1969: 46).

In spite of everything, there was a prevailing sensation that the situation could have been worse. There was some good fortune; the Japanese officer in charge of relations with the Churches was a certain Lieutenant (later Captain) Tokuji (Christian name Andrew) Ogawa, who, incredibly, turned out to be a regular worshipper at an Anglican church in Japan. As Director of Religion and Education in occupied Singapore, his influence would temporarily mitigate the situation for the Church. On one occasion, he secured Sorby Adams's release from police custody, after he was arrested for communicating with fellow Australians through the fence of the prisoner of war camp. The prisoners had caught Sorby Adams's attention and asked him for cigarettes; he had just been given a box of fifty and, without thinking, he threw it over the fence, prompting an immediate shriek from the watching guard (McKay 1974: 20). Ogawa also sought, with some success, to retain the use of churches for public worship. The Japanese decided to appoint local assistants for Ogawa, choosing the acting Dean of St. Andrew's cathedral, the

Reverend Doctor Devasahayam David Chelliah (1894–1979) as senior assistant (Chelliah, papers). The Indian-born Chelliah, PhD, JP (later OBE), was also vice-principal of St. Andrew's school. He began his career in education in 1911 and would teach until 1961, by which time he was also Archdeacon of Singapore, the first Asian in the post (Diocese of Singapore and Malaya 1967: 2). As Ogawa's assistant, Chelliah was undoubtedly placed in an extremely difficult position, which he apparently executed with great tact (McKay 1974: 22). A broadly tolerant atmosphere was thus maintained with regard to religion, and the Japanese treated the church buildings of Singapore reasonably well, compared to other occupied territories. Christ Church, the Tamil Church, had been damaged during the bombing and then partially destroyed by fire, but it was not completely beyond repair. Throughout the occupation, churches would remain open, and there was relatively little interference in the actual conduct of services; preaching was severely curtailed, however, and any hymn lyrics that might be construed as anti-militarist or anti-imperialist had to be excised (Hayter and Bennitt nd: 14–26).

The bishop made good use of his freedom while it lasted, seeking to address the need for Christians to work together in the distressing circumstances. Wilson was instrumental in forming the Federation of Christian Churches (FCC) of Malaya, which called upon all Christian groups to cooperate in three ways: to hold monthly united worship, to hold regular discussions and share ideas, and to launch a joint relief project, without limits of ethnicity or belief; in the face of Japanese indifference, hardly anything was being done for the poor and destitute. Each member denomination would continue to have its own services, alongside joint Federation events; the Roman Catholics did not get involved. The FCC reflected Bishop Wilson's long-standing devotion to the cause of Christian unity (McKay 1974: 22), and it appealed to those who had long hoped for greater cooperation between denominations or even a future United, or "Universal" Christian Church, as some called it; there was now every reason to cooperate (Chelliah, papers). "Christian bodies should not have waited so long," stated Bishop Wilson, in the undated minutes of the FCC's preliminary meeting; "Christian influence [grows] when Christian bodies [express] their opinions as a body," he said. Hayter was unequivocal about their objective; "Our aim is a Universal Church in Malaya, not uniformity of worship but a united faith and an agreed order of ministry. One of the steps to such a goal is a Federation of Christian Churches" (Hayter 1991: 76). The inaugural meeting expressed its gratitude to Captain Ogawa for having suggested the creation of the FCC; he acknowledged their thanks and agreed to become Patron of the Federation's relief organization, the Social Services Committee (Wilson, papers: JLW1).

It is likely that Captain Ogawa's enthusiasm for the FCC angered his superiors. At the Federation's United Service of Christian Witness, at St.

Andrew's cathedral, on Whit Sunday, May 24, 1942, Ogawa read the Bible reading, in English no less, but he seems to have suddenly refrained from participating in future services after that (Wilson, papers: JLW1). Bishop Wilson and his small team were grateful to Ogawa for the ostensible freedom they had enjoyed, but in reality they, their friends, visitors, and the Asian clergy were being watched carefully by the Kempeitai, or "Kempie," also known as the Japanese Gestapo, who now began to push for the internment of the bishop and his assistants (Lewis Bryan 1946: 10). Ogawa tried to appease the Kempeitai by making sure that respectful concessions were seen to go in both directions; Wilson, the FCC, and all Christian clergy demonstrated their apparent acceptance of the new political order, ensuring that all documents and correspondence followed the Japanese imperial dating system (2602 instead of 1942) or *koki*, the era referring to the mythical foundation of Japan by Emperor Jimmu in 660 BCE, and times were given in "Tokyo Time" or "TT." They even referred to the ongoing conflict by the Japanese propaganda euphemism of "Greater East Asia War" (Wilson, papers: JLW1), and "Syonan," the Japanese imperial name for Singapore, was adopted. In a landmark letter, dated March 28, 2603 (1943), writing from "Syonan," Bishop Wilson called for loyalty and cooperation with any eventual successor appointed to his office, should he suddenly be replaced, for example, by a Japanese Anglican bishop (Chelliah, papers).

INTERNMENT AND TORTURE

The date of Wilson's conciliatory letter marked the end of his year of freedom. The clergy had made an effort to cooperate, but it was not enough to placate the Kempeitai, and their go-between Ogawa had been posted to Sumatra (he would survive the war and even manage to attend a reunion with Bishop Wilson in Singapore). The last straw for the Japanese concerned a ten-meter-high tree in the garden of Bishopsbourne, a flame-of-the-forest (*butea monosperma*), which was in danger of falling. Wilson had it cut down, to the horror of the Japanese area commander, who was described as devoutly religious; the commander's specific religion is not clear, but he apparently considered the cutting-down of the flame-of-the-forest, revered as sacred tree, to be murder (McKay 1974: 26–27). Wilson, Hayter, and Sorby Adams were evicted from Bishopsbourne, and, on March 27, 1943, the Japanese informed them that they were to be interned in forty-eight hours' time. The bishop acted immediately to reinforce the local clergy, ordaining a young Eurasian, John Handy, deacon and priest on the same day, and assigning him to St Hilda's, Katong, while he continued to work at the Chinese Bank by day. An ethnic-Chinese deacon, Gwok Koh Muo, was ordained to the priesthood, and the Reverend Doctor D. D. Chelliah was placed in temporary charge of the diocese (Chelliah, papers).

Then, the bishop, Hayter, and Sorby Adams joined the other expatriates in Changi prison, which had been designed for six hundred local prisoners and was now crammed with three thousand Europeans (Thompson 1951: 652–53). Wilson apparently decided to add humor to the occasion and strode proudly into Changi wearing a top hat, but this comic touch was not appreciated by the internees; it may stand as an example of Wilson's eccentric side, and also of his ability to completely misjudge a situation (McKay 1974: 28). Apart from the terrible overcrowding and inadequate food, life had so far been almost tolerable in Changi (Hayter 1991: 137–54). The camp's clergy were led by the archdeacon, the Venerable Graham White, OBE; Jack Bennitt, Bernard Eales, Eric Scott from Penang, G. B. Thompson, and Colin King kept Church members busy with ministry activities, and cooperation with the other Churches' internees was good. Services were initially allowed and there was a little Communion wine available, but after a while various substitutes had to be experimented with; blackcurrant jam, raisins, and even sticky palm sugar, known as Gula Malacca, were boiled and bottled for use at the altar. Intinction, or dipping, was used for Communion, not only as a method of conserving the stock of "wine" but also as a means of preventing infection; Dr. Patricia Elliot, though elderly and frail, carefully monitored basic hygiene in the camp. Communion bread was made from small amounts of rice flour, maize flour, or tapioca, whenever any of these were available (Lewis Bryan 1946: 12–13). This bearable situation did not last; on October 10, 1943, hundreds of Kempeitai descended upon the camp, in what would become known as the "double tenth" incident, due to the date. They began a months-long reign of terror, starting with ransacking the camp. Dozens of internees were dragged away into "special custody" at Kempeitai headquarters (the YMCA building) without explanation, sometimes in the middle of the night. The resulting state of terror dispelled the last remaining vestiges of physical and emotional well-being (McKay 1974: 13).

One week into this ordeal, on October 17, Bishop Wilson was dragged away to be tortured and interrogated, for hours at a time, over two days and three nights. He was kept tied up in crippling positions, as the Kempeitai tried and failed to extract a confession from him, eventually leaving him in a state of unconsciousness for three weeks, before the torture resumed (McKay 1974: 13). The pretext for all this was as follows; throughout his year of relative freedom at Bishopsbourne, Wilson had supposedly organized a vast espionage network, covering half of Southeast Asia, and he was now trafficking money in and out of the camp to finance it, while coordinating this enormous operation by means of a short-wave radio. The Japanese admitted that they failed to locate this radio, though they practically destroyed the camp in their search for it. This espionage story, it became clear, was founded upon some small grains of evidence; there was at least one hidden radio receiver, not a transmitter, in Changi camp, supplying prisoners with news from outside. The radio that was known about was in the hands of a man called Dermot Victor Prittie-Perry (1908–44). Many internees, including Wilson, did indeed have money smuggled in and out of the camp, as there was no other way to acquire basic medicines and foodstuffs (McKay 1974: 25–26). It was against camp rules to handle money, but it was practically unavoidable; many funerals were being conducted, and rolls of money would often be found secreted in the clothes of the deceased. There was a broader context to the persecution, however; real Allied intelligence operations were scoring major successes at that time, coupled with daring sabotage attacks on Singapore harbor, and the Japanese were left dazed and humiliated. The "double tenth" provided an outlet for their frustration, with real events providing a flimsy excuse (Hayter and Bennitt nd: 15–17).

Perhaps because of the perceived affront to their pride, the Japanese considered it a particularly heinous offense to hear Allied broadcasts, by whatever means, independent of any potential for espionage. Authentic war news contradicted Japanese propaganda, and the resulting loss of face for the Japanese, with their version of events exposed as lies before a defeated enemy, could unleash terrible reprisals; some of the worst atrocities committed by the Japanese across Southeast Asia were linked to the supposed crime of radio ownership. The Japanese occupation forces were not, fortunately, uniformly brutal; they ranged from incompetent or indifferent to frustrated and cruel, but the Kempeitai appeared to be a breed apart. It was they, above all, who were obsessed with tracking down clandestine radios, punishing mere possession with callous disproportion. Another piece of vital context for understanding these events is that some of the Japanese were beginning to accept that there was no way they could win the war. By late 1943, the accumulation of Allied naval victories in the Pacific had convinced the more astute Japanese that it was simply a question of when and in what circumstances they would lose. Ordinary Japanese officers resolved to just keep the peace and stay alive, but the Kempeitai still could not be reined in (Gullick 2013: 72). Singapore residents imprisoned in Sumatra saw clear signs that many of the Japanese had accepted defeat; at Palembang, a camp shop was allowed, and penniless prisoners received credit and loans from local traders, agreeing to settle accounts after the war. It was tacitly understood by all sides, in other words, that the British and Dutch prisoners would soon be in a position to access their funds at home and pay them back (Wardle 1984: 79).

At Changi, other prisoners singled out after the double tenth incident endured similar treatment to the bishop, spending up to seven months tied up in filthy overcrowded cells or cages, irrespective of age, gender, or state of health. They could not lie down, they had no blankets, and bright lights burned overhead day and night. They had no belongings except the clothes they were wearing at the moment of being arrested. The single toilet provided the only drinking water, and dysentery was soon rife. Dermot Prittie-Perry, identified as the main radio offender, was executed. Friends outside the camp were also at risk; Anglican teacher and volunteer medic Elizabeth Choy Su Moi (later PBS, OSS [Order of the Star of Sarawak], OBE) (1910–2006) and her husband, Choy Khun Heng, had started their own clandestine relief network straight after the surrender. They secretly supplied camp inmates with medicine, food, clothes, mail, and, at even greater risk, radio parts. Betrayed by an informant, Choy was lured to Kempeitei HQ after her husband was arrested; she was detained, stripped, and beaten, but never broke under torture. The Choys were internationally hailed as heroes after the war and decorated by several states (Hayter 1991: 156–67). Incredibly, Bishop Wilson found the courage to hold a semblance of a church service between interrogations, celebrating Holy Communion with grains of burnt rice passed through the bars, and he also managed to administer a Baptism, using toilet water, while other prisoners kept watch (Hayter and Bennitt nd: 21–24). In May, 1944, the bishop was finally allowed to rejoin the other civilian prisoners, now transferred to the internment camp on Sime Road; he was fifty-seven pounds (twenty-six kilos) lighter than when he was arrested. Food was scarcer than ever, and the Japanese employed their usual tactic of stealing the Red Cross parcels. Prisoners were forced to dig, not only in order to grow vegetables but also to construct escape tunnels for the guards; the Japanese were openly planning for the day when they would lose the war (Thompson 1951: 652–53).

AN UNEASY PEACE

August 14, 1945 finally brought the Japanese capitulation, and the official surrender was fixed for September 2. In Singapore, amid the relief, the scale of the Church's suffering became apparent. To the very end, the occupiers had been hostile and suspicious toward local clergy, while ordinary Christians lived in fear and trepidation. The Japanese had detained and executed large numbers of young ethnic Chinese for being considered potential rebels, with many Christians among them; vile tricks and ruses had been employed to foment interethnic discord, hoping to goad Malays into attacking Chinese settlements (Chin Peng 2003: 127). The Japanese had monitored influential Christians, Church leaders, and community leaders, so Chinese Christian leaders were considered a multiple threat. The Church's losses were heartbreaking, and it was not until the war's complete end that the full stories emerged. Shortly before the fall of Singapore, a number of women missionaries, mostly nurses and teachers, had managed to get last-minute places on departing ships, and more than a dozen of these had quickly been bombed and sunk. A flotilla of Japanese ships, it was now understood, lurked in the Banka Straits with orders to sink refugee ships and provide no help to survivors. Signalers in the Dutch East Indies tried to warn Singapore about the flotilla, but the signals officer in Singapore had already fled, taking the signal code book with him. Gladys Olga Sprenger, an SPG missionary who had been head teacher of St. Mary's, Kuala Lumpur (*SDM*, vol. XXVI, no. 95, August 1934: 28), and Evelyn Simmonds, a medical missionary working at St. Andrew's hospital, both drowned in the sinking of the *Vyner Brooke,* on or shortly after February 14, 1942, just hours after escaping from Singapore. In a sense, Sprenger and Simmonds were fortunate compared to others on board the *Vyner Brooke* who managed to swim or float ashore to Sumatra; a Japanese death squad, commanded by a notorious war criminal, was waiting on the beach to assault and torture the survivors before massacring them (Wardle 1984: 76–77).

The *Mata Hari* was also attacked in the Banka Straits but was not sunk, being taken as a prize of war instead. The passengers were dropped off to be interned at Muntok, Banka Island, including the Reverend Victor Wardle of the Mission to Seamen. After being sent for a time to Palembang, the men were moved back to Muntok, which was rife with beriberi, in its wet and dry variants, and with malaria, including the irreversible cerebral malaria. Throughout his internment, Wardle held services and kept hopes alive, including his own hopes of seeing his wife and infant daughters again, but he died on January 4, 1945, aged forty-seven, after languishing in the camp hospital for six months (Wardle 1984: 94–96). Exactly one week later, Evelyn Mary Parr, who had been injured in the sinking of the *Kuala* but had survived, also died at Muntok, aged thirty-eight. Oxford-educated Mrs. Parr was a Red Cross nurse from Singapore and the wife of the Reverend Alfred Cecil Parr. Back in Singapore, Parr himself was last seen being taken prisoner while serving as chaplain to the First (Singapore Volunteer Corps) Battalion, Straits Settlement Volunteer Force. He was transported with his unit to work on the notorious Thai-Burma railway, where he died of amoebic dysentery at Hellfire Pass on June 24, 1943, aged thirty-seven (Lewis Bryan 1946: 18). Those who had remained to be interned in Singapore also counted their losses; Archdeacon White died at Sime Road camp on May 8, 1945, VE Day in Europe and less than four months after his wife, Georgina, had also died; both of them were sixty years old. They were remembered as a wonderfully supportive influence among their fellow prisoners, despite their own suffering. White's secretary had also been killed during the initial bombing of Singapore. Friends recalled how hard they had tried to persuade the Whites to get out of Singapore before the occupation, but they had insisted on staying (McKay 1974: 30).

In his sermon at the service of thanksgiving, on September 23, 1945, Bishop Wilson found reason to be grateful, noting that the war had at least not ended with a second bloody battle for Singapore, as had been widely expected (Wilson, papers: JLW1). There was also gratitude for local Christians who had remained at restricted liberty and who had discreetly kept the Church going, maintaining networks and holding services when possible, increasingly without distinctions of ethnicity or denomination. These actions contributed to a coming watershed for the local Church, in which mixed-ethnicity services, previously discouraged by British policy, would become the norm (Chia 2021: 125). Some church buildings had been looted and misused by the occupiers, but most of them were structurally intact and few suffered serious damage. The congregations, for the most part, had held together and kept some kind of worship going. The schools, however, had been completely taken over by the Japanese; the buildings were damaged and stripped of materials, books and equipment had been stolen or destroyed, and three years' worth of filth covered the walls, floors, and ceilings. But the skills to rebuild the schools were available; at the diocesan meeting held at Sime Road Camp on August 22, 1945, Bishop Wilson announced his intention to oblige liberated teachers to go home and recuperate, but every one of the diocese's women workers was determined to return to work immediately (Wilson, papers: JLW2). This included the formidable Dr. Elliot, who oversaw the reopening of St. Andrew's hospital and died just five years later in 1950 (Thompson 1951: 653–55).

The collapse of Japanese rule did not mean the immediate physical departure of the Japanese, and there was a tense interim period after the surrender, while everyone waited for the arrival of the Allies. There was little choice but to rely in part on the communist-run Malayan People's Anti-Japanese Army (MPAJA) resistance forces to maintain order. MPAJA leaders tried to assert themselves as the true liberators and assume civil power; British special forces officers, working clandestinely with the MPAJA, managed to limit these ambitions, but only just (Gullick 2013: 70). The MPAJA and CPM badly wanted a voice in government, which the British, especially in the context of early cold-war international uncertainty, were not going to allow. The CPM's priority therefore switched to a new campaign of liberation, to rid Malaya of the British, beginning with exerting influence over the labor unions. The immediate postwar power vacuum presented a real danger of unrest (Chin Peng 2003: 121–23); "The intermediate time between war and peace is most trying to our nerves and temperament," stated Bishop Wilson, and the atmosphere in Singapore would remain tense for some time (Wilson, papers: JLW1).

The British Military Administration (BMA), established by the returning British, sought to allay security concerns, but rampant inflation was also engulfing Singapore and Malaya. As prices multiplied by several hundred percent, the BMA's decision to increase wages by only a third was met with outrage. On October 21, seven thousand dock workers went on strike; aside from the wage dispute, it was evident that many ships were carrying weapons to arm the Dutch against Indonesian independence fighters, with whom the Singapore dock workers were in solidarity. On October 25, more than twenty thousand people filled Singapore's Happy World amusement park for the launch of the Singapore General Labor Union (SGLU), which represented a number of workers ten times greater than the number of attendees. The SGLU declared support both for the strikers and for the anticolonial struggle taking place in the Dutch East Indies. The BMA drafted Japanese prisoners of war and British army units to break the strike, and when the bus drivers also came out on strike, the BMA deployed British conscripts to drive the buses as well. They succeeded in breaking the strikes, but relations with the public were damaged; while purportedly bringing peace to Singapore, the BMA appeared to have remilitarized it (Chin Peng 2003: 138–41). On the mainland too, hunger marches and strikes drew thousands, and the BMA's firm response led to tragedy; at a huge demonstration in Perak, British troops fired on the crowds, killing at least thirteen. The BMA was only intended as an interim administration and was designed to last six months. Original plans had focused on the likelihood of at least three months of combat to retake British Malaya, but events at Hiroshima and Nagasaki demanded a quick rethink (Gullick 2013: 62). BMA rule ended on April 1, 1946, with the creation of the separate Crown Colony of Singapore. With unrest ongoing and the likelihood of further strikes, the British targeted the perceived root of the problem, the CPM, by suppressing several leftwing publications. The CPM, under increasing pressure, moved its activities to clandestine mode and stepped up its efforts against the British. Once again, the clouds of war gathered (Chin Peng 2003: 141–43).

Amid this volatile atmosphere, Bishop Wilson faced a massive staffing problem. Of the fourteen European clergy who were in the diocese at the time of Wilson's arrival in August 1941, only a handful remained; three had quickly resigned and therefore avoided the Japanese invasion, three had died during internment, two (ex-internees) chose to retire or not to return to the diocese for personal reasons, and the possible return of three others, all of them ex-prisoners of war or ex-internees, was delayed because of lengthy medical procedures. Clergy of Indian and Chinese ethnicity had done great work during the occupation, but a just retirement was rapidly approaching for several of them, and one of them had died of natural causes shortly before the Japanese surrender (Hayter and Bennitt nd: 33). Wilson himself was in dire need of rest, recuperation, and medical attention, and he left Singapore for a year's furlough. He would nevertheless be kept busy and even overworked during his furlough and beyond (Mak 2022: 100–101). Wilson carefully responded to letters, including many from ex-prisoners of the Japanese and, heartbreakingly, from parents and spouses of those who were missing or dead. Numerous such letters are preserved in his personal papers, held by the Imperial War Museum. He replied to Ada Prittie-Perry, mother of Changi inmate Dermot Prittie-Perry, on October 30, 1946, describing her late son's courage and selflessness as he spread life-giving hope via his secret radio receiver, which ultimately resulted in his execution. Wilson wrote of his faith being strengthened by the situation; "The nearer I was to death, and I came very near, the more certain did I become of the living presence of those who had passed from this life" (Wilson, papers: JLW4). Well-deserved peace may have been attained by those who had died in Singapore, but for the living there was still a long way to go.

CONCLUSION

British Malaya, its state of preparedness for war, and the surrender at Singapore constitute a controversial history, and the Church, which found itself on the front line when reality caught up with Singapore, has been absent from many historical accounts. Anglicans' ability to marshal, coordinate, and deploy its resources, especially human resources, made them invaluable in the battle for survival. With focus and courage, clergy, missionaries, staff, and churchgoers provided vital services at huge personal risk, in a vast test of their convictions and characters. With the higher leadership interned, the Church was forced to improvise and diversify, going beyond conventional roles such as teachers and nurses, working without the expatriate assistance and direction that had previously always been relied on. The Church had to both accept and enact long-overdue changes in practices and outlook, combatting the isolationism and sectarianism that had taken root. In a context of enormous hardship, seeds of a future Church were planted, with the forging of ecumenical partnerships and the breaking-down of barriers within congregations. Mixed-ethnicity services already existed but they had never been the norm across the diocese, until the war made them inevitable. These developments were all the more remarkable for taking place under the hostile gaze of the Japanese, who actively sought to stamp out any nascent solidarity between ethnic groups, aiming to exploit prejudices and stoke interethnic distrust, especially to the detriment of the resilient ethnic-Chinese community (Harper 1999: 184).

There would always be a certain amount of mutual wariness and even segregation, perhaps, both in Church and society in general, and this was probably beyond the Church's control; the occupation was not the first time that the ethnic-Chinese community had been discriminated against, and language barriers obviously remained, but multiethnic services and Asian leadership were at least set to become the norm. In a spiritual sense the war was arguably the making of the modern Church, but the physical and emotional pain endured by so many of its members was catastrophic. Materially, the Church's buildings, property, resources, and finances had suffered too. Most church buildings in Singapore survived intact, but several were stripped of valuables and furniture, others were used as sauce factories and rice stores or just looted and filled with garbage. Hospitals and schools were emptied; books, furniture, even pianos and window frames disappeared for ever, often in petty acts of retaliation by the Japanese.

The Second World War took a terrible toll on the Anglican Church in Singapore, but it survived; the bonds binding it together were stretched to their limits and, in the process, those bonds were strengthened. Individuals from many sectors of the Church community had an opportunity to put their faith to the test, especially after the internment of the non-Asian clergy. They began from a situation of dependency on clergy from outside, whether Europeans (mostly British) and Australasians for their learning and resources, or clergy from other parts of Asia for their cultural acumen and resourcefulness. No one was predicting a sudden end to this dependency in the postwar Church, but local clergy and lay leaders had proved themselves during the occupation, not merely keeping the Church going but breathing new life into it; "Many [Anglicans] found, [possibly] for the first time, a real fellowship and community of interest in their church membership. This was due in a very large measure to the work of the [local] clergy (Hayter and Bennitt nd: 16–17, 33–34)." It was a far cry from the Church of immediately before the war, disappointed and dispirited over the surprise appointment of Bishop Wilson, and there were fears that the Church might regress into its former state of unease. Wilson's arrival had actually been divisive at a historic moment when unity was required; "How can a Church that is not itself at peace bring peace to a world at war?" Wilson himself had asked despairingly in 1940 (Wilson, papers: JLW3).

The eccentric Wilson soon redeemed himself, winning considerable respect during the war, locally and internationally; "He has certainly helped to write a fresh page in the history of the Church in times of suffering and persecution," wrote Bishop Cecil Horsley of Colombo (Wilson, papers: JLW3). Wilson not only forgave his torturers but also, in some cases, converted them (Mak 2022: 97). The stories of smuggling, radio-transmitting, and supposed large-scale espionage operations, masterminded by Wilson and other Church members, remain difficult to evaluate. Authors and eyewitnesses have admitted varying degrees of truth to some aspects of the allegations, but it seems clear that the Japanese "double tenth" campaign was fundamentally vindictive. For the first full year of the occupation, the bishop and his two assistants enjoyed a surprising amount of freedom, thanks to the unexpected presence of an Anglican protector among the Japanese officers. This special treatment was probably controversial among the occupiers, and it seems that hardliners eventually got their wish and interned the priests. This coincided with a series of humiliating Allied victories in the immediate vicinity of Singapore, which clearly relied on intelligence and espionage. If the Japanese truly believed that Wilson was such a dangerous and powerful spymaster, however, it seems very strange that the dreaded Kempeitai just decided to stop investigating him one day. They could have simply executed him, of course, just as they executed others, but it appears that the Japanese wanted Wilson to live, with scars, burns, bruises, and broken ribs to show for it.

Besides his injuries, Wilson emerged from the war with a vision for the peacetime Church, and he remained committed to further cooperation, integration, and localization. At a diocesan chapter meeting held at Sime Road Camp on April 14, 1945 (meeting location: "Outside Hut 131"), Bishop Wilson proposed that proficiency in Malay should henceforth be required of all clergy, except those nearing retirement age; this was unanimously agreed upon (Wilson, papers: JLW2). Malay had long been acknowledged as the lingua franca of daily business, but its usefulness in Church circles had not always been fully accepted (Wardle 1984: 27). Numbers of ethnic-Chinese and ethnic-Indian (especially Tamil) clergy looked set to increase, postwar, and the first senior leaders from these communities were already waiting in the wings (Ward 2006: 269–70). There were, predictably, some skeptics, both within the Church and beyond, who were already fearful of the implications of greater localization of the Church, not to mention its eventual decolonization, and who would have liked to slow the process down. Some emphasized the "slow but steady" nature of Church reform across the centuries, but none of the skeptics could deny that local leaders were to be taken seriously. Men and women who had witnessed the war first-hand tended to be pragmatic and progressive on matters of the Church's future, and fully localizing the Church became a shared postwar priority.

All across colonial Asia, it took the Second World War to inspire widespread appreciation of local Christian clergies, and Singapore's Anglican Church was no exception. The Anglican Church in Burma, by comparison, had already made more progress toward things like local leadership and multiethnic services, and without these the Burmese Church would most likely have disappeared during the war or collapsed afterwards, when foreigners were expelled from independent Burma (Ward 2006: 242). Singapore also looked ahead to an independent future, and a definitive switch to all-local clergy would ideally be agreed on and implemented by that time, with all that this implied. While enabling various advances, the war had also halted a number of prospective missionary initiatives in the Diocese of Singapore, especially among underserved and unreached communities, and these would also remain as pending tasks for the future. Just as there appeared to be scope for reactivating these projects, however, the prospect of another war appeared on the horizon (Ng 2009: 11–12, 57–64). The implications of an imminent armed struggle for national independence increasingly clouded all the issues faced by the Church, whose links to Britain were still strong; the question of colonialism and its legacy was unresolved then, as it remains today. The Anglican Church could not easily escape the fact that it had always been widely perceived "as a sort of society existing to further the political aims of the British" (Taylor 1983: 275). This rather acerbic appraisal may serve as a stark summary of the whole experience of the Anglican Church in Asia up to that point. It is a summary that is both bleak and difficult to dismiss, and it seems to affirm the colonial Church's readiness for urgent reinvention or consignment to the past.

Chapter Six

"More Fruitful and Urgent Tasks"
The Postwar Church amidst Conflict, Controversy, and Merdeka

The experience of war in Singapore had drawn together, as never before, people from different faiths, denominations, and ethnic groups, in the cause of survival. Postwar, many Christians felt a strong desire to continue working together for the common good, and this resonated deeply with Bishop Wilson (McKay 1974: 106). He agreed to chair the new Malayan Welfare Council, which was set up by the interim government in continuation of the Churches' ecumenical social work during the war. Apart from the large number of military personnel stationed in Singapore, however, the European population was greatly reduced, so not only was it impossible for the Church to staff all of its chaplaincies (though the forces chaplains helped), the smaller European community contributed less, materially speaking. The challenges facing Singapore were numerous; rising cost of living, shortages of goods, wage freezes, strikes, and an out-of-control black market, while the return of soldiers patrolling the streets evoked wartime. In remote areas, whole villages were found to be in the grip of sickness and hunger, causing troops arriving from Europe to draw crude comparisons with the liberation of Belsen (Gullick, no. 1, 2014: 66). Interethnic relations were still potentially volatile, and politically there was great uncertainty, all adding to the air of unease. Throughout British Malaya, citizens who had held things together through to the Japanese surrender now aspired to a socially just future, independent of all foreign occupiers. Britain, impoverished by the war, was open to reevaluating its involvement in the colonies, but the global picture in the late 1940s was becoming more complex by the day, and there were not going to be any easy solutions (Chia 2021: 126).

Across Southeast Asia, the years following the Second World War saw a mixture of bloodless and not-so-bloodless processes of separation from the colonial powers, such as those in Indonesia, Burma, and Vietnam. Events in Burma highlighted an aspect of decolonization that was not lost upon Malaya and Singapore's Christians, namely that for many parts of Asia, the transition to independence would be stewarded by the majority ethnic and religious group of the particular country. Most of these countries had an active Christian minority with ties to the outgoing colonial power, and the future status of Christians under the dominant groups was to some extent uncertain. This quandary would play out for Christian minorities in the newly independent India, Pakistan, and Ceylon (Sri Lanka) which, like Singapore, Malaya, and Burma, had, and still have, notable historic Anglican communities. Christians in these former British colonies faced varying degrees of difficulty arising from the militancy of dominant non-Christian religions, whether Islam, Buddhism, or Hinduism (Jarvis 2021: 7). Singapore, apart from being tiny compared to those other states, faced a somewhat different situation; its largest constituent group, the ethnic Chinese, was religiously heterogeneous, and although they were to some degree united by shared values, they were generally tolerant of all faiths (Chin 2017: 84–87). This was a well-established situation; the ethnic Chinese, by some calculations, had already been the largest ethnic group in Singapore for over one hundred years (Saw 1969: 41–42). The situation was more problematic across the Causeway, where years of non-Malay immigration now placed the mainland Malays in imminent danger of being outnumbered; they feared becoming an underprivileged minority in their own land (Chia 2021: 126). As a result, ethnicity-based political alliances were formed, and the region was gripped by political tensions with religion and ethnicity at their center (Jarvis 2022: 130–31).

As mentioned above, Christians aspired among themselves to achieve closer cooperation between different ethnic groups. In a population of many ethnicities and languages, it had never been easy to achieve a real sense of Christian unity or fellowship that went beyond the immediate congregation; the typically Anglican combination of diverse ethnic composition and rigid institutional structure surely did not help. Before the war, European-, Indian-, and Chinese-oriented congregations tended to be sectarian in character, whether deliberately, out of practicality, or dictated by circumstances or convention, but during the Japanese occupation many of these divisions were broken down. The Reverends John Hayter and Jack Bennitt believed that divisions had been part of the fabric of the prewar Church; "We all worshipped at the same altar in the house of God, but we were not so sure about all eating at the same table when we got outside," they wrote; "We . . . took too little interest in each other, did not take enough trouble to overcome [language] barriers . . . We were not active enough in social service, and were too absorbed in activities inside the Church to play our full part in the life of the community" (Hayter and Bennitt nd: 6–7).

This was quite a damning indictment of the colonial Church, but Hayter and Bennitt blamed a lack of passion and conviction rather than ethnic prejudice. As denominations interacted more and observed each other's strengths and weaknesses, support for a "united front" of Christians grew, in the hope of more effectively working and witnessing as a single minority community. The wartime Federation of the Christian Churches acted as a model, with ecumenical cells at local levels giving expression to Christian views in each place and carrying out relief and welfare activities. This was in addition to major ecumenical projects being discussed, such as the launch of a joint theological college. The small size of the Anglican Church had always meant that a theological college of its own was unrealistic; clergy had always either been brought in, ready-trained, from Britain, Australia, New Zealand, India, or Hong Kong, or recruited locally and sent overseas for ordination training. Effective and lasting theological education provision would have to be the product of ecumenical cooperation, and thus Trinity Theological College (TTC) was opened in October 1948, for both male and female students. Bishop Wilson was greatly supportive (Mak 2022: 90–92); it was a joint effort of the Methodists, Anglicans, and Presbyterians, the inaugural teaching staff comprising five Methodists, three Anglicans, and one Presbyterian (*Straits Times* 1948: 5). Also in 1948 was the reopening of St. Andrew's hospital, in a new location, with Muriel Clark directing the training of local nurses, and Dr. Gordon Keys Smith, an Australian, in overall charge (Thompson 1951: 654–55).

DIFFICULTIES IN ADJUSTING TO POSTWAR SOCIETY AND CHURCH

The diversity of the Church was increasing again, with Hindi and Urdu being added to the daily used languages, largely because of military units stationed there (Wilson, papers: JLW3). The population of Singapore saw its most intense swell so far, on top of an already-high annual increase rate, with lower mortality, higher fertility, and new settlers arriving from the mainland. This coincided with various push and pull immigration factors, notably political upheavals and expulsions taking place in other countries (Saw 1969: 40). Singapore was braced for a new influx of Chinese immigrants, prompted by the unfolding revolution in China. As the Church knew very well, events in China had dictated the flow of immigrants into Singapore and the region for well over a century, but the prospect of further demographic changes was now tinged with concern for British Malaya's already-delicate ethnic balance. The surge in Malay nationalist sentiment made the threat of intercommunity violence very real; not that the Malay community was growing, just the opposite, it was shrinking in proportion to the others. Church leaders were eager to help keep the peace, but they worried that the Church's voice may be being rendered irrelevant; political discourse increasingly sought to exclude the religious dimension, and moral questions were rapidly becoming the preserve of secular forums, worldwide. Enmity between religions, meanwhile, and the politicization of some religions, was growing at the global level, making the Church's struggle to remain relevant feel more complex and more urgent (Hayter and Bennitt nd: 32).

Some argued that only complete organizational unity, a huge step beyond ecumenical cooperation, could facilitate Christians' full participation in postwar society, and the idea of creating a "united" Christian Church resurged. This was encouraged by success stories in newly independent India, where, with the gradual demise of the colonial-era Church of India, Pakistan, Burma and Ceylon (CIPBC), Protestant Churches merged to form a single Church of South India (CSI). Church unions have been considered compatible with Asian religious approaches, which tend to minimize denominational differences and prioritize common ground, emphasizing religion as values to be lived rather than rules to be adhered to (Gomes and Tan 2019: 216–19). Among the region's senior Anglicans, however, including Bishop Wilson, visions of Church unity did not usually include denominational mergers (Mak 2022: 104; McKay 1974: 106). Church union would be debated and eventually rejected in Ceylon (Sri Lanka), where Wilson's friend, Cecil Douglas Horsley, was Bishop of Colombo; Horsley, visiting Singapore, advised Wilson to form an Anglican Province of Southeast Asia instead, and as soon as possible (Wilson, papers: JLW3). Visions of greater unity were also manifesting themselves at the national and regional political levels. 1948 saw the creation of the Federation of Malaya (FoM), replacing the failed Malayan Union of 1946, and consisting of the Malayan mainland states and territories. This administrative arrangement, alongside the separate Crown Colonies of Singapore and British Borneo, would last until independence from Britain. The separate creation of the Crown Colony of Singapore in 1946 was a shrewd move; firstly, it acknowledged the sensitive demographic differences between Singapore and Malaya and gently promoted the idea that a union of the two would never work (which was arguably proven accurate in later years); secondly, it enabled the British goal of nurturing a special relationship with Singapore, with a view to maintaining military and naval bases there for as long as possible after eventual national independence. The FoM was of secondary interest, strategically (Gullick 2013: 65).

In this politically and ecclesiastically sensitive context, Bishop Wilson's announcement that he would resign and leave Singapore for good came as a surprise, which was compounded by Wilson's strangely timed decision to suddenly start pushing for the evangelization of the Muslim Malays. The

November 1948 issue of the "Cathedral Courier" newsletter reported on a speech given by Wilson, soon to be widely quoted, in which he argued for aggressive and surreptitious missionary efforts to convert Malays throughout the newly formed FoM. The speech was immediately leaked to the British authorities by Captain T. P. Coe, MC, retired long-serving official of the Malayan Civil Service, former Director-General of Posts and Telegraphs, and former president of the Kuala Lumpur YMCA (*Malaya Tribune* 1930: 8; 1931: 8; 1937: 11, *Straits Times* 1939: 14). "I think the best way [of evangelizing the Malays] is by quiet infiltration. . . . There will be little result for years and years but the seed needs to be sown," Wilson had said; "if [the Malays] can only get over their prejudices and learn to see Christ as He is, many would respond wonderfully" (TNA FCO 141/7399: 244/48; [Extract from Speech by the Bishop of Singapore]; 261/48; [Hugh Patterson Bryson letter]). The reaction from all quarters was swift; "Christian work among Malays 'unwise'" the *Singapore Free Press* reported on December 2, 1948; "Muslim leaders in Singapore . . . stressed that 'any effort by the Christian missionaries in that direction would only add fire to the communal differences which we are trying our best to avoid'" (*Singapore Free Press* 1948: 5).

Government officials scrambled to prevent the foreseeable catastrophe arising from Wilson's alarming and ill-timed statements. It was the brink of a diplomatic disaster, to be sure, but with the potential to turn far worse. Responses from senior British officials of the Malay states, tactfully renamed "British Advisers" (BAs) since the creation of the FoM, are collected in a now-declassified file at The National Archives (TNA), designated FCO [Foreign and Commonwealth Office] 141/7399 and formerly marked "Secret." "It has always been understood that there should be no active steps to convert the Malays to Christianity," one official observed, "though I cannot find any written agreement to the effect. It was, I understand, a gentleman's agreement" (TNA FCO 141/7399: January 7, 1949). Other BAs agreed; "a tacit understanding" had decreed that all British organizations, including Church ones, should operate non-religiously regarding the Malays, because such missionary ambitions would "likely lead to embittered feelings" and "strong reactions" (TNA FCO 141/7399: November 20, 1948). It is clear that this had long been the colonial government position, but it is less certain that the Church was always happy with this "gentleman's agreement." In the early years of the diocese, Bishop Ferguson-Davie, writing under the heading "Muslim Work," had lamented that "A non-missionary Church [is] a decaying Church," though he warned that converting the Malays would never be easy and that specially qualified personnel would be needed (*SDM*, vol. II, no. 6, February 1912: 8).

There was another danger lurking, beyond potentially embittered feelings. W. C. S. (Wilfred Charles Stewart) Corry (later CBE), BA in Pahang, described the political situation as a "witches brew" and warned that missionary work aimed at the Malays could be interpreted as a deliberate destabilizing plot by the British, whose servant Wilson was supposed to be. It would pour fuel on the two hottest challenges facing the British at that time; anticolonial communist activism and militant Malay nationalism. "The American Methodists and the Church of Rome might get away with it but not the local head of the established Church of England," Corry commented (TNA FCO 141/7399: December 21, 1948). Corry's opposite number in Kedah, one of the most devoutly Muslim states, confirmed that Islamic zeal was increasing in tandem with surging nationalism, and Malay evangelization attempts would only succeed in stoking resentment, he concluded (TNA FCO 141/7399: December 5, 1948). It was hoped that Wilson's successor, Henry Wolfe Baines (1905–72), the fourth Bishop of Singapore, might adopt a more politically sensitive attitude, but until Wilson actually departed, the BAs were advised to "keep a look out for [the] start of missionary work [aimed at the Malays]." The Acting Colonial Secretary, Hugh Patterson Bryson, MC, a former Changi internee, warned the BAs in January 1949 not to attempt to dissuade Wilson, who was not easy to deal with ("We could never hope to convince [him]"), but to just wait until Baines's arrival instead. W. A. (William Alexander) Gordon-Hall (known as "GH"), the BA of Negri Sembilan, wrote that "the bishop is, as Mr. Bryson says, a stubborn man . . . I suggest that if we can prevent the substance of the speech becoming public property before he goes, we may be able to let the matter rest." Charles Robert Howitt, Acting Chief Secretary of the FoM, enjoined the officials to "watch and pray" that Wilson's successor would find "more fruitful and urgent tasks" to occupy his time than attempting the conversion of the Malays (TNA FCO 141/7399: December 2, 1948).

The BAs' responses, drawing on decades of experience in the region, offer revealing insights into how the Churches' work was viewed. The type of missionary work being suggested by Wilson, they believed, was a "futile and dangerous enterprise" anyway; any conversions achieved would be socially unacceptable, hazardous for the converts themselves, and counterproductive for the missionaries. Recent attempts by American missionaries to convert indigenous communities had angered the Malays and led to them restricting access to the indigenous reserves (TNA FCO 141/7399 Sheet 1: January 7, 1949). Some newer missionaries, the BAs believed, were trying to "buy" converts' allegiance, employing aggressive economic tactics, such as buying up failing Malay businesses "in characteristic American fashion." What kind of Muslims would be lured into converting for material gain, the BAs asked rhetorically; "There will never be any 'rice' Christians [here]." This comment may have somewhat underestimated, or been ignorant of, the extent of poverty among rural Malays, but the conclusion was the same; the

Anglican Church must stay out of this "hornet's nest." Some officials did admire Wilson's zeal, while others pointed out that the Church did not have the resources to seriously act upon the bishop's proposal anyway (TNA FCO 141/7399; 261/48).

THE KAMPONG BARU MISSIONARIES

Bishop Wilson's longing for more aggressive missionary work would be satisfied, in a roundabout way, though not with regard to the Malays, and the opportunity arose out of unexpected circumstances. 1948 saw Singapore and Malaya plunged into a protracted internal conflict that would shape the destinies of the countries involved and accelerate the end of British rule. Ever since the CPM (Communist Party of Malaya)'s strikes and demonstrations of 1945–47 were suppressed by British forces, a guerrilla war had been brewing, and in June 1948 the insurgency began. It was soon christened the Malayan Emergency (1948–60), because the British, cynically or shrewdly, wanted to avoid the use of the word "war" whenever possible, even though Britain would deploy at least five times the number of troops in Malaya as it committed over the duration of the Korean War (Chin Peng 2003: 10). Some secretive and secluded rural settlements, or kampongs, became part of the communications and supply network for CPM guerrillas; it was believed that the guerrillas were dependent on these communities to feed and house them, as they made their way up and down the complex terrain of the country. In 1950, a new British commander, Lieutenant General Sir Harold Rawdon Briggs (1894–1952), resolved to cut off these supply lines by eradicating the kampongs and forcibly displacing the inhabitants into camps; Anglican missionaries and others would be called upon to play a significant and controversial role in this Briggs Plan, which deeply impacted the future of Christianity in the region. Unlike some other civil wars taking place across Southeast Asia, the Malayan Emergency was not a religious conflict. In the Burmese conflict, for example, religious identity acquired political and military expressions, whereas in the Malayan Emergency the opposite was true; a political and military struggle would have a religious dimension deliberately generated and teased out of it.

The divergent destinies of the Church in Singapore and Malaya must be understood in the light of events in the kampongs. The English translation "village" is inadequate to convey the significance of "kampong"; it means a community as much as a physical settlement, characterized by self-sufficiency and independence, but also insularity and isolation. The early British colonial authorities did not know how to approach the kampong phenomenon. They wavered between instinctive distrust and attempts to purchase the kampongs' cooperation, and both approaches contributed further to their marginalization. Later, urbanization and poverty forced generations of small traders, subsistence growers, and recent immigrants into newer outskirts kampongs, occupying an ill-defined hinterland between jungle and town. During the Second World War, numerous kampongs became foci of resistance to the Japanese and offered support to Allied secret operations. They were anti-Japanese, but they were frequently anti-British as well, only temporarily united with the Allies in a common cause (Spencer Chapman 1977: 85).

The Briggs Plan displaced an estimated half a million people from impoverished kampongs on the fringes of the jungles, in an attempt to neutralize their presumed potential for participating in, or actively supporting, the insurgency. These rural civilians, labeled "squatters" by the authorities, were overwhelmingly of Chinese ethnicity and poor. At the start of the Emergency, whole communities had been rounded up and "repatriated" to China, whether they originated from there or not, but the victorious revolution in 1949 abruptly put an end to this option. Under Briggs, the displaced would be transported to hundreds of so-called new villages or *kampong baru*; in reality internment camps, complete with guards, random searches, and barbed wire (Federal Legislative Council 1950: Council Paper no. 14). Conditions, sanitation, and food supplies inside the camps were deplorable (Leary 1995: 42–43). Anonymous informers were used to implicate detainees, who had only a symbolic right of appeal and no opportunity to challenge or cross-examine their accusers (Gullick, no. 2, 2014: 64). This scheme affected an incredible 10 percent of the FoM's population, stripping them of their civil rights overnight (Newsinger 2013: 219). The euphemistic term "new villages" may be interpreted as heavily ironic if not downright cynical; the Briggs Plan was nothing less than the armed detention of half a million civilians, charged with no crime. The scheme clearly resembled a punitive campaign against an entire ethnic group, from which, indeed, many of the guerrillas came. The treatment of the detained half million fueled enormous resentment, and the Briggs Plan was set to backfire by actually justifying and encouraging support for the CPM.

The High Commissioner, Sir Henry Gurney (1898–1951), and his successor, Sir Gerald Templer (1898–1979) decided that neutralizing material support for the insurgents was not going to be enough; they had to actually win sympathy for the British cause from within the camps. As Christians themselves, Gurney and Templer saw the potential to achieve this by sending in missionaries to provide education, healthcare, and social assistance (TNA Colonial Office [CO] 1951: 537/7270), and the recent expulsion of more than three thousand missionaries from China would provide a plentiful supply. Gurney was assassinated in a guerrilla ambush in October 1951, but the missionary plan went ahead, having found support at the highest levels of government in London (TNA CO 1950: 717/203/3); the extent of the government's financial backing would ultimately remain secret (Harper 1999: 185). Such overt government-sponsored missionary intervention in foreign territory, for political and military ends, was unprecedented in modern times, though historically this was, of course, far from new; colonial authorities had always looked to missionaries for broadly political support. In Singapore and Malaya, Christianity was seen as having played an integral part in building and educating the nation, moderating colonial society, and keeping a lid on potential strife. Even so, it was surprising to find, in the middle of the twentieth century, such a clear and anachronistic intersection of colonial self-preservation and evangelistic ambition (Lee 2013: 1978–79).

This extraordinary scheme was, of course, all unfolding within the Diocese of Singapore and just across the Causeway from the island itself, which, after the initial phase, was no longer the focus of the insurgency. Singapore was, however, the organizational base and arrival hub for the missionaries; at its height, the scheme involved around four hundred missionaries from more than a dozen missionary agencies, working in three hundred and thirty-three camps. They represented sixteen different Churches and twelve global Christian denominations, comprising American as well as European, Australasian, and Chinese missionaries (TNA CO 1952: 1022/379; CO 1952: 717/209/4; Lee 2013: 1977–78, 1991–2003). The Anglican Church was the first to embrace the call for kampong baru missionaries (TNA CO 1952: 1022/379). Anglican missionary societies provided the second-, third-, and fourth-biggest cohorts, with the interdenominational China Inland Mission (Overseas Mission Fellowship) in first place; the bulk of the participation was therefore unmistakably Anglican (Hood 1991: 152). Some missionaries were attracted by the opportunity to work in previously unreached areas, while others appreciated the anticommunist dimension of the scheme, seeing it as a crusade against a great evil (TNA CO 1950: 717/209/3).

Some missionaries, however, were troubled by the apparent return to complicity with colonialism and infusing missionary work with a political agenda, however justifiable that agenda may have appeared (Harper 1999: 184). Some Anglicans were especially concerned about being branded, once again, as agents of Western imperialism, and about seeing their genuine humanitarian efforts in the camps being dismissed as a Trojan horse (TNA CO 1951: 717/209/4). The influx of missionaries and the potential conversion of non-Malays to Christianity had implications for the delicate demographic situation; the missionary scheme was easy to perceive as a plot to engineer or "rig" the ethnic-religious balance at the last hurdle before national independence, by manufacturing a surge in the number of Christians (Harper 1999: 184). Politics aside, and considering the extent of ethnic-Chinese involvement in the Church, the missionaries' alignment with this effectively anti-Chinese campaign looked like very poor judgment. Ethnic-Chinese membership of the Anglican Church was hugely significant, and it would be profoundly damaging to the Church's long-term vision to be perceived as anti-Chinese. These were not even the only concerns for the Church; the government, in its enthusiasm, had opened the door to missionary groups quite indiscriminately, bypassing ecclesiastical protocols. The traditional mainstream Churches, including the Anglicans, were alarmed by the arrival of newcomer groups, such as the Southern Baptists and Chinese Evangelicals, whose fundamentalist preaching and eccentric worship styles shocked the "old guard" missionaries (Lee 2013: 1988–96).

Anglicans had justifiable concerns about how their involvement in the Malayan Emergency would be perceived, and the impact remains difficult to evaluate (Newsinger 2013: 219). A few Church leaders rejoiced that their welfare provision had "inoculated" the people against the "disease" of communism, but the kampong baru internments had demoralized and humiliated the rural ethnic-Chinese population horrendously. The experience eroded their fragile sense of national integration, made them fearful of future community endeavors, and further isolated them within their immediate ethnic group; this was the opposite of the Church's declared ethos (Harper 1999: 185–88). The Church had seized the opportunity to preach to people who had an incentive to listen and no real choice, especially if they wanted to access things like education and healthcare; they had been systematically bullied, disoriented, disenfranchised, and, in the process, made ripe for conversion (Harper 1999: 184). This was borne out when most of the now-permanent new villages where missionaries had worked ended up retaining a lasting Church presence (Lim and Fong 2005: 128–39). Rarely has there been, in the modern history of Christianity, a more literal and distasteful case of missionaries having a captive audience (Jarvis 2022: 118).

DEBATES AND DEVELOPMENTS: THE STATE OF THE CHURCH FACING NATIONAL INDEPENDENCE

Missionary opportunities would continue to present themselves in connection with political, economic, and social upheavals. The infrastructure of British Malaya was transformed in the early twentieth century, particularly the railway network. The railway boom, and its impact on urban development, produced new, marginal communities, as often occurs with rapid urbanization. In areas of urbanization, development ran parallel to the development of the railways, and this development often dictated where Church missions should focus. Today's Church of Our Saviour (COOS), now based in a renovated former cinema on Margaret Drive in Queenstown, Singapore, began as a mission on Alexandra Road, where ethnic-Indian railway employees were housed. From a handful of struggling railway workers in the 1950s, the worshipping congregation at COOS has ballooned to more than four thousand, and the church supports missionaries working in twelve countries. Other new parishes dating from the same period include the Church of the Good Shepherd (COGS) on Dundee Road, which was Queenstown's first Anglican church. Services at COGS were initially in Cantonese and Mandarin, due to the large number of ethnic-Chinese worshippers, with English-language services beginning in the early 1960s. In the 1970s COGS planted the Chapel of the Resurrection (COR), which in turn planted several churches, and the number of COGS congregations eventually rose to fifteen. St. Peter's in Serangoon Gardens (SPSG) began as a house group in the 1950s, and the current church is a complete rebuild dating from 2001. Like many parishes in Singapore, St. Peter's is a product of the vision and outreach of St. Andrew's Cathedral, though it has been an independent parish since 1966 (Green 2001: 80–95).

By the middle of the 1950s, the disparity between Singapore and Malaya was evident; Singapore was readier for national independence than Malaya, though both entities were still widely presumed to be facing some sort of common future. Given the uncertainty, it seemed fortunate that Bishop Henry Wolfe Baines proved to be adaptable and receptive to change; when faced with the influx of missionaries after expulsion from China, for example, Baines welcomed evangelical organizations such as the China Inland Mission (Overseas Mission Fellowship) and the Church Missionary Society (CMS) to establish themselves in Singapore. This was significant in a High-Church stronghold like Singapore, in the days when churchmanship counted for a lot. Apart from broadening the spectrum of worshipping traditions, Baines also pushed for the appointment of an Asian assistant bishop (Straits Budget 1956: 8). His request was granted in 1958 with the appointment of Bishop Roland Koh Peck Chiang (c.1909–72), who became the diocese's first ethnic-Chinese and indeed first Asian bishop. Born in Sandakan, North Borneo (Sabah) in 1908 or 1909, Roland Koh had converted to Christianity from Buddhism (*Church Times* 1958: 7). As Singapore and Malaya's destinies continued to diverge, Koh's episcopal ministry straddled both societies, as Assistant Bishop of Singapore and Suffragan Bishop of Kuala Lumpur. Koh would later become the first ever Malaysian diocesan bishop, for the Diocese of Sabah (formerly Jesselton). Koh, like Baines, supported the arrival of evangelical and non-denominational missionaries in Singapore (Ward 2006: 269–70).

Ecumenism and Church union were still hot topics, despite never being met, historically, with unreserved enthusiasm in Singapore, and there was no higher ecumenical aspiration than a united Singaporean-Malayan or Southeast Asian Church. The possibility of an India-style united Church for

Singapore and Malaya were debated during the 1950s and 1960s, and the Anglican South East Asia Church Council (SEACC) was launched to provide a forum for debating what kind of joint future the regional Church, or Churches, would have. With most of Southeast Asia in the 1950s and 1960s embroiled in unrest or conflict of some kind, however, it was often difficult for local Christians to see why Church unity issues mattered; there were so many more pressing things to deal with. Also, extolling the value of unity was a difficult thing to sell to Christian minorities across Southeast Asia, who often struggled to feel a sense of unity or belonging in their own societies. For many ethnic-Chinese citizens, whatever sense of community and cooperation they did experience had been sorely eroded by the atrocious kampong baru scheme. This resentment largely escaped Bishop Baines and other leaders, incidentally, who considered the Church's contribution to the kampong baru scheme to be a success. Baines continued to welcome Chinese missionaries to minister freely to the ethnic-Chinese in evident good faith, and he mused that a future Southeast Asian regional Church might be primarily an overtly Chinese-diaspora Church (Straits Budget 1960: 5).

Singapore and Malaya were developing at different paces and with different visions, increasingly relativizing their elements of common heritage. Anglican leaders tried to manage the two Church communities' growing differences in worship and theology, but also in influence and demographics; Christians were much better represented in Singapore than on the mainland, and Singapore generally had a better grip on its internal intercommunity tensions. Shared history would remain important for Southeast Asian Anglicans, but the points of difference and divergence, which were not all new, mounted in the run-up to Singapore's national independence and beyond. Anglican institutions, traditionally, never rushed to conform to secular political realignments, but the wide-ranging implications of independence could not be ignored (Ward 2006: 22–24). Singapore and Malaya still formed one diocese, however, and a unifying, united Church was still held up as an ecumenical objective for all of Southeast Asia to strive for. SEACC discussions revealed, however, that the sense of united endeavor previously promoted by the colonial Church lacked substance, and the region's national Churches found that they actually had little in common with each other (Jarvis 2021: 119–22).

Exploring the possibility of an ecumenical united Church also revealed theological disagreements that tended, rather disappointingly, to follow ethnic and national divides. Presbyterian clergy of non-Asian origin, for example, asserted the sacramental validity of their ordinations in the face of its rejection by Anglicans, and they were strongly opposed to the idea of being re-ordained in order to join a united Church. Asian Presbyterian clergy, on the other hand, considered this to be nitpicking over minutiae and clinging to the past. Across denominations, clergy demographics had changed significantly by the late 1950s, and Church leaderships comprised a growing proportion of forward-thinking ethnic-Indians and ethnic-Chinese, who tended to appreciate the need for give-and-take in ecumenical work. They were comfortable with English, the lingua franca of ecumenism, and some of them had direct experience of Church union in India. Despite all the disagreements, there was at least a general acknowledgment that religious belonging was complex, and more likely to mature, grow, and express itself in diverse ways rather than exclusive ones. This was accompanied by a consensus in favor of moving toward full Asian ownership of the Churches (Roxborogh 2018: 288–310). Southeast Asian Anglicans had essentially inherited a colonial Church, with conventions, concepts, and structures that were no longer fit for purpose; even some resistance to mixed-ethnicity services still persisted, though it had been waning since the 1940s (Ward 2006: 269). The SEACC continued to pursue a future, single "Church of the Province of South East Asia" as an autonomous part of the Anglican Communion; not a united Church but a purely Anglican venture instead, and this would eventually become a reality three decades later (Straits Budget 1960: 5).

ONE DIOCESE, TWO MERDEKAS, AND A PROPOSED "GREATER MALAYSIA"

In 1955, Singapore was granted partial self-government in internal matters, but not in foreign policy. This was the start of Singapore's Merdeka or national independence process, definitively bringing the colonial era to an end. The following year, Singapore's Chief Minister David Marshall (1908–85) petitioned Britain for complete self-government, threatening to resign if his appeal was rejected. Parliament did indeed reject the bid, citing the recent resurgence of communist activism, civil unrest, and labor disputes in Singapore. Marshall duly resigned, ceding to Lim Yew Hock (1914–84), who launched a crackdown on radical groups, trade unions, and leftwing politicians. Britain approved of Lim's approach and resumed talks, leading to self-rule for the new state of Singapore, agreed on April 11, 1957 and ratified by Parliament the following year. Elections for Singapore's new Legislative Assembly were held in May 1959, with Lee Kuan Yew (1923–2015) becoming the first Prime Minister of Singapore.

Meanwhile, the Federation of Malaya (FoM)'s own Merdeka arrived on August 31, 1957. The FoM's national independence arrangements were viewed by many as ethnically divisive, but although the Malay majority had finally asserted itself, this came with a clear statement that the newly independent FoM was not going to be an Islamic state. Non-Malays, after all, may have been a minority, but they were, and still are, a very substantial one;

the uneven distribution of ethnic groups also meant that the Malays were not guaranteed an effective majority in all places. Most mainland Malays, furthermore, were still rural and poor, and their future prosperity was not a given. The "Malay rights" movement had long since appealed to the authorities for measures to safeguard Malay interests, vis-à-vis the economically and educationally advantaged (relatively speaking) ethnic-Chinese and ethnic-Indians, but the British had never effectively addressed these concerns. The Churches' general silence on this issue looked eerily like official Christian indifference to the Malays' plight, which was nothing new; Malays had long felt subjugated by the followers of an unsympathetic religion. Now, Christians and other non-Malays on the Malayan mainland contemplated their future under Muslim majority rule with apprehension. Numerous individual British, Australasians, and others who had settled or been born in British Malaya saw themselves as a continuing part of the new society, post-independence, but their real status was up for a complete revision. Church leaders shared their worries, but took care not to overpublicize their fears (Roxborogh 2014: 62; 2018: 300–301). Balancing all of this would now be the task of the new Independence Constitution of the Federation.

Bishop Baines found himself leading a Church split between two different countries, each facing a different challenging scenario, each with pressing political concerns. Ethnic, religious, political, and legal questions were intertwined with each other, with serious implications for both nations' Christians, though Singapore's situation was less ethnically and religiously divisive (Hedlund 2010: 77). In the run-up to Merdeka, Baines had been eager to emphasize the Church's role as "a community in which people of all races can mingle and speak the truth with one another without reservation . . . a forum for political opinions . . . representing all shades of opinion on Merdeka and its problems" (Straits Budget 1956: 10). Now, Baines and his fellow Anglican Church leaders hoped that the new constitution for the post-Merdeka FoM would be robustly secular, guaranteeing not only the freedom to practice a religion, but also addressing matters such as an individual's right to change religion, and what the precise parameters for proselytization would be. Bishop Roland Koh sought to understand the extent to which the Church could be held accountable if a Muslim were to acquire a Bible or start attending church services of their own accord; could this be considered disseminating Christian literature, preaching to Muslims? Koh's questions went unanswered, and these crucial issues were left to the later deliberations of decentralized religious and state authorities. The Independence Constitution, nevertheless, came as a relief, and Baines advised against contesting it. He urged Malayan Christians in exclusively ethnic-Chinese or ethnic-Indian contexts to face reality and prepare for the future, by learning about Islam, engaging with Malay culture, learning Malay, and seeking more interaction with the Malays themselves (Roxborogh 2014: 90–91). In April 1960, Bishop Baines departed from Singapore, ending his tenure of eleven years, to become bishop of Wellington, New Zealand, where he would die in office.

The contentious interethnic relations issues outlined above were far from being Malaya-only concerns, because the question of Singapore's integration into a future united Malaysia was still wide open. In the meantime, the Anglican Church decided to express its equal responsibility to the two separated nations by renaming the diocese; from February 6, 1960 it would be known as the Diocese of Singapore and Malaya. This decision served to acknowledge the diocese's cross-border role, while simultaneously suggesting the Church's endorsement of the two nations' perceived joint destiny. Despite Singapore's successful Merdeka process, leading figures in Singapore, Westminster, and Lambeth still envisaged a united future with the FoM. The prevailing sensation was that more could be achieved in unison, within one federation, with Singapore retaining the maximum degree of autonomy in its internal affairs, as it had done in its first short period of partial self-rule. This model of a joint future with Malaya would eventually be voted on by referendum, but before then the British Colonial Office began to tentatively lay the groundwork for a grand federation of states, paying considerable attention to the religious aspects and counting on the active involvement of the Anglican Church. The declassified documents relating to this secret plan are held by The National Archives (TNA) in London, in the collection CO (Colonial Office) 1030/1019: Greater Malaysia (proposed): religious aspects [marked "Secret"] 1960–62: no. FED 59/4/028.

The core religious premises of the proposed "Greater Malaysia" were quite predictable; religions may be practiced in peace and harmony, but individual states would be "enabled" to limit missionary work among the Malays. This harked back to the conventional "hands off" policy or "gentleman's agreement" with regard to Islam, which dated back to the Pangkor Treaty and was reiterated in the 1948 Federation of Malaya Agreement (TNA CO 1030/1019: 3, 32, 90). The complex multireligious solutions of Indonesia and India were cited as examples to emulate. Defining Malays as being Muslim by default was resisted by the British government, as this would appear to defeat the religious freedom clause and place Malays who convert away from Islam in an impossible position (TNA CO 1030/1019: 41, 92); it is widely asserted that this is precisely what later came to pass (Whiting 2010: 9–12). Integrating Borneo into "Greater Malaysia" presented an inverse problem; while it would probably be necessary to recognize Islam as the official religion of the whole proposed Greater Malaysia, this would be harder to justify in the Borneo states, which had relatively small Muslim populations. Anglican leaders, having considerable influence in Borneo, pointed out that freedom of religion must mean freedom from state or federal religious control, with no special protections for any one group (TNA CO 1030/1019: 46–47, 59–66, 77–79).

All of these concerns were shared by Singapore's Church as well as civic leaders, and as the prospect of a greater united Malaysia grew more realistic, the shape that the new proposed federation was taking already worried many Anglicans (TNA CO 1030/1019: 46–47). Singapore held a referendum on September 1, 1962, to choose the terms upon which it would join with the FoM and the Borneo states to form Malaysia; the winning option would see Singaporeans receive automatic Malaysian citizenship, while Singapore would retain autonomy in internal affairs, as it had done in the first Merdeka period. Singapore was all set to join, but the Borneo problem was still unresolved. The Anglican Church was then unexpectedly called upon to play a part in smoothing the transition to a united Malaysia. The UK High Commissioner to Singapore and Commissioner General for Southeast Asia, the Earl of Selkirk (1906–94), wrote to the Colonial Office on October 16, 1962, stating that the right person to go and allay Borneo's fears was Bishop Koh, as he was a highly respected Sabah-born ethnic-Chinese Christian whose reputation and influence therefore extended across several concerned communities. James Wong (1900–1970), Bishop of Jesselton (later Sabah) disputed Koh's ability to intervene effectively, however, on the grounds that Koh was only a suffragan bishop with no real power (TNA CO 1030/1019: 62). Nevertheless, Koh was willing to help, and he suggested that some prominent non-Muslims from Borneo should make a goodwill trip to the Peninsula as well. He pointed out that similar gestures from the Muslim leadership were so far lacking, but non-Muslims were apparently eager for any chance to demonstrate their loyalty (TNA CO 1030/1019: 55–56). With Koh's help, the deal was made, but Singapore's cautious membership of Malaysia would last for less than two years before finally succumbing to a variety of disagreements; these included party political rivalry, differing visions and aspirations, the unfulfillment of Singapore's expectations with regard to autonomy, and, predictably, the handling of intercommunity relations.

The Church continued to manage its own transformation within the evolving political reality. When Bishop Baines left Singapore in 1960, he did not know who his successor would be, but he speculated that it may at last be an Asian (Straits Budget 1960: 5). The answer ("not yet") came with the arrival, from Britain, of newly consecrated Kenneth Sansbury (1905–93) as head of the renamed Diocese of Singapore and Malaya. The postwar years had largely silenced those who had previously doubted the effectiveness of local leadership, but in the early 1960s, most of the region's Christian denominations, including the Anglicans, were still largely dependent on foreigners (Ward 2006: 269–70). Some Asian nations, arguably overzealous in their efforts to decolonize, severely restricted the presence of foreign missionaries or expelled them altogether (O'Connor 2000: 154–55). Even in the absence of such measures, the campaign to "nationalize" local clergies was underway across Asia, viewed as the final stage in transforming still partly segregated colonial Churches into wholly locally driven entities. This could not just be done with the stroke of a pen, however, as governments seemed to think, and as the age of foreign leadership came to an end, foreign involvement would not disappear overnight.

For all its shortcomings, foreign leadership had at least acted as a sort of equalizer, being neither Chinese nor Tamil nor Malay, and not privileging one of those groups over another as a matter of policy. Even when foreign Church leaders disparaged the locals, they tended to disparage them more or less equally, without acknowledging any hierarchy among the local ethnicities. Ethnic differences, like the finer points of theological differences, were of little concern in practice and carried quite trivial connotations; Chinese Christians were seen as more conservative and European Christians were considered more liberal, but this was nothing to fall out over (Roxborogh 2014: 82–103). Local leadership, as it expanded, tended to emphasize the ethnic identity of each congregation, because the leader almost always belonged to the same ethnic group as the congregants; as before, churches could easily be divided into ethnic-Hokkien, ethnic-Fuzhou, ethnic-Cantonese, and ethnic-Tamil congregations. The postcolonial reality would effectively require congregations to contextualize twice; firstly, by managing the interface of their own language, values, and culture vis-à-vis Christianity, and, secondly, by managing the interface of all of the above vis-à-vis an emerging national culture and identity, and evaluating how those elements might be received in a plurireligious context. Singaporean Christians' experience of Christianity in its great diversity was set to broaden enormously, as the newly independent state, with its institutions, began to revolutionize its whole way of engaging with the world.

CONCLUSION

"Colonialism" in the words of CPM leader Chin Peng "was past its expiry date" (Chin Peng 2003: 10). The same idea, expressed in different ways, spread through the British colonial world in the years after the Second World War. Anglicans faced the question of what would become of their Churches, the Churches of the empire, as both the sociopolitical and ecclesiastical structures supporting them were dismantled. Across Southeast Asia and parts of the Indian subcontinent, Anglican Churches adjusted to unprivileged minority status in challenging situations of majority ethnic rule, while the Churches in India compromised on theology and polity to create larger "united and uniting" Churches. Moves in favor of a similar united Church for Southeast Asia, which had always enjoyed some cautious support, did not get very far, but ecumenism was recognized as an unavoidable priority. There were pressing practical reasons for Christians and their organizations to work together; preserving a socially useful role for the Churches, and maintaining a Christian voice in national affairs and moral questions, in the context of global secularization and majority non-Christian control, was not something that numerous small minority groups could do alone. The same was true of the Churches' practical goals, such as the long-standing ambition of opening a theological college for Singapore; the late 1940s was still a troubled time to be sure, but the cooperation, resources, and skills available for opening the college seemed as good as they would ever be.

Singapore's Anglican Church benefited from a generation of local clergy whose leadership skills had been tempered in the furnace of the Second World War, and then further honed in postwar unrest and upheaval. Less than three years after the war, in fact, came the communist insurgency. For whatever reason, whether for public relations or simply, as is widely believed, for insurance purposes, the British refused to call it a war. The ethnic dimension of this conflict led the British to victimize the most prominent constituent community of the Church in Singapore and Malaya, the ethnic-Chinese. The ethnic-Chinese community's prior experience of persecution was widely acknowledged; the Japanese had victimized them too, considering young, resilient, Christian Chinese males to be a triple threat. Some believed in retrospect that even the disproportionate bombing of Chinese districts by the Japanese had been deliberately orchestrated; the ethnic-Chinese community was concentrated in Singapore's downtown (Wardle 1984: 59). Some timeline-altered interpretations of the kampong baru missionary scheme describe the Church as identifying a "need" to minister to the internees, which ignores the fact that the scheme was first planned as a political and military strategy, without consulting the Church but deciding to utilize the Church. Politicians and generals, holding fast to colonial values, turned to Church leaders just when these were feeling unneeded and irrelevant in a rapidly evolving pluralist society and a rapidly secularizing postwar world. The British famously aimed to "win the hearts and minds" of the kampong residents, commissioning Christian missionaries to go in and exorcize communist sympathies, but the plan was hopelessly flawed; the sudden arrival of government-sent missionaries in the deplorable camps was greeted with suspicion, and the missionaries themselves were often uncomfortable about being seen, once again, as mere religious delegates, or pawns, of British colonialism (Newsinger 2013: 219). From any dispassionate or impartial perspective, the so-called new villages were neither security measures nor social experiments; they were concentration camps, and the participating missionaries were largely aware of the moral quagmire they were wading into (Roxborogh 2014: 78–84).

The Church had accepted a gamble, to play a leading role in the British Empire's "last stand" in Malaya; from some perspectives this politicized the Church, as well as both cementing and complicating its identification with marginalized rural and suburban communities, many of which were ethnic Chinese. It may be surprising, or simply a testament to people's resilience, that most of the new village camps evolved into permanent, mostly ethnic-Chinese settlements, and they are today home, collectively, to well over a million people, with a significant Christian population (Ng 2009: 4). This somewhat unexpected outcome completed a bizarre and controversial journey that united colonialist fervor, cold war politics, missionary enterprise, and, longer term, lasting evangelization. Understandably, therefore, this period was seen as a time of mixed blessings for the last incarnation of the colonial Church; in many day-to-day respects it had changed little, and it was struggling to keep up with the fast pace of change. It is perhaps fair and logical to talk about a Church in terms of having its own aspirations, as any national project also does, and the Diocese of Singapore was watching as two sets of aspirations present within it, those of its Singaporean and Malayan territories, diverged dramatically. For the Federation of Malaya, the pressures arising from the politics of ethnicity and the struggle for internal security made the 1950s a fight for survival, but also a fight for identity. Meanwhile, conventional church plants addressed the massive population increase taking place in Singapore.

Singapore may be too small and too cosmopolitan to meaningfully talk about marginal groups or marginal organizations, and the Anglican Church, with its key communities and high-profile institutions certainly cannot be called marginal; the Church's role in the development of Singapore's new, shared national aspirations was not in doubt. This placed the Church in a paradoxical situation with no obvious way out; the bulk of the territory of the diocese, led from Singapore, faced an issue that Singapore itself did not face. Malaya, but not Singapore, witnessed the accession to power of a nationalist majority ethnic-religious group, with far-reaching implications for the Christian minority. Church leaders in Singapore, being somewhat insulated from the tensions, risked being seen to take the critical matter of Christian-Muslim relations lightly. Long-established convention ruled out any attempts to convert the Malays, but the question of evangelizing "all those who have not heard the gospel" (Diocesan Call to Evangelism 1963), with or without a specific mention of the Malays, was tactlessly resuscitated by successive bishops every couple of decades. This indicates an enduring naiveté in the Church's practical approach to relations with the Malays, and this may have mirrored a certain nationwide naiveté with regard to Singapore's decision to be part of Malaysia. Both nations were extremely pluriethnic and plurireligious, but their different compositions and dynamics were considered sufficiently irreconcilable for the British to have separated the two countries back in 1946 (Gullick 2013: 65). Both nations professed a commitment to freedom, equality, and democracy, but it would remain difficult to shake off prejudicial perceptions of "Chinese" Singapore and "Muslim" Malaysia.

Chapter Seven

"The Deepening and Renewal of Her Spiritual Life"

Tension and Transformation in Singapore's Anglican Church

The Anglican Church in Southeast Asia reorganized, and in 1963 three dioceses emerged from the previous two; the somewhat incongruous joint Diocese of Singapore and Malaya, under Bishop Sansbury, was joined by two new dioceses in Borneo, Kuching and Jesselton (Sabah). Following its short-lived union with Malaysia, Singapore became independent on August 9, 1965, and the need to finally appoint an Asian diocesan bishop was increasingly obvious (Sng 1980: 268). The historic appointee would be Joshua Chiu Ban It (c.1921–2016), a native of Penang, who was consecrated at St. Andrew's Cathedral on All Saints' Day, 1966, and would henceforth lead the joint diocese. The Diocese of Singapore and Malaya, consisting of West (peninsular) Malaysia and Singapore, had been ambitiously named to emphasize both the distinct character and shared destiny of the two territories, and it was now ripe to be split in two. These were all important steps toward the future Church of the Province of South East Asia (PSEA), with the outline of its four-diocese composition already clear by the mid-1960s, but it was also clear that the Church's reorganizations struggled to keep up with the pace of change (Hedlund 2010: 77).

As independent Singapore began to discern its destiny, the island nation's Christians tried to envisage their future within the new national pluriethnic and plurireligious social experiment. Far from marking only differences with their fellow Singaporean neighbors, Christians would increasingly find that their moral concerns and social aspirations were shared across multiple communities. Institutionally, the Anglican Church would also begin to harmonize with the national ethos of pluralism, recognizing that the Church itself had historically integrated the "best" elements of East and West. Singapore continued to function as a point of reference for the wider region's Anglicans and other Christians, reaffirming its historic role as a welcoming base for missionaries, boasting notable Christian institutions and a stable Christian community of its own (Lim et al. 2006: 58). Anglicans maintained a high profile amidst the Christian community of Singapore, though they were still in overall third place among the denominations. Assessing membership was always a challenge, however, partly because of a fluctuating number of regular attendees who never actually formalized their membership (Jarvis 2022: 3–5). Singapore's Anglicans were still overwhelmingly ethnic-Chinese with a significant ethnic-Indian, especially Tamil cohort, and the Church took pride in its high degree of interethnic harmony; most services still used one of the three main Church languages of Chinese, Tamil, or English, but Church activity was fundamentally multiethnic (Straits Budget 1960: 5).

Apart from the imminent separation of the joint diocese into two dioceses, it was not immediately clear what the implications of Singapore's political separation from Malaysia would be for the Church. Those with an eye on history noted that Anglicanism tended not to conform automatically to political realignments; upon the creation of the United Kingdom, for example, proposals to unite the English and Scottish Churches were rejected, and British colonialism had been expanding for a century, with the Church in tow, before Anglicans began to think in terms of a proper international communion. Times had clearly changed; the two new dioceses in Borneo, for example, were created entirely in response to the new political situation, in which local communities that were mainly Christian began adjusting to life under national Muslim-majority rule. In light of this, the ecclesiastical break between Singapore and Malaysia seemed inevitable. It came as no surprise when the regional Church reorganized again in 1970, establishing the new Diocese of West Malaysia, under Bishop Roland Koh, with the Diocese of Singapore becoming a separate diocese once more. Bishop Chiu would continue to lead the newly separate diocese until 1981. After 1970, the story of the Anglican Church in Malaysia definitively becomes a related but distinct story alongside that of the Anglican Church in Singapore. Relations would remain close and cordial, but Malaysia had an increasingly different set of challenges to face (*Straits Times* no. 1, 1972: 15).

A sense of urgency to adapt to the new context gripped the Churches and Christian community of Singapore. In the face of previous shared challenges, such as the need for a theological college, ecumenical cooperation had been effective, and the Malayan Christian Council (MCC) had existed since 1948. When Singapore became independent in 1965, the MCC was renamed the Council of Churches of Malaysia and Singapore (CCMS), before splitting in the mid-1970s to become separate bodies for each country; the National

Council of Churches of Singapore (NCCS) and the Council of Churches of Malaysia (CCM). Internationally, the Churches cooperated with the East Asia Christian Conference (EACC). The EACC was founded in 1957 as a regional ecumenical organization representing up to fifteen national councils and numerous denominations, committed to working together in mission, leadership development, ecumenical engagement, and social justice. The CCMS and its successor organizations represented mainstream Churches and also maintained relationships with the National Evangelical Christian Fellowship and the non-member Roman Catholic Church. Ecumenical work successfully connected diverse Christian groups in Singapore, but local identities and community characteristics continued to assert themselves (Roxborogh 2014: 32–33; 2018: 288).

Singapore in the late 1960s and early 1970s was still in an uneasy phase of postcolonial reorientation. The Anglican Church was committed to supporting the ongoing national transition, while internally adjusting to being led by an Asian bishop for the first time. Bishop Chiu was in his forties, Penang-born, ethnic-Chinese, but "English educated," to use a loaded phrase that almost functions as an ethnic designation in Singapore. When he first arrived in Singapore, Chiu's background and ethnicity endeared him to many, but difficulties arose; Chiu was young, liberal, and ecumenical, which contrasted with the mostly conservative ethnic-Chinese community (Lim et al. 2006: 60). The courteous, well-educated new bishop was also seen as weak, not a natural leader, and prone to being manipulated (Green 2001: 7–10). Chiu searched for a way to assert his credibility while also diverting people's attention toward something constructive. In 1967 he launched a three-year diocese-wide Bible study program that became the successful "Know Your Scriptures" campaign; Chiu aimed to boost Bible literacy among Church members and emphasize Bible study as the most important aspect of Church participation (Diocese of Singapore and Malaya 1967: 3). Many of the difficulties faced by Chiu early in his tenure were beyond his control, as the effects of Singapore's troubled transition from British part-rule to full independence only began to be felt during this time. The Church's long-established privileges disappeared, and access to resources, amidst an overhaul of the Church's relationship with international missionary organizations, was significantly reduced. Suddenly, it seemed, Asian Christians would have to look to each other for support, resources, and motivation.

Singapore entered a phase of intensive industrialization, and it was in this context that the Singapore Industrial Mission (SIM) began in 1966, based in the Jurong district, heartland of the nation's new urban-industrial vision. SIM was supported by the CCMS and the EACC. Bishop Chiu served as vice-chair of the social justice-oriented EACC from 1968 to 1969 and as acting chair from 1970 to 1973. Through its link to the EACC, SIM was connected to a wave of similar industrial missions being launched across Asia. These activities would sometimes be interpreted as expressions of Asian liberation theology, but the concern for social justice and enthusiasm for workers' missions were not new in the Anglican Church. Since the advent of the mass industrial society, successive Lambeth Conferences have promoted workers' missions in the context of the Church's "social mission and social principles [and] the ideals of brotherhood which underlie the democratic movement" (Davidson 1920: 327). SIM was therefore part of a fairly unradical Anglican tradition, but it caused alarm in Singapore government circles and annoyed the state-endorsed labor unions, eventually leading to SIM and its affiliated civic center being ordered to close in 1972. This was, no doubt, a hurtful, embarrassing, and arguably unnecessary rebuke for Bishop Chiu and the others involved. It was precisely at this low point in his tenure that Chiu came into contact with the charismatic renewal or Pentecostal movement, while attending the World Council of Churches' "Salvation Today" conference in Thailand. While meditating on his recent demoralizing experiences in his Bangkok hotel room, Chiu found himself filled with an overwhelming joy, and he began spontaneously praising God in English, Chinese, Malay, and, lastly, in some unknown and unrecognizable language; he was "speaking in tongues," in Pentecostal terminology, for the first time. Soon after, he received his "baptism in the Holy Spirit" and, by the time he returned to Singapore, the leader of the Anglican Church was entirely reoriented toward Pentecostalism (Goh 2010: 59–60).

PENTECOSTALISM IN SINGAPORE: ORIGINS, CIRCUMSPECTION, AND THE ANGLICAN PERSPECTIVE

References to Pentecostalism, the charismatic movement, and charismatic renewal tend to be broadly interchangeable, with "charismatic" often being the preferred term for Pentecostal worship when integrated into the older institutional Churches. Worldwide, Pentecostalism has been described as a "global cluster of movements" with various "streams" and "waves"; terminology that challenges traditional breakdowns of Christianity into denominations and communions (Lim 2015: 213). There is no denying Pentecostalism's overwhelming influence in Singapore, where it appears to sit in harmony with the social, political, and cultural landscape of the modern state, typically, or perhaps stereotypically, appealing to young, urban, ambitious, English-educated, ethnic-Chinese citizens (Chin 2017: 3). Pentecostal or charismatic worship, often with the use of audiovisual technology and contemporary music, and typically featuring dynamic and energetic pastors, has become almost synonymous with Christianity in Singapore over the past five decades. The attraction of articulate, well-groomed leaders, vibrant rock-concert-like worship, and having many young, convivial fellow worshippers to pray with is arguably not difficult to appreciate (Chong and Hui 2013: 3).

Much more than just a worship style, however, Pentecostalism comprises a theology, an ecclesiology, and a worldview that all have evident appeal. Pentecostal churches are sometimes accused of being overly focused on numbers and finances rather than on spiritual development, or of distorting the gospel to emphasize prosperity and achievement, but their success in attracting new members appears to be unrivalled. They can be criticized for shunning mainstream Churches and rejecting traditional Christian doctrines, but they may by the same token be praised for successfully adapting their ministries to match the tastes, needs, and lifestyles of their audience (Goh 2005: 16). Undeniably, the Pentecostal boom has been key to the ongoing transformation of Southeast Asian Christianity. The common assumption that Pentecostalism in Southeast Asia is purely a recent, Western-imported phenomenon is mistaken, however, as is the perception of Pentecostalism worldwide as a creature of the 1960s and 1970s; independent Pentecostal groups were active in several parts of Asia during Pentecostalism's first global wave in the early 1900s (Lim 2015: 213).

The emergence of Pentecostalism around the world was first met with cautious but mixed reactions in Anglican circles, with aspects of the movement being counted among "dangerous tendencies in contemporary thought" (Davidson 1920: 325). "There are many members of the Church," the fifth Lambeth Conference, in 1908, noted, "both clerical and lay, in the United States, in Great Britain, and elsewhere, who practice 'Spiritual Healing' in one or other of its modern forms" (Davidson 1920: 392), pointing out the spread of "ministries of healing . . . in severance from [healing's] context in the Christian creed" (Davidson 1920: 308–9). Lambeth was very careful not to completely alienate those who were drawn to these new practices, acknowledging that "the strongest and most immediate call to the Church is to the deepening and renewal of her spiritual life" (Davidson 1920: 325); the conference affirmed that it "would not wish to say a word in disparagement or discouragement of those who may be pioneers in a new branch of service, but it believes it would for the present be unwise to depart from an attitude of watchfulness and reserve. . . . [The] evidence would [need to] be tested properly . . . by trained scientific experts." The jury, in other words, would remain out, and "those who claim to exercise these 'Gifts of Healing'" would receive neither endorsement nor condemnation for the time being. The cautious language almost speaks for itself; these healers must beware of "the temptation," the conference stated, "to wander into the dangerous ground of occultism and spiritualism" (Davidson 1920: 392–93). Sensing that bishops would need to have something to offer to these potential "pioneers" of healing, the conference recommended the provision of new prayers, for pastoral use, for the restoration of health, which would be "more . . . direct than those contained in the present Office for the Visitation of the Sick" (Davidson 1920: 325). This gesture certainly demonstrated that the matter was being taken seriously.

When Pentecostal-oriented groups based in China and Ceylon (Sri Lanka) began sending missionaries to other parts of Asia in the early 1920s, they may have been surprised to find that Singapore was already primed for elements of Pentecostalism. The *Singapore Diocesan Magazine* of February 1922 reported on a healing mission taking place in Singapore, featuring "remarkable cures," while dutifully emphasizing, in line with Lambeth's guidance, that regular prayer and Holy Communion were still the best forms of "real help" (*SDM*, vol. XII, no. 45, February 1922: 2). The success of this healing mission led to the immediate launch of a monthly healing service, with laying-on of hands, to be held at St. Andrew's Cathedral on the first Friday of each month at five o'clock; the cathedral was, the *SDM* reported, "crammed with sick persons" for the inaugural service (*SDM*, vol. XII, no. 45, February 1922: 11). The "way of renewal" had already become part of the diocese's vocabulary (*SDM*, vol. XXVI, no. 94, May 1934: 14). Two American Pentecostal missionaries of the Assemblies of God arrived in Singapore in 1928 after being expelled from China. Finding few gaps in the mission market by that stage, they opened a Cantonese-language school and called in more missionaries from Canton (Guangdong) to staff it, foreshadowing the much bigger influx of expelled missionaries that would take place after the communist rise to power (Mathews 2019: 272–74).

The real Pentecostal breakthrough in Singapore, particularly in Anglican circles, would occur a few decades later still, when Anglicans joined clergy from other mainstream denominations, and from the fringes of those denominations, in embracing Pentecostalism. This embrace was not instant or universal; on November 2, 1972, the *Straits Times* warned of "An unhealthy cult spreading among [the] young." The article described semi-clandestine meetings being held in homes and on school premises, featuring frenzied chanting, screaming, and assorted hysterics, with young people bursting into tears and whimpering; "some even [ended] up talking a lot of nonsense," it was reported (*Straits Times* no. 2, 1972: 13). The mainstream Churches expressed their reservations and fears over the use of "bongo drums and other devilish devices" (Green 2001: 5). These reservations began to dissipate after the conversion to Pentecostalism, while still leading the Anglican Church, of Bishop Chiu; this provided the movement with a unique institutional credibility boost, but it still did not look like the beginning of something particularly influential or consequential (Sng 1980: 288–89). Pentecostalism gained ground gradually, sometimes through the open endorsement of mainline denominations, sometimes through the stealthy inclusion of Pentecostal practices in mainstream services, and perhaps most notably through the foundation of new independent churches, all helped by numerous ecumenically minded individuals who were involved in more than one of these processes (Mathews 2019: 272–74).

The number of Protestant Christians in Singapore would increase dramatically in the fifty years after 1970, rising from 2 percent to 10 percent of the whole population, and this 500 percent increase applied equally to Anglicans (Johnson and Zurlo 2017: 49–51). While this remarkable growth suggests an increase in the appeal of Christianity generally, it is inevitably linked to the spread of Pentecostalism in particular. Around one-third (approximately one hundred and twenty) of Singapore's churches are Pentecostal, with Assemblies of God being the largest expressly Pentecostal denomination, comprising around fifty churches and about twenty-five thousand adherents. Most of Singapore's independent churches are Pentecostal. There are several "megachurches" with Sunday attendances ranging from ten to well over thirty thousand, beating all of the mainstream denominations (Mathews 2019: 271; Gomes and Tan 2019: 227). It follows that most conversions to Christianity in Singapore take place within charismatic and Pentecostal churches, especially independent ones. The mainstream, traditional denominations that have most effectively handled the transformation of the Christian community and benefited most from the surge in Christianity's appeal are predictably the ones who embraced elements of charismatic and Pentecostal worship and theology, notably the Anglicans and Methodists. The fact that Singapore's older mainstream Churches, including the Anglicans, keenly embraced charismatic and Pentecostal worship and theology may seem strange, because they had generally been associated with forms of Christianity that would be considered liturgically traditional and theologically liberal. As mentioned above, however, forms of Christianity that were deemed liberal, which could be interpreted as synonymous with radical or liberationist, became targets of suspicion in the context of Southeast Asia exhausted by three decades of anticommunist tension and conflict. Christians had lost confidence in and distanced themselves from the term "liberal" and its now-negative connotations, but it is also necessary to consider how that word was previously employed (Goh 2010: 54–56).

The colonial Churches in Southeast Asia were considered liberal in the sense that they peacefully accommodated a broad range of expressions, including conservative and less-conservative congregations. Being liberal did not contradict the Anglo-Catholic, High-Church, SPG influences that drove the development of the Anglican Church in Singapore; the Church of England historically appointed moderate or liberal colonial bishops of "mild [but] firm churchmanship" in order to defend the middle ground and integrate those on the wings (Wilson 1863: 7). This strategy kept the peace for many decades, as long as the essentials of theology, Church order, and Scripture were seen as non-negotiable. During its relatively short lifetime, Anglicanism had already experienced many upheavals; the Anglican "way" emerged to indicate adherence to a clear set of core beliefs and practices, while being tolerant and accommodating of difference, which recognized the fact that the Anglican Church was an unapologetic inheritor of multiple traditions. Theologically speaking, this could certainly be called a liberal approach, combining reality-based practice and intellectual flexibility while safeguarding core values (O'Donovan 2008: 7).

In recent decades, critics have tended to accuse theological liberals of abandoning core values precisely in the name of realism and flexibility, calling liberalism a "theological deviation" and even a "disease" (Sng 1980: 184). The truly liberal approach, however, as understood in former times, was compatible with the view of Anglicanism as a bridge between contrasting and opposed traditions within Christianity, balancing the Protestant reformers' zeal for the gospel with ancient Catholic order and sacraments, maintaining that middle path or via media (Ramsey 2009: 175–88). Anglican matters as such are somewhat relative here, though; compared to Western Christianity, Southeast Asian Christianity in general developed a looser attachment to denominational identity, and expectations of denominations and allegiance to denominations do not impinge greatly on the Pentecostal phenomenon in the region. Then, in timely fashion, fluidity with regard to denomination appeared to be endorsed by the 1968 Lambeth Conference, which affirmed "open" access to Holy Communion for all those baptized according to a Trinitarian formula (Green 2001: 5). It may therefore be mistaken to view the rise of Pentecostalism in Singapore, though rightly called a conservative movement, as a clash between "wings" of the historic Church or Churches; it is, rather, a form of Christianity that trumps denominational allegiance and other Church issues with absolute Biblical authority, to which alone allegiance is owed (Lim et al. 2006: 59).

PENTECOSTALISM IN SINGAPORE: NATIONAL, INTERNATIONAL, AND CULTURAL ASPECTS

Explanations for Pentecostalism's success in Singapore have generally emphasized its cultural congruency with young, ambitious members of the ethnic-Chinese community. These young professionals see in their church, it is argued, traits and qualities that they themselves would like to attain; being pragmatic, action-based, and focused on problem-solution-results, but this explanation only reaches so far. Previously, attempts to explain the appeal of pre-Pentecostal Protestant Christianity in Singapore pointed to the rejection of traditional religions' superstition in favor of rationalism, which was tied to the diffusion of Western worldviews through Church-provided English-language education, and this theory remains influential. This is, however, a limited explanation that does not particularly help to explain the success of Pentecostalism, whose growth did not coincide with the expansion of Western education. Pentecostalism's beliefs in omens, visions, and prophecies, furthermore, clearly do not represent a rejection of older religious traditions; they imply, rather, a reconnection with ancient religious ideas, not their rejection (Goh 1999: 89–90). Pentecostalism promotes strong spiritual and spiritualist notions that chime with the Asian worldview and its acceptance of the basic reality of the spirit world; it is a form of Christianity that emphasizes supernatural occurrences, and these, rather than doctrines or deeds, are seen as the ultimate (but not the only) keys to salvation. Pentecostalism's focus on signs, miracles, and powers can be seen as compatible with traditional Chinese cosmology (Mathews 2019: 275). As compelling as these explanations may be, they contrast with Singaporeans' own stated reasons for being drawn to a particular church; "doctrinally sound teachings" and "a deeper experience of God" were the most popular reasons given in a major survey (Chong and Hui 2013: 12).

Cultural and spiritual compatibility arguments, while containing apparent truisms, still only go a certain distance toward explaining the success of Pentecostalism in Singapore. Practical factors, such as Singapore's geography and infrastructure, have also contributed to the success of the movement; distances in Singapore are short and manageable, making large gatherings in one location feasible. Singapore was also established early on as a global travel hub, which allowed leading international preachers to make stopovers there, to motivate and inspire worshippers, and to connect them to the wider Pentecostal world. The Pentecostal movement in Singapore thus profited from powerful international connections, but it resisted falling back into the type of dependent relationships with the West that mainstream Churches inherited from the colonial era (Mathews 2019: 279–80). The fierce independence of Asian Christians surprised observers from America, understandably seen as Pentecostalism's homeland, because Americans are less likely to imagine that they too have been perceived as an imperialist power (Wickeri 2021: 50). Pentecostalism today is not only mostly non-Western, it impacts the West through so-called "reverse mission" (Bretherton 2019: 8–10); it remains a persistent error to see Asian Pentecostalism as wholly derived from or dependent on American or other foreign influences (Goh 2010: 55).

The Asian Pentecostal boom may be seen partly as a repudiation of imposed Western Christian forms of worship, and this could be an aspect of its appeal; Pentecostalism's process of integration may bring it closer to being seen as

Asia's "own" Christianity. This could be vigorously debated, but the fact is that certain enduring and controversial elements of popular belief and religious practice across Asia, such as charms, trances, chanting, exorcisms, and possession, have more chance of finding expression within Pentecostalism than in older Western and European forms of Christianity (Lim 2015: 226). The EACC, seeking to enable the expression of "Asianness" in religious practice, argued that there were no traditions or beliefs that automatically did not belong in Asian Christianity; since the Christianity introduced by the colonial powers was politically tinged and biased, nothing could be reliably cast aside as unchristian just because the colonial Churches had rejected it (Goh 2010: 61–63).

The keys to Pentecostal success are not all historical, however, and much depends on the dynamics of the movement as it operates, particularly its focus on outreach. Each church member is encouraged to bring a non-member to events, thereby potentially doubling attendance with new faces and sending out a powerful message of visible church growth; this can be great publicity as well as effective evangelization. Once inside, the new attendee finds that the cell groups and prayer circles are quite intimate affairs, allowing for personal attention and expression; the newcomer is valued and listened to. When the newcomer progresses to becoming a member of the church, they discover a high degree of democratization; ministry roles are accessible and encouraged, gifts of preaching and glossolalia (speaking in tongues) are not reserved to a caste of clergy or leaders. This can mean inclusion for the socially excluded, empowerment for those who aspire to lead, and a more coherent experience for those who already have positions of responsibility in the outside world. Leadership is not dependent on extensive theological education or endorsement from traditional institutions; practical skills, interpersonal skills, and gifts such as oratory and motivating tend to be valued more highly than qualifications or ordinations. Husband and wife teams of pastors are quite common; women hold formal leadership roles in Pentecostal churches while older denominations are still debating, resisting, or rejecting the idea (Mathews 2019: 277–79). These features have exposed Pentecostal churches to accusations of disregarding Christian theology or rewriting it courtesy of their own Bible colleges, whose credibility is boosted by accreditation from international Pentecostal institutions (Lim 2015: 227).

Pentecostals are sometimes accused of being intolerant bigots who irritate other faith groups with their aggressive proselytism, but it is worth noting that Christians in general are shown to interact poorly with other faiths, even in the context of the world becoming ever more religiously diverse (Zurlo et al. 2022: 74). Pentecostals are vocal and visible, and this has been described as a countercultural win for all Christians in Singapore; Christianity is now more openly and more loudly practiced there than ever before, but the long term effects of this ostensible achievement are clearly debatable. If Pentecostals' militant behaviors were to develop more explicitly political expressions, as has happened elsewhere, then concerns about Pentecostalism would also evolve (Gomes and Tan 2019: 218; Mathews 2019: 290). Pentecostalism's conservative reputation appeases many of those who might otherwise see it as extreme, and its approach to the Bible is presented as being simply literal rather than fanatical, offering plain-language verse-referenced justifications for a spirituality that emphasizes supernatural occurrences. Pentecostals may seem intransigent, but the ease with which Pentecostalism has been adopted by mainstream denominations appears to contradict the movement's reputation for inflexibility. Pentecostalism has been boosted by its integration into traditional Churches rather than weakened; ecumenical engagement has improved, and Pentecostal ministers increasingly attend courses at TTC and other mainstream seminaries. Pentecostalism is also more diverse than it often appears, and perceptions of one monolithic movement can be misleading. Diversity may not be wholly positive for Pentecostalism; the proliferation of churches, groups, cells, leaders, publications, channels, and Bible schools, it is argued, demonstrates disunity and disorganization, as the movement's rejection of the historic denominations' stale uniformity translates into rejection of the principle of Church unity as well (Lim 2015: 227–28).

PENTECOSTALISM IN SINGAPORE: FAITH, ASPIRATIONS, AND PROSPERITY

Singapore is usually ranked as the second or third richest country in the world, somewhere between Qatar and Luxembourg, with Ireland, Norway, Switzerland, and Macau also contending. Singaporeans seem to have an insatiable appetite for economic advancement, and this is far from just cliché or rhetoric. Singapore is truly a nation of millionaires; with at least one in thirteen people currently counted in this group, the number of millionaires has doubled in the last five years and it is set to double again by 2030. This astonishing success has made wealth, and the handling of wealth, one of the central questions for studying Christianity in Singapore (Gomes and Tan 2019: 213). It may come as little surprise that Singaporean churchgoers tend to be generous givers; Anglicans, for example, donate about 10 percent of their income to the Church. There may be a transactional aspect to this giving, however, and Christians generally expect spiritual blessings in return. Terence Chong and Hui Yew Foong's landmark 2013 survey of Protestants in Singapore showed this to be true for 75 percent of megachurch attendees, and not only that; 67 percent of them expected material blessings in return for their donations as well as spiritual ones. This was shown to be true for only 18.5

percent of Anglicans. Seventy-two percent of megachurch attendees believed that the financial success of their church was evidence of God's blessing upon it, and 46 percent of Anglicans agreed (Chong and Hui 2013: 12–13).

Aspiration is serious business in Singapore, encapsulated in the "Five Cs" of car, cash, condo, credit card, and country club membership, forming an unapologetic materialist mantra. The all-out pursuit of the Five Cs has been criticized, by Singaporeans themselves, as the unedifying side of Singapore's aspiration culture, as material success has superseded all other indicators of personal achievement. Whether this is true or not, religion certainly remains a significant factor in people's lives, with at least 80 percent of the population affiliated with a religion. There is no necessary contradiction here, scholars agree, especially when the religion itself is redirected toward theologizing, encouraging, and actualizing material ambition. Numerous churches have done just that, it is argued, and their ability to reconcile wealth accumulation, materialist culture, and career success with Christian theology may make Christianity the sixth "C" (Gomes and Tan 2019: 233–35). It appears to be an attractive combination, and Christianity is now the fastest-growing religion in Singapore, but this combination gives rise to accusations of prosperity theology at its crudest. Prosperity theology, or the prosperity gospel, consisting of the divine bestowal of wealth and success in return for worship and obedience, remains controversial and disputed, even among those who endorse it. The uncomplicated transactional element has been said to motivate many conversions; followers of traditional Chinese religions, dissatisfied with unresponsive deities silently ignoring prayers, have turned to a religion that noisily promises concrete results (Green 2001: 96–100). If promoting, promising, and pursuing wealth accumulation have indeed become the deciding factors in Singaporean religion, then Christianity's boom is arguably nothing to be emulated or envied (Gomes and Tan 2019: 233–35).

Megachurches' prosperity-focused blend of gospel and capitalism draws tens of thousands of Sunday attendees, especially, it seems, from the English-speaking and -educated elite, who seek a religion that resonates with their personal, spiritual, and material aspirations (Kuo 2016: 22). Megachurch teaching appears to diametrically oppose the social gospel of the historic Churches, whether Protestant or Catholic, which promoted humility, simple living, and freedom from material temptation. New Christians, it seems, are absolved from the old Churches' meager offerings of an austere and sacrificial gospel that prioritizes the poor, the distressed, and the sinner. Instead, they are guided toward a dynamic and entrepreneurial religion that prioritizes the fulfillment of their personal goals. In its defense, the newer theology does at least represent a genuine turn away from a countercultural religious prospectus that was, after all, imported into Asia without invitation, but it would be a mistake to overlook the elements of continuity with colonial

Christianity. The intersection of Christianity with capitalism, the conflation of mission priorities and market priorities, and their combined power to shape the Church's identity and destiny, are absolutely nothing new, as the colonial history of Southeast Asia amply demonstrates. Prosperity theology's innovations may be seen as further steps in the continuing paradox of the secularization of Christianity, and this is consistent with the past rather than a break from it (Gomes and Tan 2019: 234).

This is also not the first time that the role of the gospel of Jesus Christ has been inverted; instead of gospel values standing in prophetic criticism of inequalities and injustices arising from capitalism and the markets, the gospel is instead understood and interpreted in the light of consumerist, capitalist values. Perhaps the most galling aspect for many Christians, however, has nothing to do with critiquing capitalism; prosperity theology appears to provide theological justification not just for wealth accumulation but also for the flaunting of extreme wealth, as an overt sign of God's blessing and in direct proportion to how much faith one has (Gomes and Tan 2019: 234–35). It is clearly easy to dismiss this transactional form of Christianity, exemplified by Singapore's megachurches but also present or influential across mainstream denominations, as nothing more than a false gospel, a religious scam, and destructive to true Christianity. Such an assessment, however, fails to see the phenomenon as a quite valid example, however distasteful it may be, of how Christians have managed to contextualize the gospel in an environment where concerns about personal wealth and personal success are understandably close to people's hearts. Singapore is, after all, a very expensive city, and finances inevitably feature significantly in the thoughts of people who may be separated by only one or two family generations from poverty. Many of the small island's goods and services must be imported or outsourced, so Singaporeans are also unavoidably business-minded, which is nothing new. In an exceptionally fast-paced, fast-changing urban nation, it is understandable that meeting immediate spiritual needs takes precedence over rigorous theological reflection (Kuo 2016: 22).

PENTECOSTALISM IN SINGAPORE: POLITICAL-THEOLOGICAL CONSIDERATIONS AND PERSPECTIVES

Chong and Hui's study found that members of mainstream Churches, especially Anglicans, were more likely to participate in politics and engage in public debate than other Christians. This may indicate confidence derived from a history of enfranchisement, and from cultural capital accumulated as members of a long-established English-speaking tradition. Members of

Pentecostal megachurches displayed the opposite trend, preferring to disclose their views privately; this has been described as the compartmentalization or privatization of religion. This tendency varies from issue to issue, with some issues being considered right to campaign about publicly, though often corporately rather than individually. Anglicans perceive a more seamless connection between Church and secular engagement, while megachurch members see the link between the spiritual and the material as a personal matter (Chong and Hui 2013: 22–23). An example of this may be seen in the contrast between a traditionally liberal critique of corporate sin such as colonialism and a personal focus on the "fallen" nature of the individual colonialist in need of salvation (Goh 2010: 61–63). It would be an oversight, however, to assume that there is no political dimension to Pentecostalism; as well as being one of the most vibrant and sizable streams of world Christianity, it is arguably the largest social movement of the past two hundred years, as concerned with questions of power, privilege, and Church-world dynamics as any other tradition. It differs considerably from classic political theologies, however, in emphasizing Christianity's being essentially at odds with the world; it presents this as an antagonistic relationship rather than stressing contiguity between the Church and the world. It is, nevertheless, similar to other political theologies in acknowledging democracy as the desirable and normative form of political order (Bretherton 2019: 8–10).

It is widely acknowledged that Pentecostalism replaced liberal Christianity because, above all, it was better equipped to reconcile the emerging priorities of Singapore; its timing was propitious, coinciding with Singapore's industrialization and "nation-building" program (Goh 2010: 59). Singapore's nation building was distinct from some other Asian nations' similarly worded projects, because Singapore's leaders eschewed ethnic-nationalistic narratives of a special or "true" people of the island, and they did not resort to idealized retellings of a glorious past. Instead, the founding vision of Singapore openly acknowledged that it was a former colonial port with a population of more or less recent immigrants and an admittedly negligible collective memory. Anticolonial sentiment was still quite tangible, but Singapore's priorities were progress, prosperity, and fresh engagement with the global economy, not the settling of old scores with the British, the world, or any group within its own society. The new state's initial demands upon the individual were forthright but not invasive; active citizenship, economic pragmatism, responsible asceticism, and social diligence. Singapore's leaders made no claims about chosen peoples, religious primacy, or global ideologies with Singaporean characteristics, but they did frame their vision in terms of traditional, conservative, and shared Asian values; aspects of these, such as honoring elders and community before self, resonated with Confucianism and Christianity equally (Gomes and Tan 2019: 216). The ideology of shared Asian values, as it became, has been described as a deliberately emotive strategy for disarming calls for greater democratization and social justice, making it easier for the government to condemn such calls as subversive and unpatriotic (Goh 2010: 57). In the polarizing context of Cold War Southeast Asia, in fact, such talk could be instantly labeled as communism (Lim et al. 2006: 69–70).

The Singapore Industrial Mission (SIM) and its supporter the East Asia Christian Conference (EACC) had been caught in this trap, and a closer look at this history is warranted. For some time after the independence of Singapore, the EACC continued working toward the indigenization and contextualization of liberal and liberation theology to produce a socially engaged Asian theology. In the late 1960s and early 1970s, while many Christians globally were seeking to limit old state powers, postcolonial Southeast Asian societies were discovering and developing positive functions of government for the first time. Asian liberal theologians urged Christians and non-Christians to engage with authority, consider the sources of authority, and examine relationships to authority (Goh 2010: 60–63). This exercise in evaluating authority would come to symbolize the theological conflict ahead; the Biblical literalism of the Pentecostals was based on not questioning authority at all, and although this applied primarily to Biblical authority, it was conducive to a habit of not questioning governments either (Lim et al. 2006: 62). The new Singaporean state, meanwhile, was alerted to liberal Christianity's potential for encroaching upon its turf. Liberal theologians expressed support for nation building in principle, but they intended to have their say on how it unfolded; this was not part of the government's vision, and Church-politics separation became its unspoken goal. The EACC was admonished, the SIM was suppressed, and the government took its first steps towards regulating religion (Goh 2010: 60–63).

In 1973, after the suppression of the SIM, Bishop Chiu stood down after five years in the leadership of the now-discredited EACC, at which time he suddenly, fully, and openly turned to Pentecostalism. The EACC, post-Chiu, reacted with horror to the rise of Pentecostalism, seeing it as inward-looking, growth-obsessed, personality-driven, and obsessed with demons, tongues, and the second coming. Chiu announced the arrival of charismatic renewal in the Diocese of Singapore, preferring this more usually Roman Catholic phrase to "Pentecostalism." "Praise and prayer" and "prayers for healing" became the default services at St. Andrew's Cathedral and other Anglican churches (Goh 2010: 60–64). Chiu gradually stopped sending ordination candidates to TTC for their studies, preferring small Pentecostal Bible colleges instead (Lim et al. 2006: 61). The EACC accused the Anglican Church of turning into a heretical, fundamentalist sect, catering only to the rich, young, and upwardly mobile. The conflict was not denominational, however; both liberals and Pentecostals were evenly distributed among the mainstream Churches. Roman Catholics suffered most from the collapse of liberal Christianity; they would go from outnumbering Protestants two-to-one to being outnumbered by the same ratio. Catholics filled the social theology void left by the suppression of the SIM, but in 1987 the police violently descended upon them with accusations of a Marxist conspiracy. The Catholic hierarchy bent over backward to appease the government, and international protestations came to nothing, thanks to the then-pope's zero tolerance of leftwing views. The threat of a Marxist uprising was a fairly obvious ruse, but this final clampdown on liberal Christians allowed the government to justify its agenda of excluding religion from social discourse and asserting its own monopoly of the public square. Liberal Asian Christianity, the narrative went, obstructed the national project and offended the ongoing renaissance of shared Asian values (Goh 2010: 56–66, 71–72).

In the same year as the crackdown on Catholic social activism, 1987, the old EACC, now renamed the Christian Conference of Asia (CCA), was expelled from Singapore. The government admitted that it had only just made the connection between the CCA and the old, banned, SIM, a mere two decades late (Goh 2010: 71–72). Anglicans and Methodists obediently repudiated the expelled CCA, apparently uniting themselves to the decisive rejection of liberal Asian theology, but they did so with mixed feelings. No one, in fact, had reason to celebrate the ever-widening void between Church and state. After all, the Anglican Church's cooperative attitude towards the government, alongside its early acceptance of Pentecostalism, had paid dividends; new parishes were built on the strength of the new order, bringing the diocese's total nearer to twenty. These included St. James's in the Holland Village area, the Chapel of the Resurrection (COR), originally founded for the students and staff of St. Andrew's junior college and today the hub of numerous church plants, and Yishun Christian Church (Anglican) (Green 2001: 80–95). Pentecostals unequivocally welcomed the expulsion of the CCA and the Church-politics split that it implied; earthly concerns were, after all, relativized in Pentecostal thinking, because Christ has already defeated the Devil, though they continued to vociferously support Singapore's nation-building program (Goh 2010: 75–76). Reveling in Billy Graham's prophecy that identified Singapore as the Antioch of Asia, many began to imagine Singapore at the center of a triumphant march of Christianity across the continent. They began to see the emergence of Singapore in holistic, spiritual terms, starting with its foundation by Raffles, as willed by God; "from survival to success, and from success to global leadership; not just in the natural but also in the spiritual realm," in the words of Bishop Moses Tay, Chiu's successor (Goh 2010: 80).

CONCLUSION

There would seem to be little in the early, middle, and later colonial history of the Anglican Church in Singapore to explain the Church's eventual reorientation, over the course of just one generation, as a global bastion of literalist, conservative, Pentecostal Christianity. The often-heard throwaway comment that all of Asia, a mere sixty percent of the world's population, is "naturally" conservative is far from satisfactory, and although the comment is widely accepted as a truism in Asia itself, it is a truism that poses more questions than it answers. A number of factors combined to prepare the ground for the Church's Pentecostal reinvention, especially the decades-long journey towards local leadership, the effective development of lay leadership, and renewed emphases on Bible knowledge and youth work (Green 2001: 5). Talented new Church leaders were highly influential in their engagement with both the nation-building project of independent Singapore and with Christians' evolving postcolonial priorities; they listened to the emerging consensus of shared Asian values and blessed it. The Cold War overshadowed the reshaping of postcolonial Southeast Asia, and Singapore's political leaders were understandably determined to remain distant in all senses from the various minor and major conflicts taking place around the region, but this defensive attitude fostered a certain internal intolerance. The atmosphere became polarizing; Christians found that their civic concerns, social activism, and experiments in workplace ministry risked appearing ideological, and this could easily label them as communist sympathizers (Lim et al. 2006: 69–70). In reality, Christians in former colonies were usually too savvy, too wary, and too disillusioned with foreign domination to give much credence to the Soviet-aligned option (Pieris 2004: 256–57).

Christianity in Singapore faced an uncertain future and an insecure one, outside of a narrow range of possibilities. Only morally conservative, socially neutral, politically disengaged, and expressly state-cooperative models of Christian worship and outreach, it seemed, would flourish in that atmosphere. Privately lived religion, expressed publicly but cautiously, was the formula to follow, rather than publicly lived religion with a parallel private dimension, and any incursions by religion into the realm of the political would be dealt with severely (Lim et al. 2006: 69–70). The private-public dynamic is often perceived as a standoff in Pentecostal thinking, mirroring the standoff between the Church (the sacred, the holy) and the world (the profane, the debased). Political discord is inevitable, the thinking goes, but Christians are concerned with the spiritual rather than the structural; personal conversion, which translates into dutiful, democratic citizenship, is seen as the true Christian motor of change (Bretherton 2019: 117). Thus, Christians in Singapore began to focus on policing internal, personal morality rather than pursuing externals like social justice or identifying corporate sin. These revised understandings of the relationship between the political and the religious, and of the void between the two, coupled with the obedient citizenship that these understandings promoted, seemed to complement each other; general economic growth and increasing individual well-being, for example, served to inspire and justify the spread of prosperity theology. The shift in religious thinking appeared to be working (Lim et al. 2006: 69–70).

Singapore's national renewal was therefore matched by renewal in the religious arena, especially for the country's fastest-growing religion, Christianity. The Church's embrace of Pentecostalism in those circumstances was not especially incongruous, since the Pentecostal movement has long been recognized as one of authentic social transformation, whose early leading figures emerged from situations of slavery and oppression. Pentecostalism is a movement with teeth, not just smiles, feeling called to proclaim Christ in particular places and times and to proclaim how to live in those particular places and times. It is confident enough and potent enough to eschew the fixity and inflexibility of historical Christianity, flourishing instead in contexts of spontaneity and the ad hoc, which explains the movement's reluctance to concretize its structures and pursue organizational unity. With good reason, Luke Bretherton described Pentecostalism as "a multifarious, mercurial, intercultural, and global phenomenon that lacks a clear canon, an identifiable set of key thinkers, and specific institutional expressions and sociopolitical forms" (Bretherton 2019: 116–21). In terms of future challenges facing Pentecostalism in Singapore, they may be similar to those facing all denominations; growing pressure to stay relevant, the need to navigate increasingly complex social and political sensitivities, and, perhaps to a lesser degree than most Christian groups, the problem of an aging membership. There are also the perennial challenges of conducting outreach, doing witness, and effectively engaging interreligiously, all within rapidly evolving social relationships. All Churches, furthermore, face the challenge of renegotiating their "spaces" in the future (Lim 2015: 226); wariness of institutions and doubts about organized belief may spread in the context of Singapore's huge shift to a knowledge economy, increased isolated working, and growing individualization in the pursuit of a chosen lifestyle (Mathews 2019: 281–88).

Three Singaporean clergy, the Reverend Lim Leng, the Reverend Andrew Lee Tuck Leong, and the late Reverend Doctor Yap Kim Hao, two Anglicans and a Methodist, applied a faith-development analysis to the Singapore Church's trajectory. They explained that the colonial Church reached a moderate level of development, being broadly liberal but not combative, promoting an undemanding personal faith characterized by freedom and inclusion. From there, Lim, Lee, and Yap suggested, the Church in Singapore has regressed to a lower level of faith development and risks regressing further. The Church has grown numerically at the cost of reverting to a one-dimensional, mythic-literal faith, according to these clergy, discouraging reflection and refusing to admit nuance, even considering these to be illicit. The thesis of Christianity's compatibility with traditional Chinese religions, which are part of the fabric of Southeast Asian life, can be better understood, Lim, Lee, and Yap explained, when Taoism (or Daoism) is also identified as a mythic-literal belief system consisting of signs, spells, and dueling deities. Pentecostalism often emphasizes signs and omens, such as the rise of globalism, the liberalization of the Church, the foundation of the state of Israel, and it makes much of the "dueling deities" of acceptance and rejection of homosexuality. Literalist Pentecostal Christians may be unaware that "liberal" Churches are also on a trajectory of development, and just as the Church in Singapore was not always conservative, neither were the Western Churches always liberal. The degeneracy of a Church from one perspective is the next step in its faith development from another perspective. Western Anglican Churches may certainly be perceived as having made mistakes, but they are not incapable of self-criticism, including with regard to their colonial past and its legacies. Western Churches, for their part, must realize that disparaging the literalist Biblical interpretations of global south Christians only reanimates the zombie of colonialist superiority, which has not been dormant for very long in the grand scheme of things. The fact that north and south happen to find themselves at different developmental stages according to one method of analysis in no way justifies the denigration of authentic transcendental and spiritual maturity, developed over millennia, of people who genuinely trust in things like healing, exorcism, and miracles (Lim et al. 2006: 58–67).

Pentecostalism's distinctive coalescence within mainstream Christianity, exemplified by its seamless integration into the Anglican Church, is indicative of its great resilience; complex contexts of ethnic and religious plurality, intolerance, and even the persecution of Pentecostal Christians, have apparently only ever strengthened Pentecostalism's resolve (Goh 1999: 89; Lim 2015: 214). Even so, the movement's departures from traditional Biblical interpretations have cost it the long-established support of some Anglicans, who increasingly call for a more moderate, gentle, and more accurately gospel-oriented Christianity (Goh 2010: 82–83). Pentecostalism helped to push the liberal, social gospel off the Christian stage in Southeast Asia, but it has yet to succeed in reconciling, within itself, the diverse gospel callings to be spiritually liberated but socially engaged, and its followers mostly shrink from full participation in politics and civics (Chong and Hui 2013: 22–23). Pentecostalism's biggest future pitfalls are therefore most likely to be found in the gray areas inherent to the movement itself. Focusing on signs, prophecies, and sensational experiences may not work its magic forever, and people may become frustrated with Pentecostals' withdrawal from "corrupted" and "fallen" society, not to mention the movement's frequent schisms, rivalries, and internal conflicts. Pentecostals might decide to halt their withdrawal from society and apply their legendary pragmatism to social and political matters; this would be a high-stakes game that would risk alienation, disillusionment, or, possibly, government displeasure. Showing their social and political cards could force Pentecostals to choose between a rightward shift to theocracy and a leftward shift to radical activism (Goh 2010: 82).

Understanding Pentecostalism's success in Singapore calls upon observers to look beyond the various "compatibility" theses to appreciate the movement's potential for accommodating and expressing an individual's needs, aspirations, and identity, but also their politics. As decolonization progressed in the 1960s and 1970s, once-dominant liberal Christianity declined. For a time, the old colonial Anglican Church remained broadly liberal, devoid of extremes, and no militant stances were expected from its members. The Church was historically fairly progressive with regard to education, ethnicity, and gender, but only in keeping with the progressive, philanthropic wing of the old civil society, and its progressive credentials were often assumed rather than displayed (Lim et al. 2006: 60). Anglican liberalism withered as Singapore's independent government consolidated its authoritarian style of rule. Cold War panic led to "liberal" being reinterpreted as "left" and indicative of Marxist sympathies. As the government suppressed liberal Christian movements from the 1970s onwards, conservative Pentecostalism advanced, benefiting from newly acquired connotations of progress and acceptability. In understanding the rise of Pentecostalism, the most significant thesis of compatibility is not about compatibility with Chinese philosophy or folk religion, but compatibility with the capitalist development-driven ethos of the new Singapore (Goh 2010: 54).

Chapter Eight

"Indifferent to the Agenda of the Western Theological Intelligentsia"

Singapore's Anglican Church: Realization and Realignment

Getting a clear picture of today's Anglican Church in Singapore calls for a range of themes to be taken into consideration, such as the Church's engagement and self-understanding within hypermodern, multicultural Southeast Asian society and its roles and relationships within Asian Christianity, global Christianity, and global Anglicanism. The preceding chapter probed the Church's complex engagement with Pentecostalism, or charismatic renewal, over recent decades, while this chapter will more closely examine the Church's outward relationships and interactions with broader debates during that same period, from the 1970s up to the present day. While this chapter's focus may be largely outward-facing, the reality of the current situation for Christians and the particular experience of being a Singaporean Anglican must be considered. Today's Church is in many senses the living heir to the old English colonial Church described in previous chapters, and it is reasonable to ask what the modern Church retains from this experience, if anything, and to identify what it has discarded, and why. While assessing the impact of this colonial inheritance, the Church's other inheritance must also be considered; it is co-heir to the worldwide Anglican patrimony, part of a significant and arguably fragmenting global communion, and Singapore has its own responses to the Anglican Communion's divisions and controversies. Perhaps more pressingly than any global, regional or specifically Anglican considerations, the Church simply strives for continuity, relevance, and effectiveness, much like any other old, traditional organization embedded in a uniquely dynamic, developed, and fast-changing society. The Church cannot exist in a state of oblivion, isolated from the economic, political, and social whirlwind surrounding it, and must engage.

The break-up of the old Church of India, Pakistan, Burma, and Ceylon (CIPBC) in 1970 signaled a new era of opportunity and renewal for the region's Churches, including Singapore's. Skeptics, especially in the rapidly secularizing West, may have interpreted the demise of the territorially vast CIPBC as a defeat for global Christianity, or at least the British Empire brand of it, but something more complex was taking place; Christianity in the West may indeed have been declining, but an evangelistic boom was beginning in many former colonies (Cox 2008: 9). Across Asia, Churches were adjusting to new societies, reimagining their relations with other institutions, developing voices on national stages, and breaking down denominational boundaries, and for the Anglican Church in Southeast Asia, reorganizations presaged the launch of a future multinational regionwide Church. Two big takeaways from these events, for Singapore, were that old denominational expectations and distinctions could be safely breached, in order for the Church to survive, remain relevant, and flourish, and that supporting the government's national developmental vision may secure a share in the resulting stability and other fruits (Green 2001: 4–6). These became the guiding principles for the Anglican Church in Singapore, especially when the influence of Pentecostalism began to pervade, and the government's nation-building project became more determined and demanding of obedience. As vital as such realizations were at the national and regional level, however, they only tangentially affected the uncertainty facing global Anglicanism, which stood on the brink of an identity crisis.

Anglicanism, objectively, has quite successfully adapted to and kept up with social change over the last fifty years, but whether this is to be applauded or deplored is a matter for heated debate. The 1970s saw the first real waves of women's ordination in the Anglican Communion (there had been isolated precedents) and the practice gained momentum in the 1980s, leading to its widespread adoption by the 1990s. The early two-thousands saw the initial recognition of homosexuality and same-sex relationships, including for clergy, followed by the push toward acknowledging same-sex unions more broadly, and greater acceptance of complexity in matters of gender and identity. These developments have met with considerable organized opposition, including the formation and growth of rival Anglican ecclesial bodies calling for a halt to the revolution and offering orthodox "havens" for conservative Anglicans to worship in. For these opponents, changes in the Church's positions do not just stem from an ill-considered desire to keep up with the times; they are radical departures from core, Biblical principles and unalterable Christian morals. These liberalizing moves, critics assert, displace the Bible from the center of Church authority and subvert Christianity's two-thousand-year tradition.

Of all the contested issues, women's ordination was the great watershed for many Anglicans, but in Asia's conservative Churches the range of responses has been more varied than might be expected; it is rarely a simple yay or nay. In India, the two united Churches of the Anglican Communion do ordain women, though in practice their work appears to be limited to certain ministries considered suitable for women, with restrictions on public preaching. In Burma (Myanmar), the Church does not currently ordain women, though it accepted the idea in principle as early as 1973. Some Churches in Asia, such as Malaysia's, have expanded the range of non-ordained ministry roles, beyond the colonial-era two-role formula of clergy and catechists, with positions of responsibility, though not priesthood, open to women as well as men. To address the question of a specifically ministerial role for women, orders of non-ordained "deaconesses" were created in both Malaysia and Singapore, where Pentecostal thinking was moving the Church toward recognizing a wide range of gifts and ministries that cannot be conferred sacramentally anyway. This approach may have circumvented two potentially vexatious issues; embittered relations with other members of the Anglican Communion on the one hand, and cultural conflict with neighbor faith groups that restrict the roles of women on the other (Koepping 2011: 31–32).

Making decisions informed by sensitivity to neighbors of different faiths unites Anglicans in Singapore, Malaysia, and Burma with their fellow Anglicans in Bangladesh and Pakistan, who refrain from ordaining women so as not to further alienate or provoke the national religious majority. Internationally, the conservative Anglican movement, in its various forms, tends to enable rather than mandate opposition to women's ordination; opposition is a common rather than a universal or required stance, for example, among affiliates of Gafcon, a network of traditionalist Anglican Churches that emerged from the 2008 Global Anglican Future Conference (GAFCON). No crisis over women's ordination erupted in Singapore, where the Church's embrace of Pentecostalism challenged the customary Anglican importance given to priestly ordination, largely defusing the issue. It is interesting to note, however, that colonial-era Singapore was home to leading exponents of women's ordination, including the Reverend Henry T. Malaher and Bishop John Leonard Wilson (*The Times* 1959: 6), and that the latter's daughter, the late Reverend Canon Doctor Susan Cole-King (1934–2001) was among the first women to be ordained in the Church of England (Mak 2022: 105–6).

Chapter Eight

THE CHURCH IN SINGAPORE UNDER THE LEADERSHIP OF MOSES TAY

After the last remaining British armed forces personnel departed Singapore in the early 1970s, they left behind a church building, St. Peter's, situated on Admiralty Road, in the northeastern corner of Singapore. In 1977, the government of Singapore offered it to the diocese, which placed it under the care of St. Andrew's Cathedral. The first services held there were charismatic "prayer and praise" services, like those conducted at the cathedral. The Reverend Canon Frank Lomax, the British vicar of St. Andrew's, began a regular Holy Communion service, assisted by a chaplain of the still-present New Zealand armed forces. As a mere mission outpost of the cathedral and despite a less than stellar location, the church attracted new converts, and a committed congregation began to grow. In 1978, the Reverend Doctor Moses Tay Leng Kong, Dean of Singapore, was sent as priest-in-charge to St. Peter's, where he oversaw continued growth until 1982, when he became Bishop of Singapore. In the 1980s, St. Peter's was forced to vacate the original building, leading to a joint construction agreement with the Lutheran Church and a new name, Yishun Christian Church, with "(Anglican)" and "(Lutheran)" branches. The new name reflects the church's origins; Yishun is an alternative spelling of Nee Soon, the name of the vast British cantonment of colonial times, retained in the name of Nee Soon Road and the present-day Nee Soon Camp of the Singaporean armed forces. Yishun Christian Church was formally dedicated and consecrated on May 29, 1987, by Bishop Tay, with Bishop Daniel Chong representing the Lutherans.

If today's Anglican Church in Singapore may be said to have been shaped by one person more than any other, that person is probably Moses Tay Leng Kong. He was born on June 14, 1938, in Tangkak, Johor, then in British Malaya, the fifth of seven children in a family of Christian immigrants from China. The Tays were greatly influenced by the eccentric and extraordinarily influential Chinese evangelist John Sung (or Song) (1901–44) whose preaching tours included Malaya and Singapore (Sng 1980: 176–77). After the 1949 revolution, the Tays lost their savings, banked back home in China, with which they had planned to educate their children. Despite this setback, Moses would be the first member of his family to attend university. Before that, he found himself in a tiny Protestant minority at a prestigious school, St. Francis's Institution, where he faced Roman Catholic "indoctrination" until his vicar moved him to the Anglo-Chinese School, and then to the High School in Melaka. He studied medicine at the University of Singapore and practiced medicine in Malaysia for eight years prior to ordination. Tay served as Dean from 1974, under Bishop Joshua Chiu Ban It, before succeeding him as Bishop in 1982. He was Singapore's seventh Bishop and second Asian bishop, and he later became the first Archbishop of the new Province of South East Asia (PSEA) (Tay 2009: 5–6, 34–57).

Tay's commitment to Pentecostalism was at least as intense as that of his predecessor, whose influence Tay did not deny; Bishop Chiu had favored sending ordination candidates to Pentecostal Bible colleges rather than the traditional Anglican-supported TTC, but Tay went further and made speaking in tongues an effective requirement for ordination (Lim et al. 2006: 61). Tay's rejection of traditional routes to ordination was viewed with wariness even by his supporters, but they felt that he redeemed himself with impressive provision of comprehensive training for laypeople. Tay strongly opposed women's ordination, citing Biblical prohibitions, at the 1988 Lambeth Conference, where he also enthusiastically asserted his charismatic credentials. Some found this disturbing, but Tay was generally effective in normalizing the charismatic tendency; "In Anglican circles," Michael Green wrote, "the charismatic movement began in Singapore" (Green 2001: 3–4, 12–20). An even more widely publicized display of Tay's zeal was the exorcism and destruction of an antique Chinese chest, remembered as having been decorated with diabolic symbols. This dramatic spectacle may have elicited shock or ridicule from some in Singapore, as it might have done anywhere, but it was not incongruous with Southeast Asian understandings of the sort of thing a religious leader might do, and it did not actually draw very strong reactions (Lim et al. 2006: 62). Visits overseas were another matter; when Tay visited Stanley Park in Vancouver in the early 1990s, he was deeply troubled by the park's totem poles, which he declared "artifacts of an alien religion [and] idols possessed by evil spirits, [requiring] prayer and exorcism" (Jenkins 2011: 157). This outburst was said to have horrified local Anglicans, but no apology was forthcoming, and Tay's attempt to arrange a return visit to Vancouver was rebuffed (Tse 2016: 104).

Some Singaporean Anglicans approached the then-Archbishop of Canterbury, George Carey, under whose direct jurisdiction Singapore still fell at the time, to express concerns about what they saw as the eradication of Anglican traditions, liturgies, and heritage under Tay's leadership. The prayer book, in its various authorized forms, was being replaced with free-form worship, they said, and altars were being removed in favor of stages for performance and preaching. The Church's carefully ordered lectionary was being ignored as ministers selected the day's readings at will, while collects and propers, they complained, were giving way to ad hoc prayers according to the inspiration, needs, and tastes of the congregation. Apparently only one white foreigner-dominated parish retained "real" Anglican worship, in addition to one regular traditional service at the cathedral. This may suggest that resistance to change came mainly from the expatriate community, but this is not necessarily true; the cathedral's British vicar, Frank Lomax, was thoroughly supportive of the charismatic renewal, and of Tay, while the cathedral's mostly ethnic-Chinese clergy were unreceptive at first (Green 2001: 6). The complaints were allegedly ignored by Canterbury (Lim et al. 2006: 67–68). If Carey's strategy was to appease Tay and tolerate whatever was necessary in order to keep him firmly in the global Anglican fold, it seems not to have worked; Tay refused to attend international Anglican events, especially those involving clergy who supported the newly emerging bone of contention; LGBT issues (Jenkins 2011: 251). Tay also refused to be involved in ecumenism, it was claimed (Lim et al. 2006: 69). The Archbishop of Canterbury's ability to intervene directly in Singapore was about to be curtailed anyway; on February 2, 1996, Tay was installed as the first Metropolitan Archbishop and Primate of the newly created Church of the Province of South East Asia (PSEA). The PSEA would feature prominently in debates around emerging hot-button issues in the Anglican Communion, broadly following Tay's line and respecting his declared goal of promoting "wholesome spirituality" (Lim et al. 2006: 58).

As the lead diocese in a new Anglican province, the Church in Singapore now had to balance the needs, wishes, and preferences of three other dioceses and several overseas deaneries against its own distinct drive, flavor, and vision. Tay would discover that the PSEA, with its three diverse and well-established Malaysian dioceses, was not quite as responsive to his leadership as his own diocese, especially considering his relatively short four-year term as primate (Green 2001: 9). This did not seem to discourage Tay, who surely realized that Singapore still had more influence over the individual Malaysian dioceses than vice versa (Lim et al. 2006: 58). Among the half-dozen countries where the PSEA was present, nowhere could boast a significant national-level Christian minority like little Singapore's, then rapidly approaching 15 percent of the population; the whole of Malaysia had only four times the number of Anglicans as Singapore, but this was enough to ensure that total domination did not ensue. Singapore's success, furthermore, should not be exaggerated; Church growth under Tay was steady but not overwhelming. The Provincial Liturgical Committee (PLC) of the PSEA bravely attempted to reconcile the significant differences in worshipping styles across the province with their Church-wide provision of resources. By 1999, the PLC, which began work immediately after the creation of the PSEA, had produced a new prayer book and a new song book, a second volume of which came out for the twentieth anniversary of the PSEA in 2016. The PLC has since focused on the development of pastoral services resources, to equip Church members in their wide variety of ministries (Province of South East Asia 2019: 4).

The influence of the Church in Singapore was felt far beyond Southeast Asia, as the culture of conservatism and contestation fostered under

Tay foreshadowed developments in what became known as Anglican Realignment. In several respects, Tay led the way, not just in standing up to the worldwide Church but also in breaking with Anglican conventions, as required, and reevaluating aspects of Anglican heritage. This attitude would come to characterize Anglican Realignment, whose most successful adherent groups are often those that break with tradition rather than conserve it. A landmark example of this came when Tay, just a few months short of his retirement, made international headlines. Two priests of the Episcopal Church in the United States, Charles Murphy and John Rodgers, had for some time led clergy in protest, citing a crisis of faith and leadership in the dispute-stricken Anglican Communion (AC). Their list of concerns was sweeping; abortion, euthanasia, divorce, sexuality, same-sex unions, and racial inclusivity. Tay, joined by Archbishop Emmanuel Kolini of Rwanda and four other overseas bishops, consecrated Murphy and Rodgers as "missionary bishops" to North America, at St. Andrew's Cathedral, on January 29, 2000, contravening AC polity and procedures. Together they established the Anglican Mission in America (AMiA) to circumvent the jurisdiction of the Episcopal Church, to be overseen by the primates of the PSEA and Rwanda (Ward 2006: 64–65). Tay then retired as planned, but continuity with his leadership priorities was assured under another non-Singaporean as the PSEA's second leader, Yong Ping Chung (1941–2022), Bishop of Sabah, and under John Chew Hiang Chea (1947–) as the eighth and first ever Singapore-born Bishop of Singapore. Archbishop Yong, with Bishop Lim Cheng Ean (1942–) of West Malaysia, as well as Bishop Chew, would be among those most vociferously opposed to the next watershed, the appointment of openly gay Bishop Gene Robinson in 2003. The PSEA declared a state of impaired communion with the Episcopal Church as a result of Robinson's appointment, and Yong became increasingly vocal in promoting AMiA (Jarvis 2022: 147).

THE CONSERVATIVE OPPOSITION INTERNATIONALIZES

Conservative Anglicans had initially taken heart from the 1998 Lambeth Conference, which not only affirmed traditional Church teaching that "homosexual practice is incompatible with Scripture" and advised against the "legitimizing or blessing of same sex unions" but also accurately forewarned of the potential for division and polarization resulting from the homosexuality debate (Lim et al. 2006: 69–75). The perceived betrayal of these 1998 "promises" transformed the Lambeth Conference, in some eyes, from a sign of hope to a symbol of despair. The consecration of the two AMiA bishops in 2000 has, with good reason, been interpreted as a rebuke to the Lambeth-oriented Anglican world and, perhaps, to the liberalizing world in general. A simple pastoral defense of the consecrations framed them as Tay responding to a cry for help from marginalized fellow Christians (Green 2001: 22). Critics have claimed that the consecrations helped to generate an insular, secretive, and sectarian traditionalist culture that proves difficult to engage with for everyone, from detractors to potential supporters. Others have argued that AMiA's actions were far from traditionalist, in casting aside centuries-old protocols, disregarding diocesan boundaries, and scorning the vital consultative process involved in selecting a bishop (Lim et al. 2006: 72–75). Ancient tradition does suggest that Archbishops are free to ordain whomsoever they please in their own province, but more recent practices have set new precedents and have long been accepted. The AMiA consecrations were a decisive move, certainly, but one that came from the top, critics asserted; the event was concocted between leaders and excluded other voices. Some observers highlighted the contrast with the appointment of Bishop Gene Robinson, which, in itself, was an open and transparent process, done by the book. The response to those critics was that due process, when followed to the letter, can produce a tyranny of its own, far more tyrannical than pragmatic leaders taking decisive action to solve a painful problem, and that there is nothing consultative about due process reaching a compromise decision that frustrates everyone (Jenkins 2011: 251–57).

Since the early two-thousands, AMiA's goal of providing alternative orthodox oversight to Anglicans in North America, in opposition to perceived liberal degeneration in the Church, has been taken up by other, broader-scope contesting groupings. These include the Global South Fellowship of Anglican Churches (GSFA), often loosely referred to as Global South or the Global South bishops. The GSFA, based in Singapore, officially acknowledges the structures and protocols of the Anglican Communion (AC), uniting bishops from more than half of the AC's forty-two Provinces, including the PSEA, in conservative-oriented discussion. The GSFA dates back to a launch meeting in Kenya in 1994, followed by a meeting in Malaysia in 1997; Singapore hosted the 2010 meeting, during the tenure of Bishop John Chew. The global Anglican conservative or orthodox movement also includes groups with one foot placed firmly outside of official Anglican structures, such as Gafcon, named after the periodic Global Anglican Future Conference (GAFCON). Gafcon (upper and lower case) refers to the movement arising from the GAFCON (upper case) conference events, and it is also referred to as the Global Fellowship of Confessing Anglicans. Gafcon's participating bodies cover a spectrum of relationships with the AC, from full membership to full separation. There is overlap between the leaderships of Gafcon and the GSFA, though the GSFA's leaders have nearly all been conservative AC primates from the global south, while Gafcon was, until 2023, chaired by the primate of the non-AC Anglican Church in North America (ACNA), Archbishop Foley Beach.

Members of this movement may not encourage the use of the term conservative, preferring "orthodox," while appreciating the need to explain "orthodox Anglicanism" to the untrained ear (GAFCON 2008: 30–41). It is a term with a long history in Southeast Asia. Three hundred years ago, the word "orthodox" was already being used to indicate the High Church tradition, of which organizations like the SPG and SPCK became flagships (O'Connor 2000: 7–8). Considering the lasting influence of these organizations in Southeast Asia, it is perhaps unsurprising that modern Anglican orthodoxy still finds an attentive audience there. From the orthodox perspective, Western or global-north Christianity may have been eroded by social and cultural revolution, but the postcolonial Churches have survived and flourished, and Christianity's center of gravity has shifted southwards. Colonial-era orthodoxy outlived colonialism, and it now empowers global-south Churches to criticize the "liberalized" global north, with an authority rooted in the tradition they inherited and preserved. The orthodox missionaries of yesteryear, who sought to establish self-governing local Churches, probably never imagined that those local entities would one day hit back at the "parent" Church, in affirmation of the orthodoxy they inherited (Cox 2008: 9–20). There is, arguably, plenty to hit back over; the AC's apparent reversals of historical stances on emotive issues are not only divisive and polarizing, but also socially and politically problematic. Bishops of the PSEA argued their case not just on the basis of the Church's traditional views on things like homosexuality, but also explained that any Church seen to endorse these moves would become a pariah in cultural contexts like Southeast Asia, and in some contexts may be seen to be endorsing criminal activity (Jarvis 2022: 147).

The temptation to view the orthodox Anglican opposition movement as a fringe group or breakaway sect should be resisted. The groupings outlined above have a reasonable claim to represent, collectively, tens of millions of Anglicans around the globe, or the majority of the world's Anglicans, a claim that is both disputed and very difficult to disprove. The movement's most prominent groups, the GSFA and Gafcon, have explicitly stated their rejection of the offices of leadership of the AC while acknowledging the special roles of Churches such as Singapore's, Rwanda's, and ACNA, looking to them as sound, modern, flourishing examples of authentic Anglican orthodoxy. This conservative consensus has helped to satisfy a broader Singaporean longing for greater international connectivity, and Singapore's Church has been correspondingly receptive to incoming ideas, especially from the United States. As a global generalization, Christian conservatives will tend to agree on issues like sexuality, gender, and the family, but they may not all buy into things like literalism, creationism, end-times events, and the prophetic significance of the state of Israel equally. One person whose conservative commitment seems to have been all-embracing is Archbishop Tay, who, in his retirement, is believed to have joined a millennium-messianic Jewish-Christian end-times community in Haifa called Kehilat HaCarmel (Lim et al. 2006: 62).

Naturally, not all Singaporeans, Christians or non-Christians, are univocal on every issue either, and not all conservative stances are guaranteed to resonate politically, even under an authoritarian government. Both public opinion and government policy in Singapore have shifted several times on issues like homosexuality, and these shifts, including liberalizing ones, have been driven at various times by Christians and non-Christians, including Muslims. In 2003, the same year as the Gene Robinson controversy, the National Council of Churches of Singapore (NCCS) campaigned for the retention of colonial laws against homosexual practices, with penalties of imprisonment, in response to signs of an imminent government shift toward greater tolerance. Some senior Anglicans, including the retired Archbishop Tay, added their voices to the NCCS's chorus, and some did not. The government's motivation in such cases has usually been interpreted as neither ideology nor religion, but simply to do what economic pragmatism requires. It has escaped no conservative Christian's attention, of course, that LGBT culture and open attitudes to sex and sexuality are very widespread across Southeast Asia, including Singapore, but this does not seem to have softened some Christians' resolve to oppose them (Lim et al. 2006: 69–75). Sexual matters are among the most emotive topics in many cultures, and disapproval often seems to stem from revulsion rather than rationale, so the core issues can be clouded. Sexuality issues have certainly exposed differences in Anglican understandings of authority, both in terms of human, governing authority and the divine authority of the Bible. For many Anglicans the question is black and white, and Biblical teaching on homosexual activity is clear. Clear it may be, others argue, but some Biblical teaching, for example on slavery and wearing veils, must be seen as time- and culture-specific, and it cannot be considered binding on today's Christians. The Bible does not usually, in fact, set out the most faithful course of action in black and white; several paths may be indicated, which challenges the faithful to evaluate them and identify the approach that most corresponds to all available sources of faith, including prayer. It is the Church's task to reconcile without compromising (Jenkins 2006: 1–4).

EXAMINING THE RIFT: BEYOND SINGLE ISSUES AND "ASIAN CONSERVATISM"

Southeast Asia's conservatism may appear to be contradicted by the fact that the region famously offers havens for progressive attitudes to sex, sexuality, and gender identity, but it would be a stereotypical Western mistake to assume that these attitudes conflict with religious values. These attitudes do not necessarily impinge upon or alienate from a person's religion, or vice versa; they are not normally intended as an affront to any particular religion, and they do not detract from the basic principles of an unspoken social contract of continuity that has taken millennia to negotiate. The colonial-era perception of "The Unchanging East" (*SDM*, vol. VI, no. 23, May 1916: 1) is still a heartfelt reality in Southeast Asia. The region's generally tolerant and peaceful way of life and the considerable success of its multifaith societies, according to this outlook, are so sacred to Southeast Asia that nothing must be allowed to subvert them. Christianity has gained so much ground in Southeast Asia thanks to its capacity to honor that delicate social balance and not to disrupt it, so whenever an apparent innovation in Christianity appears on the northern horizon, local Christians instinctively stand their ground. Western theological output, furthermore, can seem loaded with worrying neo-colonialist overtones; anything perceived as coming from a default or "true" global-north global-west perspective must and will be received with caution in postcolonial Asia, Africa, and Latin America. Within the Anglican Communion, anything that even vaguely resembles an edict or decree from Canterbury will absolutely be questioned, then contested, and probably resisted. History almost demands that this be the case.

There is little doubt that the worldwide Anglican Church still has work to do in managing the uncomfortable legacy of its colonial past; fairly or unfairly, the specters of colonial-era discrimination and exploitation still haunt the Church. Discord at the ten-yearly Lambeth Conference is frequently and bitterly blamed on the surviving vestiges of imperialist and neo-imperialist attitudes. Concerns about the persistence of deep-rooted colonial-era prejudices may in fact be more frequently raised in the debates and disputes of the AC than in any other modern-day institution. It would be unwise to brush these conflicts aside as in-house Church trivia; the AC is far from inconsequential, constituting the world's third-largest Christian communion, with the bulk of its membership in the developing world, where Anglicans and others face a bewildering array of challenges. The colonial systems as such may be gone, but there is still much to understand about how the two "sides" of the colonial debate continue to interact; this is true of religious questions of sexuality and gender, but it also affects crucial questions of resources, climate, debt, human rights, and the mechanics of postcolonial relationships themselves. Current times are witnessing a surge in popular, critical engagement with the colonialism debate and the broader question of societies with "uncomfortable" histories. It is fair to say that a significant portion of the crisis in the AC is not actually about religion or theology, though these themes, with liturgy, do have their place in the broader colonialism debate; theology and liturgy can be key to expressing and elucidating conceptions of community and identity, not to mention justice and liberation.

The situation in the AC is rightly referred to as a crisis (Brittain and McKinnon 2018: 1–4) because the organization is effectively already split; significant national and regional Anglican Churches on at least four continents already operate in defiance and repudiation of the official structures and Instruments of Communion of the AC, which include the Archbishop of Canterbury, with growing groups in other areas as well. Canterbury has, according to GAFCON IV, "failed to maintain . . . communion based on the Word of God and shared faith in Christ" (GAFCON IV 2023: 2). The rupture is readily attributed to disagreements over very modern problems, but the geographical parameters of the split in the AC clearly follow the fault-lines left behind by the previous political configuration of the globe. The colonial Anglican Churches survived the postcolonial reconfiguration of the world, but this does not mean that the former, colonial-era bases for "maintaining communion" are necessarily ones to preserve. The modern-day relationships that connect member countries of the "Anglican world" are undeniably the inheritors of the former, colonial-era relationships; indeed, the modern relationships grew out of the old, deeply problematic ones. The idea that unresolved colonial relationship issues are the real underlying cause of worldwide Anglican discord is supported by the fact that dissenting Anglican Churches do not agree, among themselves, on quite basic issues such as sacraments, liturgy, vestments, ecclesiology, ecumenism, and women's ordination, so the idea that the dissenters are or could be united by theology is not credible.

The crisis in the AC must be seen as part of the wider seismic shift taking place in global Christianity, and, as such, Anglican discord may have a slightly longer history than many people think. For several decades, the southward shift of global Christianity's geographical center has been greeted with a combination of concern and denial, with both reactions being largely due to the fact that the very conversation has been dominated by Western theologians. A few clear-sighted observers, however, saw the shift for what it is; a revolution, in which "a protean indigenous [global-south] Christianity has emerged indifferent to the agenda of the Western theological intelligentsia" (Martin 1996: 26). The "revolutionaries" do not always necessarily reject the contents of the West's theological agenda, but they do reject the West's default privilege of being the ones to set that agenda. Within the AC, resistance to the agenda of Canterbury-led Christianity does not merely echo the rejection of colonialism; it is, in itself, the outright rejection of the faintest whiff of colonialism, consciously or unconsciously betrayed in the manner and language of delivery and communication. No one, it is widely acknowledged, operates entirely independently of their inherited worldview, and there are plenty of global-north Anglican leaders with familial links to colonialism; their background, education, and views may differ surprisingly little from those of their colonial-era predecessors. This argument is, of course, a deliberately rather cheap insinuation, which, like parallel assumptions about global-south leaders' cultural hardwiring, may be vigorously refuted; no individual, from any side of the debate, should have to accept being stereotyped. Simplifying the debate never seems to help, in fact; critics and defenders alike have talked of the Archbishop of Canterbury having to "walk a tightrope" between progressives and conservatives, an image that raises innumerable further questions about how reconciliation may be achieved or indeed avoided. Reconciliation must surely include a recognition that all Churches, whether global-north or global-south, are adaptations embedded in highly contrasting contexts, with a shared goal of witnessing the gospel, the implications of which have always varied and will always vary in different settings (*Church Times* 2023: 20).

PERSPECTIVES ON THE ANGLICAN CHURCH IN SINGAPORE TODAY

John Chew retired as Bishop of Singapore (2000–12) and Primate of the PSEA (2006–12) in 2012, to be succeeded as Bishop of Singapore by Rennis Ponniah (c.1955–), a prominent figure in the GSFA. Ponniah chaired the committee that prepared the GSFA's "covenantal" document, known as the Cairo Covenant, co-drafted with Singaporean theologian the Reverend Canon Doctor Michael Nai-Chiu Poon; it was uncompromising in outlining the GSFA's aim to monitor diversity in faith and practice according to the plain, literal teaching of Scripture. Ponniah was among those who stayed away from the 2008 Lambeth Conference, in protest at the perceived betrayal of Lambeth 1998. He has also been active in the Gafcon movement and he was one of the principal speakers at GAFCON 2018 in Jerusalem. In 2019, the PSEA recognized ACNA as a fellow Anglican province and declared full communion. Under Ponniah, the Diocese of Singapore broke the ceiling of twenty thousand communicants and counted twenty-eight parishes, with congregations in countries across Southeast Asia, including deaneries in Cambodia, Indonesia, Laos, Thailand, Vietnam, and Nepal. Bishop Ponniah reported at the 2017 New Wineskins Conference that the Nepal deanery had grown to eighty-three churches and more than ten thousand members, boosted by the Anglicans' provision of pastoral support in the aftermath of the devastating earthquake in 2015. The diocese also developed strong links with the conservative evangelical Diocese of Sydney during this time.

At various points in the Church's history, especially since the Second World War, there have been attempts to address the apparent slowness of

Singapore's Christian groups to cooperate with each other, and observers have noted a reluctance of the Churches to develop constructive relationships with other institutions in society. This has often been attributed to the Churches' former protected status under British rule having engendered complacency (Roxborogh 2014: 63), while some scholars have countered that the sum of the colonial and postcolonial experiences have actually taught the Church that engaging with society is unavoidable, lest it lose its voice in the public square (Cox 2008: 9). The extent to which this engagement means that the Church should tolerate or accommodate society's values, if at all, and how this affects its relationship with sibling Churches around the world, pose burning questions for conservative Anglicans. The perception of Singaporean Anglicans' self-isolation has steadily diminished in recent decades, and today's Church engages with society at many levels, exemplified by the attainment, a few years ago, of an Anglican Deputy Prime Minister and then President of Singapore, Tony Tan Keng Yam (1940–), an active member of St. George's Anglican church. The diocese has high-level government-recognized social commitments, including ten prestigious schools, numerous kindergartens and children's centers, St. Andrew's Missionary Hospital, Singapore Anglican Welfare Council, and Singapore Anglican Community Services (SACS), among others. SACS operates ten local centers around Singapore and is devoted to mental health and supporting children with autism.

Since 2020, the Church has been led by Bishop Titus Chung Khiam Boon, the tenth Bishop of Singapore. Chung, in his mid-fifties at the time of his appointment, is a graduate of TTC and has a PhD from the University of Edinburgh. From February 2024 he is also Archbishop and Primate of the PSEA, initially for a four-year term. Chung served at St. Andrew's Cathedral for more than a decade as priest-in-charge of the Mandarin-speaking congregation, which at one point offered no fewer than sixteen worship services each weekend. Most services at St. Andrew's Cathedral are currently conducted in either English or Mandarin, but the cathedral is also home to Burmese-, Cantonese-, Hokkien-, Indonesian-, Tagalog-, and Tamil-speaking congregations. The Church, like many features of Singapore, may still be perceived as a hybrid of East and West, but the old assumption that Christianity in Southeast Asia is seen as unavoidably aligned with colonial rule and European cultural hegemony is entirely outdated and redundant. Similarly, assumptions that local Christianity is quietly resented as an instrument of neo-imperialist propaganda, or that, conversely, it has been appropriated locally only in order to subvert Western (or indeed Eastern) ideas are wholly dysfunctional. Both sets of assumptions credit Western Christianity with powers that it does not have, promoting a fundamentally colonial-era notion that Christianity in Asia is, or is perceived by locals as, a foreign imposition. The continued tension in north-to-south and south-to-west relationships within the AC may suggest some residual colonial-era bitterness, but what ails intercontinental Anglican relations more than resentment is the paucity of shared experience in contrast to the extensive shared history; the post-postmodern challenges and priorities of the so-called parent Churches are largely unrelated to Southeast Asian Christians' problems. Feigning common goals and perspectives around things like poverty and climate is unlikely to bridge the divide, especially while all disagreements are attributed by default to cultural differences, a term that is too broad and too loose to be meaningful.

The particular form and flavor of Christianity that has flourished in Singapore will be unappealing for many Western Christian observers, but the island nation's perceived moralistic, exclusivist, hardline Pentecostal brand does appear to lie comfortably in bed beside a prosperity-, stability-, and security-focused government-led consensus, so far. Both of these ethoses combine Western and Eastern values with deep suspicion of anything resembling nuance, laxity, or liberalism, which, through an understandable wish to safeguard Singapore's success formula, become synonymous with subversion. It can be easy to forget, in fact, that Singapore's plumping for Pentecostalism did not come at the end of a deliberate quest to find an inflexible, closed-minded form of Christianity to adopt; rather, it was the product of Singapore's long-established cosmopolitan character and tradition of international interaction, which generated an atmosphere of openness and receptiveness to new ideas, not intolerance. This receptiveness, combined with genuine deference for shared values, cautiousness in the face of authoritarianism, and an interest in defending hard-won national success, created favorable conditions for an Anglican-driven charismatic renewal, in harmony with an optimistic, proud, and protective spirit of independence (Ward 2006: 312–13). Defiant Pentecostalism also appeared to do a better job than its rival traditions in demonstrating that local Churches need not be imitations of the West or North (Goh 2010: 65). Just as Singapore's economic power is admired across Southeast Asia, the Diocese of Singapore's successful incorporation of Pentecostalism has been highly influential in the region's Churches (Stanley 2018: 310).

It may be commendable that an Anglican Church is so capable of evolving, accommodating, and adapting, but concerns that traditional Anglican worship, theology, and identity have been eclipsed by Pentecostal practices in Singapore have never dissipated (Blossom 1995: 403–7). Today, there is a feeling that residual Anglican identity hangs around in Singapore like a vaguely disreputable elderly relative, and even individual churches' ties to the diocese can seem begrudging; the word "Anglican" sometimes appears in parentheses, for example, and some parishes' online presences coldly describe their church as being "owned by" the Diocese of Singapore, rather than the more conventional "part of" or "belongs to." It is vital to stress, however, that the Church has moved on since the Tay era and the days of obligatory speaking in tongues. The current Church leadership appears to be aware of contentious issues around worship and identity, and there is a definite sensation that the pendulum is being pulled back in the general direction of central or central-evangelical churchmanship. Bishop Chung's long-term episcopal ministry goal may be to reconcile visions, moderate extremes, and resuscitate a broader Church model, but there are no signs of a change of stance on the big international issues in Anglicanism. Singapore's Christians will no doubt choose the best Church "vehicle" for their aspirations and callings, which may mean finding a balance between the outward-looking, socially involved, and rights-focused liberal Christianity of times gone by, and the conservative, private morality-, and conversion-oriented Pentecostalism of recent decades. The separation of private and public belief, and the confinement of religion to the private realm, so incongruous to liberal, social justice-oriented Christianity, served Singapore's national developmental goals and created a huge audience for Pentecostalism, but it is important to remember that the Church was not faced with a wide range of options. The suppression of Church movements in the 1970s, the extra-judicial detention of Church workers in the 1980s, and the enactment of legislation to muzzle religious leaders in the 1990s, ensured that the Church will never forget the consequences of contesting the state (Goh 2010: 54–58). It is far from certain, however, that Singaporean Christians consider the debate closed, as to what type of Christianity will serve them best, going forward.

CONCLUSION

In theology, worship, and vision, the Anglican Church in Singapore had already distanced itself significantly from its former identity of robust High-Church Anglo-Catholicism by the late 1950s. This was the result of an against-the-odds combination of postwar factors, including a reinvigorated international Evangelical movement, the expulsion of missionaries from China, an open-minded Bishop of Singapore, and the British government-backed Malayan Emergency mission program to "win hearts and minds." Later on, the ecclesiastical separation of Singapore and Malaysia further allowed diverse identities to develop. This separation was more than just an organizational response to political realignment, it was a recognition of the fact that the nature and needs of the Church in Singapore had always been different, were still different, and would be increasingly different in future. These two motivations were not unrelated, of course. The separated Churches, like their respective governments, faced different post-independence challenges; the Singaporean Church's willing engagement with its government's nation-building project would allow it to flourish, while the Malaysian Church's respectful compliance with its government's ostensibly multiethnic model would allow it to just survive. The Church in Singapore would be perceived as endorsing the new national plan to combine the "best" elements of East and West in social, economic, and political matters, while strictly enforcing Singapore's homegrown moral and ideological red lines.

While Malaysia's Anglicans preserved a generally conservative but quite varied tapestry of Church traditions, charismatic renewal, or Pentecostalism, took hold in Singapore and began to radiate throughout the region. None of the regional dioceses and deaneries would be left untouched by this influence; it was "not a question of churchmanship," supporters argued, "but of obedience [to God]" (Green 2001: 105). The Singaporean Church's influence became globally consequential when its leaders vigorously challenged controversial developments in Anglicanism, and more so when Malaysian and other global-south Church leaders declared solidarity with them (Ward 2006: 22–24, 312–13). As a generalization, socially and theologically conservative Anglicanism sits well with the worldview, spirituality, and shared Asian values of Southeast Asia, and despite debatable internal differences in theology, ecclesiology, appreciation of Anglican heritage, and ways of responding to global Anglican discord, this regional cultural compatibility remains a common feature of the Southeast Asian Anglican Churches. This sympathy, with its differences, helped to ensure a smooth transition from the old colonial ecclesiastical structures to eventually form a new province of the Anglican Communion, with the three Malaysian dioceses under Singapore's one diocese as the leading regional Church.

The capacity for cultural compatibility to explain Christian growth can be both under- and overestimated; the Church of England, for example, is intertwined with the lives, customs, history, and heritage of the English people, but this does nothing to halt chronic Church decline. Southeast Asian Christians appear to experience something more profound than simple compatibility; a harmonious continuity with all Asian spirituality, which tends to look beyond both the material (the written, the normative) and the theoretical (the meaning, the motivation) to the lived experience, without seeing the harsh dividing lines so typical of the Western mindset. This harmonious continuity is not total, unswerving, or provable with hard science, but it is tangible enough to govern the Southeast Asian Churches' engagement with the rest of the Anglican world and to generate affinity with other postcolonial Churches of the global south. Like them, Anglicans in Singapore have evaluated the colonial Church inheritance on its merits; the colonial-era missionaries, with their various flaws, are not repudiated but thanked, for bringing the Gospel and for believing in the ability of local people to build, sustain, and run their own Church (Cox 2008: 21). The experience of integrating the

Church into Asia, and of Asians into the Church, ultimately led to the conclusion that localization must be full and authentic, not only in the theology and ecclesiology adopted and adapted, but more importantly in the practice and mission of a truly local Church (Phan 2000: 218).

Modern Singaporean and Southeast Asian Anglicans no longer look to colonial times for lessons on how to run their Church, of course. There is both more domestic interaction with (and movement between) other Christian denominations than previously, and more international interaction, which is not confined to the old Church networks and trimmed-down mission societies. Anglicans hailing from diverse Christian and non-Christian backgrounds are exposed to multiple global Christian influences and input. Singaporean parishes plant churches at home and overseas, commission missionaries, and provide aid across Southeast Asia. The more one looks at today's Church, the more the specter of the colonial one fades into the ether. Ethnicity, once such a delicate and divisive question, is still relevant to religious affiliation, but religion is not usually the primary identifier of ethnicity (Gomes and Tan 2019: 216); numerous factors in this multicultural, multiethnic, and increasingly mixed-ethnicity society can make ethnic-religious profiles redundant (Goh 2005: 41). Not every Singaporean does fit neatly into one ethnic group, no ethnic group is uniform in its religious adherence, and beliefs and customs from one religion frequently coalesce problem-free with the practice of another religion; these realities sound controversial in a society that values order and predictability. Singapore's Christians bear out the facts, representing a complex combination of cultures, backgrounds, and identities (Chong and Hui 2013: 2).

The Anglican Church in Singapore probably made its biggest international impact with its support of AMiA, which breathed life into Anglican Realignment and instantly cast Singapore as a key player in it. These events also hinted at the dysfunctional nature of postcolonial Church relations, as the might of the "parent Church" was seen to be defied, illustrating how the Anglican Church in Singapore had grown in confidence in the relatively short period of time since the end of empire. Singapore's clear stances sent out a message to conservatives in the West and opened up a new channel of communication; there were, the message ran, untapped sources of support in the global south, should conservative Anglicans fail to find any in the global north. The ensuing two decades of dramas and defections have served as reminders that Anglicanism has always been perceivable as rather amorphous and malleable; the Anglican Communion (AC)'s best option may be to accept its future as a loose association of Churches that celebrate common heritage and explore common values, while acknowledging enormous differences (Ward 2006: 17–18). The declared aim of the delayed 2022 Lambeth Conference was not to come to terms with the crisis, however, it was to explore ways of responding to the needs of the twenty-first century world, but there was no escape from existing, emerging, and evolving discord. Unresolved differences become tangible at international Anglican gatherings, with the ever-increasing presence of woman bishops, woman priests, gender-diverse priests, and same-sex partners and spouses accompanying bishops and clergy, some of them Anglicans and some not. For some observers, the stated aim of Lambeth 2022, responding to the needs of the modern world, points to the heart of the problem, rather than the goal, of today's worldwide Anglican Church; it has fallen into a cycle of being overly responsive to the world's demands, rather than manning the barricades of Christian essentials (Ballard and Pritchard 2006: 149).

The story of today's Anglican Church in Singapore reminds us that there are no normative versions of Anglicanism, or Christianity; there is no chief or primatial Anglican Church, and there are no junior or rookie Anglican Churches hanging onto the AC's apron strings, ripe to be cut off if they do not behave (Ward 2006: 15). Geography, with its cousin geopolitics, does have a part to play in the evolving future prospects for the Church, however. Concern for the Church in Asia sits among a multitude of critical worries; natural and man-made disasters, health emergencies, economic crises, famine, drought, crop failure, crises of water, food, and energy, exploitation, political violence, and religious persecution. None of these problems are exclusive to any one world region, of course, and recent years have revealed the vulnerability of even the most conventionally developed countries when faced with a health crisis or an environmental disaster. Governments' inability to meet basic needs, to prevent economic reversal, to quell civil unrest, and to avoid war has been exposed, virally and in real time. Churches in Asia stand at a strange and unexpected crossroads. Christian minorities have a unique perspective on the world's problems, but the hierarchy of problems can be painful to acknowledge, and people are forced to balance and reconcile survival in the world versus survival of the soul. Without spiritual safety, other types of safety are arguably transitory. Singapore's Christians may not stand on the edge of an environmental or economic abyss like many communities across Asia, and they do not face persecution or famine, but their true calling may be to motivate, encourage, and lead their fellow Christians and neighbors who do.

Conclusion

The Anglican Church in Singapore faces a number of challenges. Church growth, which once depended on Chinese immigration and mission schools, is now driven by complex individual quests for realization, fulfillment, and the need to constantly adjust created by an ever-evolving society (Sng 1980: 305). Today, the Church's schools are considered to be more than a little exclusive, catering primarily to an English-educated elite rather than the orphaned and marginalized of times past (Gomes and Tan 2019: 217). The schools' success may be a double-edged sword, as their elitism may repulse sectors of the Church's target audience; Singapore's privileged lifestyles, career opportunities, and corresponding attitudes are not universal experiences (Goh 2005: 41–44). Christianity has acquired class connotations that may not serve the Church well forever. Education and language tend to dictate class in Singapore, with English considered the language of success; around 40 percent of English-speaking households are Christian, which contributes to an image of Christianity as the religion of the "English-only" elite (Gomes and Tan 2019: 234).

The achievements of the Anglican Church and other Christian bodies are undeniable but not without parallel; religious growth in Singapore is not exclusive to Christianity. In recent years, Buddhism has grown at the same rate and sometimes faster than Christianity; young, educated, socially mobile citizens are as well-represented among new Buddhist converts as they are among Christian ones. The Church still has the potential to offer something distinctive compared to the competition, but it does not have unlimited options for diversifying in super-regulated Singapore. Unlike some of their regional counterparts, Christian groups in Singapore enjoy safety and stability but they are also forced to moderate their activities according to government directives and the national vision. The extraordinarily wide-ranging powers of the Maintenance of Religious Harmony Act 1990 (MRHA) protect faith groups from interreligious strife, but they also rule out actions that could be interpreted as interference in politics, proselytization, or criticism of other faith groups or the government. Meanwhile, Singapore's prosperity and functioning welfare system mean fewer opportunities for Christians to do aid work or poverty relief, so these ministries tend to be oriented overseas. Singapore sends hundreds of missionaries to other countries, and it also acts as a hub for mission-related organizations and events, but this "hosting and sending" ministry does not constitute a coherent "own" role for the local Church, as the real activity is not happening in Singapore, among Singaporeans. Prosperity, in other words, has enabled the Church to outwardly facilitate activities, arguably without prompting the Church to look inwards at the dangers of comfortableness and complacency; this blind spot may impede the Church's pursuit of a truly distinctive role (Goh 2005: 41–45).

ASPIRATION

Singapore is famously one of the richest countries in the world, and its six million inhabitants are perceived as having an insatiable appetite for economic advancement. According to different calculations, between one in six and one in thirteen Singaporeans is a millionaire; the number of millionaires has doubled in the last five years, and it is set to double again by 2030. The concepts of personal fulfillment and material success appear to have melded completely, and the fact that religion has such a significant role in Singaporean life, with between 80 and 99 percent of the population affiliated with a religion, can seem incongruous. A study of any one religion in Singapore must account for how that religion converses, converges, and coalesces with materialistic ambition, which is expressed as a quest to secure the Five Cs; car, cash, condo, credit card, and country club membership. Being Christian in Singapore means reconciling the gospel with this wealth culture, and the most attractive churches tend be those that most nimbly marry Christian beliefs with the pursuit of affluence. Christianity's status as the fastest-growing religion in Singapore has prompted suggestions that Christianity is the sixth "C." This form of Christianity is defended as being a salutary move away from oppressive, social obligation-focused versions of Christianity that have sometimes stifled the individual, and a move toward a personalist religion that emphasizes needs, goals, and self-improvement. It can also be seen as the ultimate secularization of Christianity, the triumph of capitalism and consumerist principles in stealthily shaping the future of all Churches and the faith they promote. Instead of the gospel prophetically critiquing the inequalities created by the forces of the market system, these forces are themselves influencing how the gospel is presented, understood, and assimilated by Singaporean Christians (Gomes and Tan 2019: 213–15, 234–35).

While Singapore's embrace of Western capitalism as philosophy, economics, culture, and mindset appears to be total and unflinching, religious aspects of the country's Western inheritance have faced more robust scrutiny and revision. One assessment describes Western Christian influence in Southeast Asia in terms of Four Cs, to contrast with the Five (or Six) Cs of materialistic aspiration; Christian theology was created in Europe, corrected in England, corrupted in America, and crammed into Asia. This assessment corresponds to a broad international consensus that Western Christian theological paradigms, criticized variously as being dualistic, individualistic, overly Enlightenment-influenced, and promoting a naturalistic worldview, are incompatible with Asian ones. In order to flourish in Asia, it has been argued, Christianity has needed to be decolonized and de-Westernized. Clive Chin, previously of Singapore Bible College, observed that this somewhat delayed resentment toward foreign religious influence coincided with the emergence of a "guilt complex" on the Western side (Chin 2017: 1–2). De-Westernizing the Christian experience, however, is not the only process of "identity cleansing" that has taken place in this context; instances of de-Sinification, including dropping the designation "Chinese" from the names of religious organizations, suggest that the process is not just about disengaging with the West but about reevaluating all outside identity markers, in pursuit of more total local authenticity (Goh 2007: 29). These concerns and sensitivities are far from trivial; the persistence of tensions between the Chinese and Malay ethnic groups, with violent clashes within living memory, has simultaneously necessitated and inhibited debate and scholarship on the questions of Singaporean and Singaporean Christian identity (Chin 2017: 84).

IDENTITY

At 75 percent of the population, the ethnic Chinese constitute the largest ethnic group in Singapore, but it is also the most heterogeneous group and always has been (Chin 2017: 3). The ethnic Chinese already outnumbered the Malays in Singapore as early as 1836 (Saw 1969: 41–42), but anti-Chinese prejudice and discrimination, under various rulers, were severely detrimental for the community. A perception and self-perception of the ethnic Chinese as an underclass were fostered, and this exposed them to criminal exploitation (Goh 2007: 38); Chinese secret societies also have a long history in Singapore (Sng 1980: 57–59). This marginalization gave impetus to Christian missionary efforts, however, making a moral rallying cry of fighting vice. Today, the significance of ethnic-Chinese participation in the Church is enormous; three-quarters of Singapore's Christians come from traditional Chinese (Buddhist, Taoist, Confucian, or mixed) religious backgrounds, and the use of many and varied Chinese dialects in religious settings is disproportionately high compared to English- and Mandarin-dominated daily life (Chin 2017: 84–85). The co-dominance of Mandarin owes much to its government-mandated use in schools, and this is likely to impact religion heavily as younger ethnic-Chinese self-perceptions drift further away from the ethnic dialects and ethnic identities of older generations. Researchers disagree on whether to list Singapore's largest religious group as followers of traditional Chinese religions in general or Buddhism specifically, demonstrating that the borders between these religions are already porous, and suggesting that both labels may actually serve better as loose umbrella terms (Musa 2023: 1; Zurlo et al. 2022: 73). None of the aspects of life in this highly diverse community are clearly delineated, in fact, whether language, culture, or politics (Goh 2007: 29). Confucianism, like Buddhism, remains influential far beyond the ranks of its actual devotees; it encourages economic ambition, equates authority with stability, and supports the ideal of national identity. Christianity is considered compatible with these Confucian principles, with the advantage that it suffers a great deal less than Confucianism from exploitable ethnic connotations (Chin 2017: 87). Clive Chin explained that the perception of Christianity as being "ethnically neutral, global, and all-encompassing" leads many to view it as an improvement on traditional Chinese religions (Chin 2017: 3).

While it celebrates its success, Singaporean Christianity may yet struggle to crystallize its contribution to that desirable national identity, amidst the broader uncertainty and ongoing debate of what it means to be Singaporean, which mirrors similar debates taking place in Hong Kong and Taiwan (Kuo 2016: 22). The Anglican Church is arguably faced with the triple task of concretizing what being Singaporean, Singaporean Christian, and Singaporean Anglican Christian mean in practice. One possibility, already hinted at above, could be for the Church to reevaluate its inward- and outward-looking roles, and seek to apply the gospel not just in personal moral questions but in social and public questions as well. The Church's extensive social and public activities are not in dispute, but advancing the gospel socially and publicly may require taking back that portion of the public square that the Church relinquished in order to appease the government and continue to exist. There may be ample opportunities to test the water, as a loose coalition of Christians and non-Christians did when they opposed the creation of major "integrated resort" casino developments in 2005; the result was predictably disappointing, but they were certainly not chastised for inserting themselves into the conversation (Kuo 2016: 21).

All Singaporeans ultimately face the same challenge; in the push to forge a credible Singaporean identity, religion and ethnicity will not be brushed aside, and the connections and tensions between the two are too many and too complex to defuse with rhetoric or platitudes (Chin 2017: 85–87). This is perhaps exemplified by the case of Singaporean Malays, for whom religion and ethnicity are inextricably linked, in an analogous situation to Malays in Malaysia, where they are the national majority. It is important to point out, furthermore, that both the ethnic-Malay and ethnic-Indian communities, like the ethnic-Chinese one, are complex within themselves and far from homogeneous (Green 2001: 2). The breadth of Christianity's appeal has been linked to its ability to act as a bridge between and within these very diverse communities, which is an extremely desirable and valuable attribute in Singapore, but the pervading sensation is that the Church has never fully explored or exploited this aspect of its social and public potential (Gomes and Tan 2019: 216–19).

VALUES

Christianity's success in Singapore is often attributed to its strong identification with family as well as with nation, and the Church will want to preserve this winning formula. Filial piety and respecting hierarchy are familiar and cherished values for the majority of Singaporeans, corresponding to the principles of personal sacrifice and commitment to community found in Confucianism. Hierarchical disposition (parents before children) and egalitarianism (community before self) are instilled into Singaporeans from a young age, and it has been argued that these values also resonate with historic Christianity's own hierarchical (clergy or elders over congregation) and egalitarian (equality within congregation) values. These ideals, furthermore, are harmonious with the concept of shared Asian values, which gained momentum in the 1980s. This concept evolved into a national political ideology and a national identity philosophy that stresses community and hierarchy over the individual; this can mean foregoing personal freedoms for the declared greater good, which takes on particular significance in authoritarian contexts. According to the Asian values ideology, the family is upheld as the basic unit and microcosm of successful society, and loyalty to the state becomes homologous with allegiance to the family. Singapore's political leaders officially endorsed this ideology in the early 1990s, regarding it as a blueprint for an emerging national self-understanding that would harness all of Singapore's qualities of survival and resilience (Gomes and Tan 2019: 216–19).

Singapore is often seen to be competing with Hong Kong for the undeclared title of Asia's World City; the two rivals share an apparently contradictory reputation for being global and modern but also inward-looking and authoritarian. Singapore's history and geography have given rise to a diverse, harmonious, and business-friendly society, but the diversity is highly regulated and the harmony is rigorously enforced (Kuo 2016: 21). Within this possible paradox lies the essence of Singapore's pragmatic rather than dogmatic secularism, and history points to an explanation. The failure of Singapore's union with Malaysia in the 1960s was tied to disagreements over the future use of ethnicity- and religion-aligned party politics, which had already served their purpose in achieving independence. Renewed interethnic violence in Singapore caused concerns over these political models to multiply, leading to the exclusion of religion from political platforms; religious political alliances were declared antithetical to national unity in a pluralist society. In its proper place, however, so the thinking went, religion could contribute to integration, social cohesion, and therefore stability; religious groups could become useful partners in nation building, and, to this day, faith-based organizations play an important role in social services and welfare provision. Religion's role is kept both vague and narrow; to do good deeds and care for others. The government is also appreciatively cognizant of religion's ability to promote values conducive to a successful economy, but Singapore's strict moral code, which seems intended to distinguish it from the decadent West, is curated by the state without religious assistance. With reason, the state's support for religion is often perceived as being self-serving (Musa 2023: 2–4). When religion's moral voice is raised, the state's priority of maintaining harmony is tested, as indeed are the boundaries of the MRHA legislation. The government has opted to listen respectfully and then impose its will, as in the aforementioned case of legislation to massively expand legal gambling. Both Christian and Muslim leaders spoke out against the plan, and the government responded; it agreed to back a campaign to discourage gambling and provide help for addicts, but the casino plan went ahead all the same (Kuo 2016: 21).

ANGLICANISM

The Anglican Church in Singapore, more precisely the Diocese of Singapore, is part of the Church of the Province of South East Asia (PSEA), which in turn is part of the global Anglican Communion. The Anglican Communion is currently gravely disunited on several issues, and this is often interpreted as a standoff between global north (often intended to include Europe and North America) and global south (which is often not intended to include Australasia). The north-south clash of perspectives is arguably a more reliable schema of Anglican discord than the conventional categorizations of liberal and conservative, into which not all conflicting viewpoints can necessarily be grouped. Liberals and conservatives have, after all, historically cohabited in the Anglican Church despite their differences, leading optimists to persist in the belief that this can be achieved once more. The division between global-north Anglicans and global-south Anglicans, however, is widely regarded as being more definitive than previous ruptures, leading some to conclude that they now constitute two separate Churches (Jenkins 2006: 1). The 2023 Gafcon IV gathering in Rwanda called for the "resetting" of the Anglican Communion due to perceived departures from orthodox teachings on sex and sexuality, claiming that instruments of unity such as the office of Archbishop of Canterbury can no longer be trusted to lead Anglicanism biblically and faithfully (GAFCON IV 2023: 2–3). While Gafcon and global south-oriented stances on sexuality may be unequivocal, the pro-orthodoxy movement is increasingly dogged by internal disagreements on basics of theology and churchmanship, including debates over the number of sacraments and the still-unresolved issue of women's ordination. Article 12 of Gafcon's 2008 "Jerusalem Declaration" appeared to recognize this impasse, pledging "to seek the mind of Christ on issues that divide us" (Gafcon 2008), but it does not seem that clarity has been achieved. The alliance around Gafcon may be faced with the same task as Anglicanism in general, to rediscover the historic Anglican distinction between what is essential and what is negotiable (Jenkins 2006: 42–67).

The north-south divide is not about to disappear, and the Anglican Communion must arguably bridge it or perish; alternatively, it may well continue in its current fractured state for many decades to come, inviting doubt as to whether it was ever very united in the first place. The north-south divide, unfortunately, is also not the only divide that Anglicans face. Organized Christianity in all its manifestations has never faced an abyss between itself and secular culture as wide and cavernous as the current one. Values, concepts, and aspirations, in many parts of the world, including the old Christian strongholds, have mutated to such a degree that the Churches' teachings seem to be constantly out of sync, bizarre, and expressed in alien language. On very emotive questions, Christianity actually offends the convictions of many individuals, generating further hostility toward the Church and religion in general. The Church's stances on issues of sex and gender, it must be remembered, did not change substantially for centuries, but society's (especially Western society's) views evolved with increasing momentum throughout the twentieth century and into the twenty-first. Some Christians see this accumulation of forces squaring up to the Church in Biblical, even apocalyptic terms, but the real historical reasons for these shifts in society's values are no mystery; the urban working lifestyle, the economics of raising a family, greater knowledge of and control over the human body, breaks with traditional support networks, the erosion of traditional community life, and the depersonalization of much human interaction through technology, have combined to transform society at its most elemental levels (McKenzie 2014: 81–84). It is against the backdrop of these experiences that much more recently developed societies, like Singapore's, have carefully orchestrated their destinies, hand-picked their moral parameters, and steel-underpinned their value systems.

The temptation to reduce Anglicanism's problem to a conflict between liberal and conservative remains, and while there is of course more to the crisis than a clash between forces of change and forces of opposition, for Christians to join one "camp" can be an emotionally charged experience, especially when the language of liberal and conservative evolves into the language of resistance, faithfulness, and pursuing truth in confusing times (McKenzie 2014: 80). In the 1950s and 1960s, all of the main Christian denominations accepted the need for adjustment to a postwar, postcolonial, and rapidly secularizing world. The old Anglican missionary societies, for example, moved away from instructing and preaching toward partnership models that recognized the legitimacy and autonomy of local, postcolonial Churches. In retrospect, a dangerous message may have been sent out; adapting to the secular world was the new priority emanating from Christian Europe, and "first world" Anglicans, still apparently in charge, were ready to compromise (Goodhew 2017: 12). The advent of women's ordination in the 1970s seemed to confirm the victory of compromise; some Anglican provinces then became more accepting of homosexual relationships, leading to the next milestone, the episcopal ordination of a non-celibate gay man. There is something unavoidably clumsy about mentioning the ordination of women and the ordination of practicing homosexuals in the same breath, but the point is perceptual; the message of the 1960s appeared to be consistent and borne out, that Christian teaching was being revised in the light of modern society's (and many modern Christians') secular values. What may be seen as unbridled liberalization, however, the result of the Church being seduced by the world (Green 2001: 103), may be seen from other angles as the Church taking effective and necessary steps in order to survive and remain at least minimally in touch with the reality that people live (O'Donovan 2008: 1–4).

FUTURE

Adapting in order to survive and compromising with the forces of the secular world in order to secure some living space is not only a familiar repertoire for a former colonial Church like Singapore's, it is the stuff of its very existence. Like many of the former colonial Churches of the global south, the Church in Singapore reached a stage of complete local leadership, inclusive of local ethnic groups in all their complexity, in a relatively short space of time; such resourcefulness and resilience will be important factors to consider when trying to foresee the Church's future (McKenzie 2014: 81–87). The number of Anglicans continues to increase globally but unevenly, which makes this growth a potential cause for celebration as well as a warning of further division (Goodhew 2017: 3). The contrast in demographics between global-north and global-south is undeniable, and if the global south stays on something resembling its current course, the future of Anglicanism remains numerically theirs. Not only is growth on the side of the global south, the global north is rapidly disengaging from Church, marriage, parenthood, and the customs and conventions proposed by traditional religion (Jenkins 2006: 2). Even so, the global-north Church arguably demonstrates no burning corporate desire to learn from the global-south Church and its successes; this reluctance seems to be hardwired, along with the usual cliché that people of the global south are just innately more disposed toward religion (Green 2001: 115).

It is difficult to imagine something resembling an amicable end to the crisis in Anglicanism. Many oppose what may be labeled a culture of compromise, but there is little evidence of compromising going on within any of the debate camps themselves, and all sides seem committed to holding firm to their positions. Progress may demand that both compromising and opposing cede to reconciling, and relevant examples may be gleaned from the history of the colonial Church. The British Parliament's brazen paternalism in decreeing Christian government for the non-Christian peoples it had colonized was matched by the cautious wisdom of appointing moderate and "mild [but] firm" bishops to govern the colonial Church, because they were the ones most likely to hold the Church's opposing wings together (Wilson 1863: 7). This was reconciliation and accommodation but not compromise, and neither side "won." This is, hopefully, what some observers have alluded to when stating that only "courageous leadership" can save the Anglican Communion (Green 2001: 22). Mild but firm peacekeeping worked for many decades, as long as the core essentials of theology, Church order, and Scripture were scrupulously acknowledged as non-negotiable (O'Donovan 2008: 4–5).

Neither Evangelicalism nor Catholicism ultimately made the greatest impact on the Anglican Church in Singapore; the bold shift toward Pentecostalism was an alienating experience for some, including clergy who were less than sympathetic to the renewal. Others, despite their doubts, managed to accept the new order, encouraged by the fact that the general boom in Christian conversions was benefiting the Anglican Church in equal measure. It was not just about numbers, of course, and the idea of a profound renewal in the Church was well supported in principle. It was an era of exciting reinvigoration but also an era of rampant challenges to Christianity, and the time-honored responses were just not considered adequate. It was a time of great contrasts for Singapore as a whole, with internal security issues and major regional instability, alongside resurging national spirit and successful decolonization. Asserting Singapore's identity, uniqueness, and dignity was a worthwhile national project, keenly shared by the Anglican Church; it may have been remiss or foolish of them not to do so. The Church was faced with a propitious moment for taking complete ownership of its own postcolonial destiny, not just by repudiating British control, which was rapidly fading into memory anyway, but rather by reconciling and synthesizing Singaporean Christians' eclectic mix of values, traditions, and aspirations better than had previously been done by the Church. Christian worship could begin to express, celebrate, and satisfy the call to Asianness, as Singapore got ready to show its renewed face to the world.

The Anglican Church in Singapore's recent history is one of adaptation to a fast-changing present and reconciliation with a less than comfortable past, and these have clearly not always been gentle processes. The Church's apparent acquiescence to often draconian government edicts can be dismaying, especially if this demonstrates that the Church has been cowed into a permanent state of capitulation by experiences of repression in the 1970s and 1980s. It may be that the cultural memory of the close relationship between Church and authorities in colonial times, and the benefits that this relationship brought, has evolved into a latent longing to replicate it, thereby stretching the limits of the Church's patience with authoritarianism. It is also possible that the Church has learned pragmatism from its environment, and now both Church and state in Singapore efficiently embody the national consensus, however that may be defined. The famous but not limitless potential for this consensus to provide stability, prosperity, and harmony has bolstered the Church's domestic credibility while controversializing its international image. The Anglican Church in Singapore is therefore presented with an awkward opportunity; while it could be self-destructive or hypocritical for the Church to challenge the status quo that it helped to establish, such an attitude could also be more faithful to the gospel of Jesus Christ and more in keeping with the Church's colonial and postcolonial destiny, to push back once more against the excesses, obsessions, and obstructions of a dominant mindset.

Bibliography

Ballard, Paul and John Pritchard. *Practical Theology in Action: Christian Thinking in the Service of Church and Society.* London: SPCK, 2006.
Bell, Daniel M., Jr. "State and Civil Society." In *The Blackwell Companion to Political Theology*, edited by Peter Scott and William T. Cavanaugh, 423–38. Oxford: Blackwell, 2004.
Blossom, Jay. "More in Common with Pentecostals Than with Canterbury: June 6, 1993, at Yishun Christian Church (Anglican), Singapore." *Anglican and Episcopal History* 64, no. 3 (September 1995); Historical Society of the Episcopal Church [403–7].
Boulger, Demetrius Charles. *The Life of Sir Stamford Raffles.* London: Horace Marshall and Son, 1897.
Bretherton, Luke. *Christ and The Common Life: Political Theology and The Case for Democracy.* Grand Rapids, MI: William. B. Eerdmans, 2019.
Brittain, Christopher Craig and Andrew McKinnon. *The Anglican Communion at a Crossroads.* University Park, PA: Penn State University Press, 2018.
Buckley, Charles Burton. *An Anecdotal History of Old Times in Singapore* [two volumes]. Singapore: Fraser and Neave Ltd. 1902.
Burgess, Anthony. *Little Wilson and Big God.* London: Vintage (Random House), 2012.
Chelliah, Devasahayam David. Papers—see National Archives, Singapore.
Chen, Kuan-Hsing. *Asia as Method: Toward Deimperialization.* Durham, NC: Duke University Press, 2010.
Chia, Edmund Kee-Fook. "Wawasan 2020 and Christianity in Religiously Plural Malaysia." In *From Malaysia to the Ends of the Earth: Southeast Asian and Diasporic Contributions to Biblical and Theological Studies*, edited by Wei-Fun Goh et al., 119–137. Claremont, CA: Claremont Press, 2021.
Chin, Clive S. *The Perception of Christianity as a Rational Religion in Singapore.* Eugene, OR: Pickwick, 2017.
Chin Peng. *My Side of History.* Singapore: Media Masters, 2003.
Chong, Terence and Hui Yew Foong. *Different Under God.* Singapore: ISEAS, 2013.
Church of England. *Reports of the Boards of Missions of the Provinces of Canterbury and York on the Mission Field.* London: SPCK, 1894.
Church Times. "Chinese Assistant Bishop for Singapore." March 21, 1958 [7].

———. "Full Faith, Less Full Freedom." January 6, 2023 [20].
Cox, Jeffrey. *Imperial Fault Lines: Christianity and Colonial Power in India, 1818–1940*. Stanford, CA: Stanford University Press, 2002.
———. *The British Missionary Enterprise since 1700*. New York: Routledge, 2008.
Davidson, Randall T. (editor). *The Five Lambeth Conferences*. London: SPCK, 1920.
Diocesan Call to Evangelism—see National Archives, Singapore.
Diocese of Singapore and Malaya—see National Archives, Singapore.
Evers, Georg. "'On the Trail of Spices': Christianity in Southeast Asia." In *The Oxford Handbook of Christianity in Asia*, edited by Felix Wilfred, 65–79. Oxford: Oxford University Press, 2014.
Federal Legislative Council of Malaya. "The Squatter Problem in the Federation of Malaya in 1950" (Council Paper no. 14 of 1950). Kuala Lumpur: Government Printer, 1950.
Ferguson-Davie, Charlotte Elizabeth (editor). *In Rubber Lands: An Account of the Work of the Church in Malaya*. London: The Society for the Propagation of the Gospel in Foreign Parts, 1921.
Gafcon. *Jerusalem Declaration*. June 2008. https://www.gafcon.org/jerusalem-2018/key-documents/jerusalem-declaration [accessed December 12, 2023].
GAFCON (Global Anglican Future Conference) Theological Resource Team. *The Way, the Truth and the Life: Theological Resources for a Pilgrimage to a Global Anglican Future*. London: Latimer Trust, 2008.
GAFCON IV. *The Kigali Commitment*. Kigali, Rwanda. April 21, 2023. https://gafcon23.org/gafcon-iv-conference-statement/ [accessed December 12, 2023].
Gillman, Ian and Hans-Joachim Klimkeit. *Christians in Asia Before 1500*. Richmond: Curzon, 1999.
Glendinning, Victoria. *Raffles and the Golden Opportunity*. London: Profile, 2012.
Goh, Daniel P. S. "Rethinking Resurgent Christianity in Singapore." *Southeast Asian Journal of Social Science* 27, no. 1. Leiden: Brill, 1999 [89–112].
———. "State and Social Christianity in Post-Colonial Singapore." *Sojourn: Journal of Social Issues in Southeast Asia* 25, no. 1 (April 2010), Singapore: ISEAS (Yusof Ishak Institute), 2010 [54–89].
Goh, Elaine Wei-Fun, Jeffrey Kah-Jin Kuan, Jonathan Yun-Ka Tan, and Amos Wai-Ming Yong (editors). *From Malaysia to the Ends of the Earth: Southeast Asian and Diasporic Contributions to Biblical and Theological Studies*. Claremont, CA: Claremont Press, 2021.
Goh, Robbie B. H. *Christianity in Southeast Asia*. Singapore: ISEAS, 2005.
———. "Singapore's 'Two YMCAs': Christianity, Colonialism, and Ethnic Fault Lines." *Crossroads: An Interdisciplinary Journal of Southeast Asian Studies* 18, no. 2 (2007) [29–64].
Gomes, Catherine and Jonathan Tan. "Christianity as the Sixth Aspirational 'C': Megachurches and the Changing Landscape of Religion, Prosperity, and Wealth in Singapore." In *Money and Moralities in Contemporary Asia*, edited by Cheryll Alipio and Lan Anh Hoang, 213–40. Amsterdam: Amsterdam University Press, 2019.

Gomes, Edwin H. *Seventeen Years Among the Sea Dyaks of Borneo.* London: Seeley and Co. Ltd. 1911.

Gomes, William H. *An Account of Saint Andrew's Church Mission from A. D. 1856 to A. D. 1887: Chiefly Compiled from the Records of Its Proceedings Kept in Saint Andrew's Cathedral.* Singapore: Singapore and Straits Printing Office, 1888.

Goodhew, David (editor). *Growth and Decline in the Anglican Communion, 1980 to the Present.* Abingdon: Routledge, 2017.

Green, Michael. *Asian Tigers for Christ.* London: SPCK, 2001.

Guilmoto, Christophe Z. "The Tamil Migration Cycle, 1830–1950." *Economic and Political Weekly* 28, no. 3/4 (January 16–23, 1993): [111–20].

Gullick, J. M. [John Michael]. "Recollections of My Time in Malaya (1945–1956) Part 1." *Journal of the Malaysian Branch of the Royal Asiatic Society* 86, no. 2 (305) (December 2013): [59–76].

———. "Recollections of My Time in Malaya (1945–1956) Part 2." *Journal of the Malaysian Branch of the Royal Asiatic Society* 87, no. 1 (306) (June 2014): [53–81].

———. "Recollections of My Time in Malaya (1945–1956) Part 3." *Journal of the Malaysian Branch of the Royal Asiatic Society* 87, no. 2 (307) (December 2014): [47–89].

Harper, T. N. [Timothy Norman] *The End of Empire and the Making of Malaya.* Cambridge: Cambridge University Press, 1999.

Hayter, John. *Priest in Prison: Four Years of Life in Japanese-Occupied Singapore.* Singapore: Graham Brash, 1991.

Hayter, John and Jack Bennitt. *The War and After: Singapore.* London: Society for the Propagation of the Gospel, no date [c. 1947].

Hedlund, Roger E. "Understanding Southeast Asian Christianity." In *Christian Movements in Southeast Asia: A Theological Exploration,* edited by Michael Nai-Chiu Poon, 59–100. Singapore: Genesis Books and Trinity Theological College, 2010.

Hood, George. *Neither Bang nor Whimper: The End of a Missionary Era in China.* Singapore: Presbyterian Church of Singapore, 1991.

Hoskins, Janet Alison. "An Unjealous God? Christian Elements in a Vietnamese Syncretistic Religion." *Current Anthropology* 55, no. S10 (2014): [S302–S311].

Imperial War Museum—see Wilson, John Leonard.

Jarvis, Edward. *The Anglican Church in Burma: From Colonial Past to Global Future.* University Park, PA: Penn State University Press, 2021.

———. *The Anglican Church in Malaysia: Evolving Concepts, Challenging Contexts, Emerging Subtexts.* Cham: Palgrave Macmillan, 2022.

Jenkins, Philip. *The New Faces of Christianity: Believing the Bible in the Global South.* Oxford: Oxford University Press, 2006.

———. *The Next Christendom: The Coming of Global Christianity.* Oxford: Oxford University Press, 2011.

Johnson, Todd M. and Gina A. Zurlo. "The Changing Demographics of Global Anglicanism, 1970–2010." In *Growth and Decline in the Anglican Communion, 1980 to the Present,* edited by David Goodhew, 37–54. Abingdon: Routledge, 2017.

Keith, Charles. *Catholic Vietnam: A Church from Empire to Nation.* Berkeley, CA: University of California Press, 2012.

Khoo Kay Kim. "The Pangkor Engagement of 1874." *Journal of the Malaysian Branch of the Royal Asiatic Society* 47, no. 1 (225). Kuala Lumpur: Malaysian Branch of the Royal Asiatic Society, 1974 [1–12].

Koepping, Elizabeth. "Hunting with the Head: Borneo Villagers Negotiating Exclusivist Religion." *Studies in World Christianity* 12, no. 1 (2006); Edinburgh University Press [59–78].

———. "India, Pakistan, Bangladesh, Burma/Myanmar." In *Christianities in Asia*, edited by Peter C. Phan, 9–44. Chichester: Wiley-Blackwell, 2011.

Kuo, Henry. "The Church in Singapore: An Ecclesiology on the Way." *The Evangelical Review of Theology and Politics* (ERTP) 4 (2016); ERTP Forum: The Church, Evangelism, and the Political in Countries of the Western Pacific Rim. King's Divinity Press; King's Evangelical Divinity School [21–23].

Leary, John D. *Violence and the Dream People: The Orang Asli in the Malayan Emergency 1948–1960.* Athens OH: Ohio University Center for International Studies, 1995.

Lee Kam Hing, "A Neglected Story: Christian Missionaries, Chinese New Villagers, and Communists in the Battle for the 'Hearts and Minds' in Malaya, 1948–1960." *Modern Asian Studies* 47, no. 6 (November 2013). Cambridge: Cambridge University Press [1977–2006].

Legislative Council of the Straits Settlements. "An Act for the Separation of the Straits Settlements from the Diocese of Calcutta [August 9, 1869]." Acts and Ordinances [1867–1886] [two volumes] [50–51].

Lewis Bryan, John Northridge. *The Churches of the Captivity in Malaya.* London: SPCK, 1946.

Lim, Leng, with Kim-Hao Yap and Tuck-Leong Lee. "The Mythic-Literalists in the Province of Southeast Asia." In *Other Voices Other Worlds: The Global Church Speaks Out on Homosexuality*, edited by Terry Brown, 58–76. London: Darton, Longman and Todd, 2006.

Lim, Timothy T. N. "Pentecostalism in Singapore and Malaysia: Past, Present, and Future." In *Global Renewal Christianity: Spirit-Empowered Movements Past, Present, and Future; Vol. 1: Asia and Oceania,* edited by Vinson Synan and Amos Yong, 213–32. Lake Mary, FL: Charisma House, 2015.

Lim Hin Fui and Fong Tian Yong. *The New Villages in Malaysia: The Journey Ahead.* Kuala Lumpur: Institute of Strategic and Policy Research, 2005.

Loh Keng Aun. *Fifty Years of the Anglican Church in Singapore Island, 1909–1959 (Singapore Studies on Borneo and Malaya Number Four).* Singapore: The Department of History, University of Singapore, 1963.

Mak, Sue Ann. "Bishop John Leonard Wilson (Singapore 1941–1949): Koinonia in Suffering." *Asia Journal of Theology* 36, no. 1 (April 2022) [89–107].

Malaya Tribune. "Untitled." December 18, 1930 [8].

———. "Untitled." April 22, 1931 [8].

———. "Canon Waddy in Singapore." September 6, 1933 [9].

———. "Lord Nuffield's Generosity." February 3, 1936 [12].
———. "Untitled." January 19, 1937 [11].
Martin, David. *Forbidden Revolutions*. London: SPCK, 1996.
Mathews, Mathew. "Pentecostalism in Singapore: History, Adaptation, and Future." In *Asia Pacific Pentecostalism,* edited by Denise A. Austin, Jacqueline Grey, and Paul W. Lewis, 271–94. Leiden: Brill, 2019.
Maughan, Steven S. *Mighty England Do Good: Culture, Faith, Empire, and World in the Foreign Missions of the Church of England, 1850–1915*. Grand Rapids, MI: William B. Eerdmans, 2014.
McDougall, Francis Thomas—see Society for the Propagation of the Gospel in Foreign Parts.
McKay, Roy. *John Leonard Wilson: Confessor for the Faith*. London: Hodder and Stoughton, 1974.
McKenzie, Thomas. *The Anglican Way*. Nashville, TN: Colony Catherine, 2014.
"Mission to the Island of Borneo." *The Colonial Church Chronicle and Missionary Journal* 1, no. 1 (July 1847) [26–34].
Musa, Mohammad Alami. "Singapore's Secularism and its Pragmatic Approach to Religion." *Religions* 14(2), no. 219 (2023) special issue: "Political Secularism and Religion." [1–13].
Nagata, Judith. "Christianity Among Transnational Chinese: Religious Versus (Sub)ethnic Affiliation." *International Migration* 43, no. 3 (2005) [99–128].
National Archives (TNA), Kew. Records of the Colonial Office (CO) etc.: CO 717/203/3; "Commissioner-General for Southeast Asia, Malcolm MacDonald, to Secretary of State for the Colonies, 28 August 1950."
———. CO 717/209/3; "Secretary, Church Missionary Society to Colonial Office, 4 September 1950."
———. CO 537/7270; "Sir Henry Gurney to Higham of the Colonial Office, 13 March 1951."
———. CO 717/209/4; "Colonial Office, London, to the Governor of Singapore, 19 March 1951."
———. CO 1022/379; "Sir Gerald Templer to Secretary of State for the Colonies, 27 September 1952."
———. CO 1030/1019; "Proposed State of Greater Malaysia: Religious Aspects. SECRET, 1960–1962."
———. FCO (Records of the Foreign and Commonwealth Office and predecessors): FCO 141/7399; "Malaya: Anglican Missionary Work among Malays in the Settlements and Generally (Migrated Archives) 1948–1952."
———. FCO (Records of the Foreign and Commonwealth Office and predecessors): From the Federal Secretariat. S[ECRET] 261/48.
National Archives, Singapore (NAS) (National Library Board). British Library V4/259; "Separation of the Straits Settlements from the Diocese of Calcutta (1869)."
———. Chelliah, papers; "Collection of various documents concerning Rev. Dr. D. D. Chelliah (1919–1963)."
———. Diocesan Call to Evangelism (pastoral letter) (April 24, 1963).

―――. Diocese of Singapore and Malaya; *Diocesan Digest* no. 48 (January 1967).
―――. *Singapore Diocesan Magazine* (*SDM*), volumes I (1910) to XXVI (1934).
Newsinger, John. *The Blood Never Dried: A People's History of the British Empire*. London: Bookmarks, 2013.
Ng Moon Hing. *From Village to Village*. Kuala Lumpur: Synod of the Diocese of West Malaysia, 2009.
O'Connor, Daniel (and others). *Three Centuries of Mission: The United Society for the Propagation of the Gospel, 1701–2000*. London: Continuum, 2000.
O'Donovan, Oliver. *Church in Crisis: The Gay Controversy and the Anglican Communion*. Eugene, OR: Cascade, 2008.
Pascoe, Charles Frederick. *Classified Digest of the Records of the Society for the Propagation of the Gospel in Foreign Parts, 1701–1892*. London: Society for the Propagation of the Gospel in Foreign Parts, 1895.
―――. *Two Hundred Years of the SPG: An Historical Account of the Society for the Propagation of the Gospel in Foreign Parts, 1701–1900*. (Two volumes). London: Society for the Propagation of the Gospel in Foreign Parts, 1901.
Peace, Richard V. "Conflicting Understandings of Christian Conversion: A Missiological Challenge." *International Bulletin of Missionary Research* 28, no. 1, 2004 [8–14].
Phan, Peter C. "Ecclesia in Asia: Challenges for Asian Christianity." *East Asian Pastoral Review* 37 (2000), East Asian Pastoral Institute [215–32].
Pieris, Aloysius. "Political Theologies in Asia." In *The Blackwell Companion to Political Theology*, edited by Peter Scott and William T. Cavanaugh, 256–70. Oxford: Blackwell, 2004.
Ponniah, Moses. "The Situation in Malaysia." *Transformation* 17, no. 1: *Suffering and Power in Christian-Muslim Relations: The Political Challenge of Islam Today and its Implications for the Church in Education and Mission* (January 2000). Sage Publications, Inc. [31–34].
Porter, Andrew. *Religion Versus Empire? British Protestant Missionaries and Overseas Expansion, 1700–1914*. Manchester: Manchester University Press, 2004.
Province of South East Asia [Church of the]. *You Are Truly My Disciples If You Remain Faithful to My Teachings*. [booklet] February 3, 2019.
Raffles, Sophia. *Memoir of the Life and Public Services of Sir Stamford Raffles* [two volumes]. London: James Duncan, 1835.
Ramsey, Michael. *The Gospel and the Catholic Church*. Peabody, MA: Hendrickson, 2009.
Rönnbäck, Klas, Oskar Broberg, and Stefania Galli. "A Colonial Cash Cow: the Return on Investments in British Malaya, 1889–1969." *Cliometrica* 16 (2021) [149–173].
Roxborogh, John. *A History of Christianity in Malaysia*. Singapore: Genesis Books and Seminari Theoloji Malaysia, 2014.
―――. "Asian Agency, Protestant Traditions, and Ecumenical Movements in Asia, 1910 to 2010, with Special Reference to Malaysia and Singapore." *Asian Ecumenical Movement; Hong Kong Journal of Catholic Studies* no. 9 (2018); Centre for Catholic Studies, Chinese University of Hong Kong [285–317].

Saravanamuttu, Manicasothy. *The Sara Saga.* Penang: Areca Books, 2010.
Saw Swee Hock. "Population Trends in Singapore, 1819–1967." *Journal of Southeast Asian History* 10, no. 1. (Singapore Commemorative Issue, 1819–1969) (March 1969); Cambridge: Cambridge University Press [36–49].
SDM (Singapore Diocesan Magazine)—see National Archives, Singapore.
Singapore Church Record Books, National Library Board, Singapore, volume one, 1838–1863.
———. volume two, 1859–1870.
———. volume seven, 1902–1915.
———. volume eight, 1917–1928.
———. volume nine, 1928–1941.
Singapore Diocesan Magazine (SDM)—see National Archives, Singapore.
Singapore Free Press and Mercantile Advertiser. "SPG in Bangkok." August 15, 1933. [4].
———. "Christian Work Among Malays 'Unwise.'" December 2, 1948 [5].
Sng, Bobby Ewe Kong. *In His Good Time: The Story of the Church in Singapore, 1819–1978.* Singapore: Graduates Christian Fellowship, 1980.
Society for the Propagation of the Gospel in Foreign Parts (SPG) Archive, Oxford, Bodleian Libraries. Letters of Francis Thomas McDougall (1848–1859): Copies of Letters Received (CLR) 72.
———. Letters of Francis Thomas McDougall and Harriette McDougall (1849–1867): MSS. Pac. s. 104 (1); MSS. Pac. s. 104 (2); MSS. Pac. s. 104 (3); MSS. Pac. s. 104 (4).
Spencer, George John Trevor. "Notes of a Visit to Penang, Singapore, and Malacca." *The Colonial Church Chronicle and Missionary Journal* 1, no. 3 (September, 1847) [88–96].
———. "Notes of a Visit to Penang, Singapore, and Malacca." *The Colonial Church Chronicle and Missionary Journal* 1, no. 4 (October, 1847) [131–39].
———. "Notes of a Visit to Penang, Singapore, and Malacca." *The Colonial Church Chronicle and Missionary Journal* 1, no. 5 (November, 1847) [168–72].
Spencer Chapman, Frederick. *The Jungle Is Neutral.* London: Triad Panther Books, 1977.
St. Andrew's Cathedral. *Report of Church Funds and of the St Andrew's Church Mission in the Year 1875.* Singapore: Mission Press, 1876.
St. Andrew's Church Mission. *Report for the Year 1881.* Singapore: Mission Press, 1881.
Stanley, Brian. *Christianity in the Twentieth Century: A World History.* Princeton: Princeton University Press, 2018.
Straits Budget. "Church and Merdeka: By a Bishop." April 12, 1956 [10].
———. "Bishop: Make a Malayan My No. 2." December 20, 1956 [8].
———. "Church Will Change Name of Diocese." February 10, 1960 [6].
———. "Poser: Who Will Be Bishop Baines' Successor?" May 4, 1960 [5].
Straits Times. "St Andrew's Church Mission." Singapore. July 4, 1863 [1].
———. "St Andrew's Church Mission." Singapore. July 11, 1863 [1].
———. "Officers Back From Long Leave." May 2, 1939 [14].

———. "New College Opened." October 5, 1948 [5].

———. "Anglican Bishop Roland Koh Dies in the US." no. 1, October 10, 1972 [15].

———. "An Unhealthy Cult Spreading Among Young." no. 2, November 2, 1972 [13].

Strong, Rowan. *Anglicanism and the British Empire, c.1700–1850*. Oxford: Oxford University Press, 2007.

Swindell, Frank G. *A Short History of St Andrew's Church, Singapore*. Singapore: Malaya Tribune Press Ltd. 1929.

Tay, Moses. *Born for Blessings: An Autobiography of Moses Tay*. Singapore: Genesis, 2009.

Taylor, Brian. *The Anglican Church in Borneo, 1842–1962*. Bognor Regis: New Horizon, 1983.

———. "Gender in Sarawak: Mission and Reception." *Studies in Church History* 34 (1998) [461–73].

The Times. "Case for Ordination of Women 'Strong;' Bishop of Birmingham." April 20, 1959 [6].

Thompson, Henry Paget. *Into All Lands: The History of the Society for the Propagation of the Gospel in Foreign Parts, 1701–1950*. London: SPCK, 1951.

TNA—see National Archives, Kew.

Trevor, George (editor). *The Parochial Missionary Magazine: Part One*. London: G. Bell / J. Hatchard and Son, 1849.

Tse, Justin K. H. "A Tale of Three Bishops: Ideologies of Chineseness and Global Cities in Vancouver's Anglican Realignment. *Ching Feng: A Journal on Christianity and Chinese Religion and Culture* 15, no. 1–2 (2016) [103–30].

Walls, Andrew F. "Converts or Proselytes? The Crisis over Conversion in the Early Church." *International Bulletin of Missionary Research* 28, no. 1 (2004) [2–6].

Ward, Kevin. *A History of Global Anglicanism*. Cambridge: Cambridge University Press, 2006.

Wardle, Betty. *Family Journal—The War Years*. Horndean: Southern Press, 1984.

West, George A. *The World That Works*. London: Blandford Press, 1945.

White, Nicholas. "Gentlemanly Capitalism and Empire in the Twentieth Century: the Forgotten Case of Malaya, 1914–1965." In *Gentlemanly Capitalism and British Imperialism: The New Debate on Empire*, edited by Raymond E. Dumett, 175–95, London: Longman, 1999.

Whiting, Amanda J. "Secularism, the Islamic State and the Malaysian Legal Profession." *Asian Journal of Comparative Law* 5, no. 1 (2010) art. 10 [1–34].

Wickeri, Phillip L. *Hong Kong's Last English Bishop: The Life and Times of John Gilbert Hindley Baker*. Hong Kong: Hong Kong University Press, 2021.

Wilson, Daniel (editor). *Bishop Wilson's Journal Letters*. London: James Nisbet and Co. 1863.

Wilson, John Leonard. The Papers of the Rt Revd John Leonard Wilson (JLW) held at the Imperial War Museum, London: JLW1; JLW2; JLW3; JLW4.

———. JLW 1: The Federation of Christian Churches of Malaya.

———. JLW 2: Minutes of Chapter Meetings at Sime Road Camp, November 1944 to August 1945.

———. JLW 3: Miscellaneous Papers.
———. JLW 4: Personal Correspondence, January 1941 to June 1960.
Winstedt, Richard Olaf. *Malaya and Its History.* London: Hutchinson University Library, 1962.
Zurlo, Gina A., Todd M. Johnson, and Peter F. Crossing. "World Christianity and Religions 2022: A Complicated Relationship." *International Bulletin of Mission Research* 46, no. 1 (January 2022) [71–80].

Index

Anglican Communion: beginnings, 46–47; colonial legacy, 163–65, 166–67; dioceses in Asia, creation of, 36–37; divisions in, 154–55, 164–65, 178–80; future prospects, 180–81; interfaith questions, early, 63–64; internal relations, early, 58–59; reorganizations in, 116, 129–30, 133–34; women's ordination, 77–78, 154–55, 157. *See also* Anglican Realignment

Anglicanism, 18–19, 47, 134, 140. *See also* Anglican Realignment; churchmanship and ecclesiology

Anglican Mission in the Americas. *See* Anglican Realignment

Anglican Realignment, 154–55, 158–62, 164, 170–71

Anglo-Catholicism. *See* churchmanship and ecclesiology

Baines, Henry Wolfe (bishop), 118, 123, 124, 126, 128

Bangkok, Thailand, 73, 79, 80, 87

Borneo, 37–38. *See also* McDougall, Francis Thomas (bishop)

Calcutta, Diocese of. *See* Cotton, George Edward Lynch (bishop); Wilson, Daniel (bishop)

Chambers, Walter (bishop), 55, 59

charismatic renewal. *See* Pentecostalism

Chew Hiang Chea, John (bishop), 159, 160, 165

Chiu Ban It, Joshua (bishop), 133–36, 147

Christian Conference of Asia. *See* East Asia Christian Conference

Christian conversions. *See* conversion

Christianity: arrival in Southeast Asia, 11–16; in Asia, study of, 6–7, 8–9; and Asian identity, 4, 123–24, 129, 141–42, 162–63, 170; belonging in Singapore, modes of, 7–8; characteristics in Asia, 3, 52, 135, 140, 141–42, 149, 162; Christian diversity in Singapore, 1, 5–6, 170; as "civilizing" influence, 51–52; decolonization of, 175; global issues in, 1–2, 164–65; growth in Singapore, 1–2, 6, 139; liberal Christianity in Asia, 139–40, 146–48; relations between denominations, 26, 35–36, 42–43, 45–46, 49, 51, 53, 67; theological differences in

Asia, 123–25, 164–65. *See also* ecumenism; Pentecostalism
Chung, Titus (bishop), 166, 168
churchmanship and ecclesiology, 16, 19–20, 53–54, 84, 123, 139–40, 168
Church Missionary Society, 19–20, 41, 123
Church of England and Anglican presence in Singapore: chaplains and churches, early, 23, 24–26; churches founded post-independence, 148, 156; developments post-Second World War, 122–23; Diocese of Singapore and other bodies, creation of, 67, 71, 72; and First World War, 75–77; languages, 45, 60, 72–74, 86–87, 115; limits of appeal, 69; membership and growth, 39–40, 41, 66, 73–74, 77, 134, 139; moral, social, and political questions, 33–34, 43–44; relations with Presbyterians, 26, 42–43; relations with Roman Catholics, 35–36, 45–46, 49, 53; relations with various denominations, 51, 53, 67, 78, 86; and Second World War, 95–98, 99–102, 102–5; Singaporean independence, response to, 128–29, 131–32, 134; visions of future Church, 34, 78–79, 89–90, 111–12, 116. *See also* Province of South East Asia
Church of the Province of South East Asia. *See* Province of South East Asia
colonialism: analysis and study of, 4, 6–7, 163–65; approaches to, varying, 13–16; attitudes to religion, 13–14; economics of, 75–76, 113; evolving views of, 76–77, 83, 89; motivations and rationale, 2, 11–12, 75–76; perceptions of local religions, 12–13, 29, 32–33; Protestant justifications of, 15–16, 29. *See also* prejudice and discrimination

Communist Party of Malaya. *See* Malayan Emergency
conversion, 6, 15–16, 27, 29, 52–53, 81
Cotton, George Edward Lynch (bishop) 41, 42–43, 44
Council of Churches of Malaysia and Singapore. *See* ecumenism

demographics of Singapore: colonial period, early, 1, 5–6, 22, 24, 25, 39, 64–66; colonial period, later, 73, 79, 85; today, 174, 175–76
Diocese of Singapore. *See* Church of England and Anglican presence in Singapore; Province of South East Asia

East Asia Christian Conference, 135, 142, 147–48
East India Company, 15–16, 35, 39, 40–41, 48, 55
economy of Singapore: colonial period, early, 25; colonial period, later, 67–68, 71, 77; and First World War, 75–76; post-Second World War, 113; today, 145, 174
ecumenism, 101–2, 113, 114–15, 123–24, 134–35, 165–66
education missions. *See* missionary work

Federation of Christian Churches of Malaya. *See* ecumenism
Ferguson-Davie, Charles James (bishop), 71, 72, 78, 79

GAFCON. *See* Anglican Realignment
Global South Fellowship of Anglican Churches. *See* Anglican Realignment

Hose, George Frederick (bishop), 57, 59–60, 61, 66–67

Kampong baru missions. *See* Malayan Emergency

Koh Peck Chiang, Roland (bishop), 123, 128, 134

McDougall, Francis Thomas (bishop), 37–38, 50. *See also* Borneo
Malayan Christian Council. *See* ecumenism
Malayan Emergency, 107–8, 119–22, 130–31
Malayan Welfare Council. *See* ecumenism
medical missions. *See* missionary work
megachurches. *See* Pentecostalism
missionary work: difficulties, 54–55; early missions, 23, 27–29, 40; education missions, 81–83, 89, 173; expansion, 56–57, 60; expectations of missionaries, 61; in Malayan Emergency, 107–8, 119–22, 130–31; medical missions, 71, 83–84; motivations, 48–49; perceptions of missionaries, 6–7, 62–63; Saint Andrew's Church Mission, 40–41, 54–55, 55–56, 60; Singapore Industrial Mission, 135–36, 147–48; understandings of mission, 52, 66
Missions to Seamen, 45, 81, 88, 95, 97

National Council of Churches of Singapore, 134–35, 162. *See also* ecumenism

Pentecostalism: appeal in Singapore, 5–6, 140–43, 151–52; arrival in Singapore, 138–39; background, 136–38; economic and social factors, 143–45; megachurches, 5, 139, 144, 145; political dimension, 145–48, 149–50
Ponniah, Rennis (bishop), 165
prejudice and discrimination, 32–33, 49, 61–62, 62–63
Province of South East Asia, Church of: and Anglican Realignment, 159, 161, 165; background and launch of, 133, 154, 157, 158; engagement with society, 166; future in Singapore, 168, 173–74, 180; languages, 166; membership and growth, 3, 7, 158, 165; in Singapore today, 3, 153–54, 165–68

Raffles, Stamford: attitudes and views, 32, 39; life, 2–3, 20–24, 29–30, 50; and religion, 3, 22–23, 28–29
Roberts, Basil Coleby (bishop), 79, 84

Saint Andrew's cathedral, 23, 24, 25–27, 42–43, 74, 166
Saint Andrew's Church Mission. *See* missionary work
Sansbury, Kenneth (bishop), 128, 133
schools. *See* missionary work
Second World War, 87–88, 93–107
Singapore: Asian values, 146–47, 149, 169, 177; Christian community, characteristics of, 133–34, 168; Churches present in, 85–86; comparisons with other states, 3, 143, 177–78; independence, 125–28; intercommunity relations, 75, 85–86, 115–16, 116–19, 175, 178; origins and early settlers, 20–22, 31–32; political realignments, 55, 58, 65–66, 116; post-Second World War situation, 107–9, 115–16; vice and crime, 35, 175; wealth, 143–44, 174. *See also* demographics of Singapore; economy of Singapore
Singapore Industrial Mission. *See* missionary work
Society for the Propagation of the Gospel in Foreign Parts, 41, 53, 56–57, 66
Southeast Asia: arrival of empires, 11–16; Christian presence, early, 17; independence movements, 113–14; origins and early settlers, 31–32; Pangkor, Treaty of, 57–58;

religions, 11–13, 31–33; and Second World War, 93–99
Spencer, George (bishop), 32–33, 34–36, 53

Tay Leng Kong, Moses (bishop), 148, 156–60, 162
Trinity Theological College, 115, 143, 147, 157

Wilson, Daniel (bishop), 18, 19, 32, 25–26, 34–36, 39–40
Wilson, John Leonard (bishop), 84–85, 94–111, 113, 115, 116–19, 155
women's ordination. *See* Anglican Communion

About the Author

Edward Jarvis, ThD, PhD, is a Fellow of the Royal Asiatic Society, a Fellow of the Royal Historical Society, and an Anglican priest. He is the author of seven books including *The Anglican Church in Burma: from Colonial Past to Global Future* and *The Anglican Church in Malaysia: Evolving Concepts, Challenging Contexts, Emerging Subtexts*.